Competition Engine Building

Advanced Engine Design and Assembly Techniques

John Baechtel

CarTech®

CarTech®

CarTech®, Inc.
39966 Grand Avenue
North Branch, MN 55056
Phone: 651-277-1200 or 800-551-4754
Fax: 651-277-1203
www.cartechbooks.com

© 2012 by John Baechtel

All rights reserved. No part of this publication may be reproduced or utilized in any form or by any means, electronic or mechanical, including photocopying, recording, or by any information storage and retrieval system, without prior permission from the Author. All text, photographs, and artwork are the property of the Author unless otherwise noted or credited.

The information in this work is true and complete to the best of our knowledge. However, all information is presented without any guarantee on the part of the Author or Publisher, who also disclaim any liability incurred in connection with the use of the information.

All trademarks, trade names, model names and numbers, and other product designations referred to herein are the property of their respective owners and are used solely for identification purposes. This work is a publication of CarTech, Inc., and has not been licensed, approved, sponsored, or endorsed by any other person or entity.

Edit by Scott Parkhurst
Layout by Monica Seiberlich

ISBN 978-1-61325-288-8
Item No. SA214P

Library of Congress Cataloging-in-Publication Data

Baechtel, John.
  Competition engine building : advanced engine design & assembly techniques / by John Baechtel.
      p. cm.
  ISBN 978-1-934709-62-7
 1. Automobiles, Racing–Motors–Design and construction. I. Title.

 TL210.B275 2012
 629.25'04–dc23
                          2011052748

Written, edited, and designed in the U.S.A.
Printed in U.S.A.

Title Page: *This Sonny Leonard–built engine is loosely based on the big-block Chevy design, but now boasts Sonny's own hemispherical chamber heads and displaces 802 ci! It's a popular engine choice with the IHRA Pro Stock crowd. (Courtesy Sonny's Racing Engines)*

Back Cover Photos

Top Left: *Cup engines such as Chevrolet's RO7 model represent the logical result of a single 4-barrel engine fully developed for its intended application. These highly targeted engines excel at pinpointing powerband placement.*

Top Right: *Precision adjustments are a fundamental part of the tuning process, but savvy builders also recognize that individual cylinders can be tuned with other methods such as varying lash and rocker ratios.*

Middle Left: *Forced-induction engines are a different story. Most of the fundamentals of torque and power production still apply, albeit with appropriate attention to the elementary rules of gas exchange in a boosted environment. With appropriate tuning, the results are usually spectacular.*

Middle Right: *Accurate deck height measurement is essential for computing the compression ratio. With or without a ring installed during mockup, the best location to check deck height is near the edge of the piston along the pin axis. This eliminates any effect from piston rocking.*

Bottom Left: *Tall, single-plane 4-barrel intake manifolds and carburetors are formidable racing attire. This Dart Big Chief spread-port intake and 1,150-cfm Holley Ultra HP aluminum Dominator pack a powerful punch when teamed with an appropriate-size, high-compression short block.*

Bottom Right: *Cam thrust on the Comp Cams belt drive is adjusted via three inclined ramps with corresponding ramps on the cover plate. As the plate rotates, cam thrust is increased or decreased depending on the rate of ramp incline.*

CONTENTS

Acknowledgments 5
Introduction 6

Chapter 1: Race Engine Planning 8
Consider the Limitations 9
Performance Objectives 15
Unlocking Hidden Power 17
How Cylinders Influence Each Other 18

Chapter 2: Torque and Horsepower 20
Volumetric Efficiency 22
Understanding BSFC 22
Where Power Comes From 23
What Influences Power? 24

Chapter 3: Cylinder Blocks 25
Grooming the Short Block 26
Block Type 26
Block Inspection 33
Machine Shop Processes 35

Chapter 4: Crankshafts 45
Crankshaft Types 46
Strength Treatments 49
Counterweights 49
Operating Conditions 51
Crankshaft Oiling 51
Engine Balancing 53
Crankshaft Dampening 54

Chapter 5: Piston Technology 56
Piston Speed 56
Acceleration 57
Piston Speed Issues 58
Selection Factors 58
Race Piston Terminology 64
Rings 65
Piston Ring Terminology 68
Ring Installation 69
Micro-Welding 69

Chapter 6: Connecting Rods 72
Rod Length as a Tuning Component 73
Connecting Rod Materials 75
Characteristics of Rod Activity 78
Rod-to-Piston Clearance 78

Chapter 7: Engine Bearings 80
Characteristics of Engine Bearings 81
Roller Cam Bearings 83
Clearances 83
Bearing Failures 84

Chapter 8: Cylinder Heads 87
Choosing a Cylinder Head 89
Valves and Valve Sizes 90

Chapter 9: Induction Systems 95
Dual-Plane Intakes 96
Single-Plane Intakes 98
Tunnel Ram Intakes 100
Plenum Characteristics 102
Mixture Conditioning 104
Surface Texturing 105
Reversion 106
Secondary Intake Considerations 106
Flow Testing 107
Electronic Fuel Injection 108

Chapter 10: Carburetors 110
Carburetor Selection 112
Exit Air Speed 113
Tuning Elements 114
Basic Tuning and Maintenance 116
Final Thoughts 117

Chapter 11: Camshafts 118
Understanding Cam Specs 119
Calculating Valve Lift 120
Finding TDC 121

    Degreeing the Cam 121
    Calculating Valve Overlap 126
    Camshaft Terminology 126
    Rocker Ratio Tuning 127
    Duration 128
    Camshaft Selection Criteria 129
    Firing Order Swaps 129

Chapter 12: Sumps and Oiling 131
    Wet Sump Systems 133
    Dry Sump Systems 136
    Oil Accumulators for Racing Engines 141
    Common Modifications 141

Chapter 13: Ignition Systems 143
    Ignition Choices 144
    Race Engine Ignition Tips 147

Chapter 14: Exhaust Systems 148
    PipeMax Header Software 150
    Step Headers 150
    Header Design Kit 152

Chapter 15: Engine Build Tips 153
    Assembly Procedure 154

Chapter 16: Engine Startup and Maintenance 166
    Startup and Break-In 166
    Maintenance Program 170
    Recommended Maintenance 172
    Engine Dyno Testing 173

Source Guide 175

ACKNOWLEDGMENTS

Engines have been an overwhelming passion for me since my earliest days. In middle school I marveled at the spectacular engines I saw in the pages of early hot rod magazines. Later as an editor at *Car Craft* and then *Hot Rod*, I was elated that I had finally achieved the opportunity to learn about, document, and most importantly, build all kinds of high-performance engines. Even then I still read and absorbed everything I could find about engines, particularly racing engines. I studied books on combustion theory, engine airflow, carburetors, exhaust systems, and all the basic math and science involved. I supplemented that with more specific books about old racing engines, exotic European racing engines, Cosworth V-8s, Offys, Millers, Formula 1 engines, and even some of the early aircraft engines used in land speed record cars like the Napier Lion, the Rolls-Royce "R" Schneider Trophy aero engines, and the Liberty V-12. My favorite book and personal bible is *The Miller Dynasty* by Mark Dees. It chronicles the amazing designs of Harry Miller whose engines dominated the early years of Indianapolis and served as forerunners to the amazing Offys.

I studied the discipline rigorously; not to ultimately acquire some sort of magic engine guru status, but to truly understand how these incredible machines work and how they are continuously manipulated to raise the power bar. After 35 years I also learned that almost everyone out there still has some unexpected kernel of knowledge that I could learn from. I also came to the realization that our grandfathers and great grandfathers pretty much had it all figured out in the early twentieth century. They already had roller bearings, roller rocker arms, four-valve heads, tuned inlet systems, and so on. They just didn't have the materials and metallurgy to make them work the way we do today. Over the years I had the good fortune to enjoy extraordinarily memorable opportunities to pick the brains of legendary engine designers and builders such as Bill "Grumpy" Jenkins, Buddy Morrison, Bob Glidden, Warren Johnson, Dick Landy, John Lingenfelter, Hans Hermann, Jim Feuling, Jon Kaase, Ed Iskenderian, and many others. After leaving the magazines and running my own performance dyno lab for a decade or so I was able to observe and absorb the ideas of many lesser known engine builders who came to test their theories. I quickly found that there are literally thousands of highly talented unsung engine builders across the nation and they all have something to contribute.

I learned that race engine building is as much an art as it is a skill. A high degree of hard-earned skill goes into the physical task of measuring, machining, assembling, and tuning a competition engine. In turn, the art of race engine building is seen in its mathematical elegance and the savvy builder's ability to contemplate and visualize the complex dynamics of high-speed racing assemblies. It's been said that Dale Earnhardt was a great driver because he could see the air and use it to his advantage. I think there are engine builders out there who can do the same thing. They see and understand an engine's airflow and how properly dimensioned flow paths can be manipulated to shape and expand power curves to best suit specific racing applications. Men of keen perception, these builders seem to possess the ability to see molecules, perhaps even atoms, and understand how to harness engine airflow for greater and greater output.

I'd personally like to acknowledge and thank some of those remarkable individuals who contributed to this book through their generous coaching, input, and support during its evolution. Many thanks indeed to Jim McFarland, my friend, long-standing mentor, personal confidant, and beacon of sanity. Kudos also to my old racing buddy Charles Jenckes who, like McFarland, is undoubtedly one of the true engine gurus. Thanks also to Tom Lieb at Scat Enterprises for reviewing and correcting my inadequacies in the crankshaft chapter. And Jeff Smith at *Car Craft* magazine for remaining the ever-enlightening sounding board for questions, tips, and recommendations. Jack McInnis at Dart Machinery provided photos, parts, advice, and considerable patience in getting this done. Thanks Jack.

ACKNOWLEDGMENTS

My appreciation also extends to Phil Elliot at T&D Machine, Chris Madsen at Ross Pistons, Scott Hall from Moroso Performance, David Basham and James Cole at BMS Machine, Bill Tichenor at Holley Performance Products, Billy Godbold and Trent Goodwin from Comp Cams, Sonny Leonard Racing Engines, Automotive Specialists, Matt Genette at Jegs Performance, Todd Ryden from MSD, Chris Raschke and Zack Kimball at ARP, Dave Secunda at Wilson Manifolds, Alan Rebescher at Summit Racing, and at least a hundred others whom I have neither the space nor the necessary intellectual capacity to recall at this specific moment. Nonetheless, I extend my heartfelt thanks to all of you.

This book barely scratches the surface of an extraordinarily complex subject, but I hope it is enough to prompt others to embrace the underlying theory and supporting mathematics that enable true power builders to pinpoint power curve shapes and placement to suit the specific needs of each individual racing application. It doesn't come easy, but the rewards often exceed the expectations. They always have for me.

INTRODUCTION

While the physical phenomena occurring within a high-speed racing engine don't necessarily approach the level of quantum mechanics, for the purpose of discussion we can almost treat them as such. Well over a century after the invention of the internal combustion engine men still puzzle over various mechanical and thermodynamic relationships that produce astonishing amounts of power from a mechanical device that is at best 20- to 30-percent efficient.

So many complicated interactions occur inside a racing engine that it can be difficult to fully comprehend the unseen dynamics that ultimately emerge as torque and horsepower. It's hard to imagine near-1-pound slugs of reciprocating metal changing direction 75 to 150 times per second or more within a collection of cylinders not much taller than large coffee mugs. It's harder still to grasp the unsteady gas dynamics and valve motion required to create and effectively harness combustion pressure when everything is moving so fast. Still, some engines are more efficient than others and for the purpose of general transportation even the most inefficient combinations are surprisingly useful.

As racing engines go, a thoughtful mix of mechanical components and fundamental tuning procedures delivers superior performance, but what is often overlooked in books of this nature is contemplation of how various mechanical components and invisible dynamic forces interact to build torque and horsepower. This book differs from most engine building books in that it concentrates more on fundamentals instead of the trick of the week. Professional engine builders tend to stick to what they know works and that is usually something that has been developed over time with careful regard to the application and what the engine is expected to accomplish. Many engine builders are surprisingly successful with less peak power than their competitors because they have become adept at positioning an engine's powerband to suit its final application.

Everyone pretty much grasps the physical processes of the four-cycle engine and we are all familiar with the common paths to power, i.e., more airflow, higher compression ratios, bigger camshafts, and so on—all tied together in a tidy blueprinted package. Millions of dyno tests have confirmed the validity of commonly accepted practices and component relationships. Why some work better than others is not always readily apparent, but the fact that some do suggests a more formidable mechanical and thermodynamic blend that begs closer examination so we might determine why they excel and how we might build on their success in the pursuit of even greater performance.

Many books have been written about various parts combinations and tuning practices, but they

INTRODUCTION

generally fail to investigate why some combinations perform better than others. Magazine dyno tests frequently compare manifolds, cylinder heads, and other components, and as soon as one prevails over the others it is pronounced superior with little explanation as to why. There is also rarely much effort to retune for individual component preferences that may favor a different spark curve, a larger carburetor, or smaller headers, any one of which or a combination of which might harvest unexpected torque and horsepower gains from an optimized blend of component relationships. The same manifold that came in second in a hasty dyno comparison may actually be superior when properly tuned to accommodate the overall component mix as it applies to the final application and track conditions. The right carburetor spacer, stagger jetting, and/or other individual cylinder tuning strategies may unleash power that might never be recognized without a more thorough investigation than the cut-and-dried A/B comparison.

By necessity a book about competition engine building covers a lot of ground, most of it related to engine component selection, blueprinting, and final assembly techniques. Fundamentals are the basis for good power, but it's important to also review some core principles governing the physical dynamics involved. Some are extraordinarily complicated at the race engine level, but thoughtful manipulation of these complex relationships often leads to greater engine efficiency and a path to more useable power than commonly thought possible.

This is not to suggest that I am some black ops guru of engine performance, but rather to share some 40-odd years of observation, dyno testing, and learning experience punctuated by carefully polled comments from top engine builders and designers who routinely probe the expanding frontiers of competition engine performance. Not quantum mechanics per se, but at the very least, the automotive equivalent of rocket science.

In an age where pretty much anyone can throw good parts and a ton of boost at an engine and make obscene power, the science of naturally aspirated engine performance continues to evolve and those who contemplate the minutia frequently reap appropriate rewards.

Much of the information offered herein also applies to supercharged and nitrous applications with appropriate regard to the specifics involved. I hope that some of this information encourages hardcore enthusiasts and engine builders to frontload the normal blueprint and assembly process with a more critical focus on the largely invisible forces at work inside a high-speed competition engine—forces that when properly harnessed and manipulated, can lead to a whole new level of engine performance and more importantly, victories in your chosen racing venue.

No single book can possibly touch on all the aspects of competition engine building as it relates to all the various applications that racers require. In this book I hope to illuminate important factors that will prompt further thought and investigation on the part of engine builders seeking to elevate and expand their efforts to a higher level that applies to any racing environment they choose.

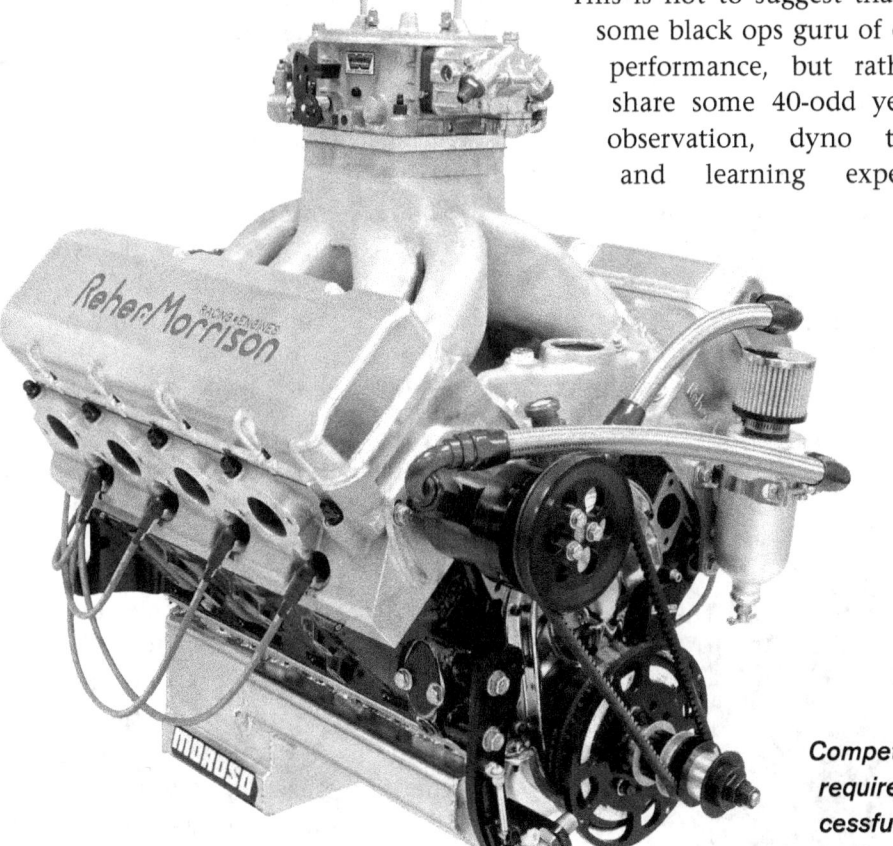

Competition engines are built to meet the specific requirements of various racing venues. The most successful ones are carefully tailored to match their final application. (Courtesy Don Cooper, Reher-Morrison)

CHAPTER 1

RACE ENGINE PLANNING

Purpose-built competition engines vary in content according to the particular requirements of their intended application. Some are built for very high RPM with a narrow powerband; others are designed for a lower, broader power range with greater emphasis on drivability and endurance qualities. All of them target operational requirements specific to their racing application and are often functionally unsuitable outside their intended performance environment. A drag racing engine wouldn't last five laps on a challenging road course like Road Atlanta or Laguna Seca, and a sports car engine couldn't hope to match the high specific output of a 10,000-rpm small-displacement Competition Eliminator engine.

Bonneville engines require some qualities of both engine types, effectively supporting what amounts to a 5-mile drag race demanding big horsepower to overcome aerodynamic drag and stout internals to endure the long, hard pull. Unlimited sprint car engines run extreme engine speeds with frequent throttling that places severe shock loads on internal parts while supercharged and turbocharged engines each have their own unique requirements that are completely different from a naturally aspirated superspeedway "Cup" engine or sportsman class Saturday night specials.

The focus of this book is primarily directed at naturally aspirated (all motor) engines, but it will be evident along the way that many of the principles also apply to boosted and nitrous applications. In every case, fundamental engine building practices are mandatory, but build content and assembly practices are very much application specific or, in many cases, rules specific depending on the type and level of competition.

Despite broad differences, all competition engines seek optimum manipulation of the properties of fuel and air to create maximum volumetric efficiency (VE) and cylinder pressure to drive the pistons and thus the car. Mechanical

Highly optimized Sprint Cup engines approach 900 hp with efficiency that rivals a Formula 1 engine. (Courtesy General Motors)

RACE ENGINE PLANNING

Unlimited applications are free to apply any and all power strategies available including massive displacement, sophisticated internal components, and highly tuned inlet and exhaust systems designed to optimize powerband positioning. (Courtesy Don Cooper, Reher-Morrison)

components are chosen according to established engineering principles and then carefully matched to achieve this goal with the specific requirements of a given application in mind. In many cases these efforts are limited by class rules or operational parameters that dictate pre-defined engine content. Hence it is prudent to list and examine all of the applicable requirements when planning a competition engine build.

Preliminary planning steps help identify potential problem areas and ensure the best possible blend of performance parts to suit the intended application. Operational requirements and sanctioning body limitations require careful deliberation prior to finalizing the parts manifest. This includes critical examination of every potential component and the assistance of home PC computer simulation programs that can help you estimate potentially ideal combinations based on prevailing rules and requirements.

Consider the Limitations

Unlimited engine combinations enjoy the best possible repertoire of race engine theory and high-performance parts. Designer/builders are free to tailor the package to perfectly match known operational requirements without regard to strict boundaries enacted to limit power and speed or to control the expense of a particular racing series.

Unfortunately, many racing venues enforce some level of restriction that suits their particular goals or racing philosophy. That's not necessarily a bad thing, as it clearly defines fixed goals for you to target. Some builders relish the challenge of wringing every last bit of power from an engine that has been administratively handicapped. Others abhor it. Accordingly, it may be useful to preface a discussion of engine building strategies with an examination of common handicapping methods to review how they might affect a particular

Competition Engine Building Goals

1. Configure Component Mix for Application Specifics
2. Optimize Engine Airflow Paths to Suit Application
3. Optimize Cylinder Sealing
4. Optimize Fuel Mixture Quality
5. Optimize Combustion Efficiency
6. Minimize Pumping Losses
7. Minimize Friction Losses
8. Position the Powerband

build. Some or much of the following may apply to a specific program.

Displacement

Racing associations often enforce displacement limits to control engine output. These rules are implemented to limit speeds in certain series or to differentiate classes for elapsed time or top speed, as found in drag racing or at Bonneville. Displacement limits are rigorously enforced, but sactioning bodies still present opportunities to optimize specific packages under the prevailing rules in some cases. When displacement is specified, but the bore and stroke combination is left open, builders often gravitate toward the largest possible bore dimension to achieve maximum breathing capability with larger valves and more effective piston area for combustion pressure to apply force against the piston top. This shortens stroke length and generally tends to raise the operational powerband (RPM).

This trend is favored because it aids breathing and reduces piston speed for greater durability. Sometimes builders prefer a longer stroke

CHAPTER 1

and a broader powerband more suitable to certain track layouts. This reduces bore size, but the final bore/stroke combination ultimately seeks the best possible compromise that accommodates the displacement limit while biased as much as possible for breathing efficiency and equivalent piston area. Drag racers lean toward big bore/short stroke combinations, while short circuit, road race, and oval track racers favor more stroke length and a lower powerband to reinforce endurance qualities and torque production for tight corners and shorter straightaways.

Once the desired powerband has been defined, PC engine simulation software (such as Performance Trends Engine Analyzer Pro or Motion Software's Dynomation 5) can often provide valuable direction in choosing the optimum bore/stroke ratio and corresponding connecting rod length. These are important considerations when planning a series-specific engine. It may be somewhat instructive to know what your competitors are doing, but don't assume that it is necessarily best for your own effort.

Through careful evaluation and computer simulation, you may identify a superior combination that takes greater advantage of other factors such as car weight, rear axle and transmission ratios, shift point RPM drop, tire size, and other contributing factors that affect the total vehicle package. Within a fixed displacement window, you have to identify the best possible bore and stroke combination for the way that the car will be driven. Whenever the rules stipulate these sorts of limitations, new opportunities often emerge.

Block Type

Aluminum blocks are accepted in many types of racing, but there are several factors to consider whenever you have a choice. Aluminum blocks are pretty comfortable in a 500- to 800-hp environment and some racers run them at substantially higher power levels. Still, many builders prefer an iron block, especially for applications that are supercharged or nitrous assisted. They feel that iron race blocks are more dimensionally stable in those high-stress environments. Block stability promotes superior ring seal and less friction, which many feel is an acceptable trade-off for any weight penalty caused by the heavier block.

Aluminum blocks have improved dramatically over the past decade or more and the current liners are very good. If you have the option of running an aluminum block, consider the weight savings versus the application carefully to determine how well it serves your needs. If weight is a critical factor, aluminum becomes attractive, but alloy blocks are a good bit more expensive. Evaluate how hard your combination is going to stress the block with RPM and high cylinder pressures and proceed from there. And don't forget to consider thermal characteristics as they apply to cooling and heat retention in the combustion space (see Chapter 3 for more details).

Bore Size

Some sportsman racing series limit cylinder bore size and in some cases even the spacing. These are typically cost measures designed to curtail the use of expensive cylinder blocks with revised bore spacing that permits larger bores while retaining desirable cylinder wall thickness and stability. Sprint Cup engines are a good example. They are displacement limited to 358 ci and a maximum bore of 4.185 inches. Cup engines previously operated with a bore spacing of 4.400 inches, but NASCAR allowed a bore spacing increase to 4.500 inches to accommodate larger bores, bigger valves, and revised valve geometry. All this is in an attempt to level the playing field among various brands. If the cylinder bore is not specified, you must choose a bore dimension that best suits the particular application as defined by airflow and combustion chamber requirements, compression ratio, flame travel, and other factors, including a specific stroke length

Iron blocks are prevalent in most racing series. Some series are limited to production blocks only, while others use dedicated race blocks from manufacturers such as World Products and Dart Machinery.

that also accommodates your operational requirements.

Compression Ratio

Compression ratio is an effective means of limiting power in some series and also curbs cost. It typically influences piston and cylinder head selection where a particular cylinder head may also be specified. When cylinder head and chamber size are dictated, piston configuration, deck height, and gasket thickness must be juggled to chase the compression ratio requirement. Short tracks frequently enforce a 9:1 rule while NASCAR engines are limited to 12:1. Unlimited drag racing and Bonneville engines often exceed 14:1 while stock class drag racers are limited to the original factory compression ratio of their particular vehicle. Compression ratio limits generally dictate flat-top pistons, which encourage efficient combustion while maintaining desirable quench to promote charge turbulence and maintain mixture quality.

Hypereutectic pistons are often specified, although forgings are permitted in some series. There is certainly less bang for the buck without higher compression ratios, but given specific parameters, experienced engine builders adjust contributing components to best suit any fixed compression ratio, particularly with an eye toward increasing the effective compression ratio via camshaft timing and effective inlet tuning to improve VE.

Crankshaft Type

Some lower-level sportsman organizations require stock cranks and rods. These are cost measures frequently accompanied by camshaft, cylinder head, and induction limits. Power is generally limited in these applications so durability issues are infrequent. In claimer racing and many drag racing classes, cast cranks, and stock rods are successfully employed without distress.

Weight limitations for the crankshaft are also common, something on the order of a 50-pound minimum in most cases. This dramatically reduces the cost of racing in these classes, but that doesn't mean you can't consider blueprinting the assemblies for optimum balance in the desired RPM range and making discreet modifications to reduce crankcase windage.

Cylinder Heads

Most sanctioning body cylinder head rules generally strive to limit cost. Many ruling bodies enforce an iron cylinder head rule with further restrictions on valve size and material, valvespring pressure, combustion chamber size, intake port volume, spark plug placement, and other contributing factors. Some rules permit bowl porting while others forbid everything including multi-angle valve jobs and back-cut valves. Classes that allow aluminum racing heads are usually unrestricted unless they involve original factory cylinder heads in a stock drag racing class.

Some racing classes limit spring diameter and configuration, retainer material, valve shape, and other factors. A careful evaluation of allowable cylinder head configurations and hardware usually extends to camshaft selection and further reflection on intake manifold and exhaust system compatibility. Choices

This 14:1, gas-ported Pro Mod nitrous piston from Ross Racing Pistons is just the ticket for big power applications. High compression ratios are still a favored path to power, but compression domes as seen here are illegal in many sportsman racing series. Flat-top or dished pistons that ensure a specified compression ratio are often legislated to limit power and costs.

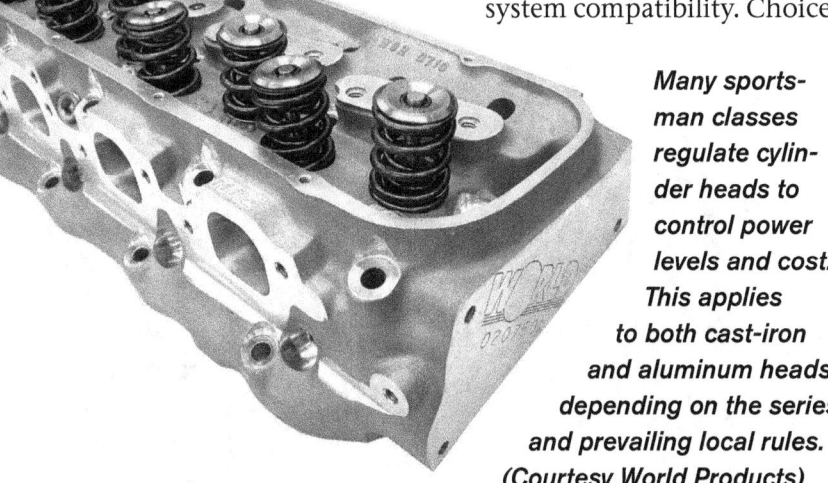

Many sportsman classes regulate cylinder heads to control power levels and cost. This applies to both cast-iron and aluminum heads depending on the series and prevailing local rules. (Courtesy World Products)

focus on achieving maximum possible VE within the stated boundaries. Savvy builders also key in on component choices and attending port volumes and valve sizes to take best advantage of transmission and rear axle gearing, tire size, and specific RPM requirements for the tracks the engine will visit most often.

Intake Manifolds

Intake manifold and carburetor restrictions are prevalent in many types of racing. They are primarily intended to limit airflow and RPM potential. In some cases more than one choice is offered and the final selection is based on which configuration generates the best VE and torque-tuning potential. That's why, where rules permit, a twin-carb, high-RPM tunnel ram is chosen over a single 4-barrel for a drag racing application, but you're not likely to see a tunnel ram intake on a road racing car.

Some classes dictate the use of a dual-plane intake, which often extends to the use of a stock cast-iron manifold. When the intake manifold is specified, all you can do is identify the manifold's characteristics and tailor your package accordingly. (Chapter 9 discusses how to map manifold characteristics on a flow bench to obtain a ballpark view of individual port strengths and weaknesses.) Once you have a clear picture of the manifold's efficiency you can evaluate potential steps to ensure its contribution to maximum performance.

Depending on other restrictions these may include rocker ratio or cam timing adjustments to individual cylinders based on individual runner flow dynamics. Or it may be addressed by manipulation of header dimensions to complement and possibly broaden the torque range dictated by the intake manifold's fixed dimensions. If allowed, carb spacers may support better mixture quality and, in the case of dual-plane intakes, staggering jetting from side to side may also provide some improvement, particularly as it relates to the lean side of the engine. Many circle-track classes also require a 2-barrel carburetor of a specified size with no modifications allowed, although repositioning of the carburetor location on the intake manifold is sometimes permitted.

Camshafts and Valve Gear

Camshafts are one of the most common restrictions. Most often a rule limitation restricts the use of roller camshafts, specifying only flat-tappet camshafts, frequently with an additional stipulation of stock lifter diameter. Some classes further stipulate hydraulic lifters only or a valve lift rule, which is typically .500 inch. Other classes factor cost by limiting racers to stock or hypereutectic pistons and other restrictions that may include OEM blocks only, iron heads, stock exhaust manifolds or spec headers, and other requirements more closely associated with "claimer"-type engine regulations.

In addition to cam type and lifter restrictions, camshaft rules may also stipulate a minimum engine-idle vacuum to control camshaft profiles. Other internal component restrictions may include stock crankshaft and connecting rods and most certainly, wet sump oiling with a stock pump and perhaps a racing-style oil pan. These engines are pretty inexpensive, but a thorough understanding of the basic limitations and potentially favorable component

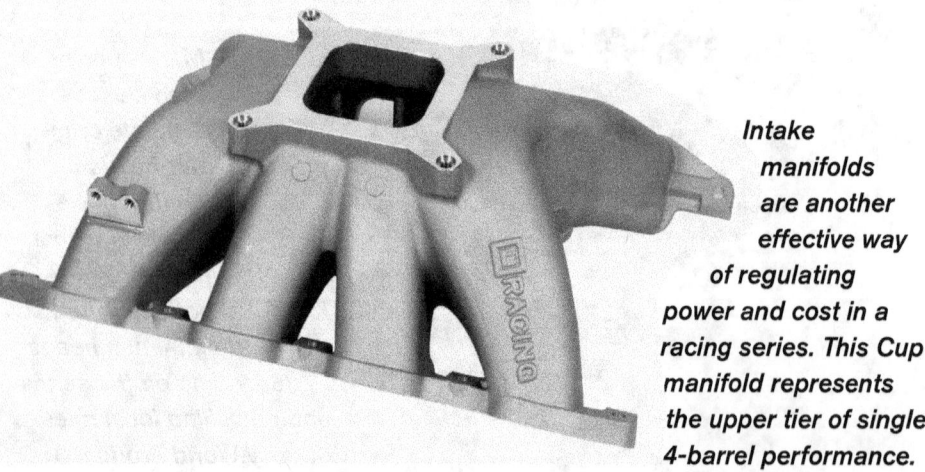

Intake manifolds are another effective way of regulating power and cost in a racing series. This Cup manifold represents the upper tier of single 4-barrel performance.

Flat-tappet cams and maximum valve lift rules are among the most common restrictions in sportsman class racing. These rules are implemented to eliminate expensive roller cams (top) and enable the use of more affordable camshafts and valvetrain hardware.

RACE ENGINE PLANNING

relationships may illuminate previously unconsidered paths to power. Think torque management and positioning within the applicable powerband.

Exhaust Systems

Exhaust systems are usually less restricted. Most often they involve a muffler requirement, stock exhaust manifolds, or possibly a spec header. Builders often consider mixed rocker arm selections optimized to provide appropriate exhaust event timing to aid cylinder blow-down if allowed.

Spec mufflers may be required and testing with backpressure readings can help pinpoint the most beneficial exhaust pipe cross-sectional area, effective primary pipe lengths, and collector sizes if headers are permitted. Modeling this on a PC simulator like PipeMax (see Chapter 14) can pinpoint the best overall dimensions. Simulators are front-loaded with all the mathematical fundamentals of engine performance. They can't always predict absolute power and torque, but they can illuminate trends according to the physics and that amounts to a pretty good road map for serious engine builders.

As long as the requirement is clearly identified in the rules, savvy engine builders always find ways to optimize within those rules. If a spec header is involved and you're not comfortable with discreetly modifying pipe dimensions, consider the possibility of different cam timing in cylinders whose intake and exhaust timing peaks differ due to unequal port or pipe cross-section or length. Like other components, any restriction on the exhaust system should be carefully evaluated for its effect on torque production and positioning and how it affects other parts of the engine package. There are usually ways to refine and assemble a more robust package even within restrictive rules.

Operational Requirements of Competition Engines

- Effective operating range (powerband)
- Minimum and maximum engine speed
- Projected torque and power peaks
- Steady state or endurance operation
- Short-duration high RPM
- Projected loading
- Gearing and shift points
- RPM drop on shifts relative to torque peak
- Track type, length, and shift frequency
- Cooling and oiling concerns
- Induction and exhaust tuning
- Fuel type
- Most prevalent gear used
- Average time in each gear

Spec engines make racing equitable and affordable for many entry- and core-level racers. Costs are reduced and power is equalized to promote closer racing. (Courtesy Automotive Specialists)

Stock-type HEI ignitions are often required in core-level racing series. Internal modifications to otherwise stock units are sometimes permitted. (Courtesy Davis Unified Ignition)

CHAPTER 1

Spec Motors

Many series call for sealed spec motors. Spec engines have their internals specified with no substitutions or modifications permitted. They are assembled and sealed by an independent source to prevent tampering. Racers purchase a complete engine package ready to run. In addition to setting a power limit, these engines stabilize cost because the supplier can build them in volume with fixed or predictable expense. They are surprisingly powerful and typically very close in power production from one engine to another.

Ignition Source

Some classes still impose a limit on ignition systems and require the use of a stock-type high-energy-ignition (HEI) distributor, for example, or a stock coil. Approved aftermarket distributors are accepted in some classes, but may be limited to those that do not require a separate ignition amplifier box. These restrictions are narrowly aimed at cost containment and in that regard they are probably a good thing for many sportsman racers.

Essential Concerns of Competition Engine Building

- Cylinder block type
- Cylinder wall thickness
- Engine bearing speed
- Cylinder bore spacing
- Priority main oiling
- Oil sump style
- Valve angles
- Pushrod or OHC
- Two-valve or four-valve
- Piston speed
- Crankcase breathing
- Engine dimensions
- Engine weight
- Bore/Stroke ratio
- Rod length to stroke ratio
- Distributor type and location
- Firing order
- Block rigidity and hardness
- Cylinder wall finish
- Piston ring seal
- Oil control
- Friction management
- Crankcase pressure management
- Heat management
- Piston area
- Valve area
- Port flow and velocity
- Runner taper
- Valvetrain stability
- Combustion efficiency

Fuels and Fuel Systems

Many organizations require a spec fuel or pump gas and may limit the type of fuel pump and fuel line size. Even these restrictions leave room for interpretation if you consider the burn characteristics of the fuel. This may cause you to re-evaluate cam timing or the ignition curve and even things like float levels, jetting, or air bleeds based on the specific gravity of the fuel, octane tolerance, and burn rate. If you have a spec fuel, request a complete breakdown of its chemical properties to include heat and energy values, burn rate, specific gravity, evaporation characteristics, and anything else you can study.

If you understand the burn characteristics of the fuel you can configure the cylinder head package and fuel strategy to extract maximum available energy. Further consideration should also be given to the size and location of the fuel supply, fuel system components and flow rates, and anticipated dynamic g-loading that may affect fuel flow to the carburetor and even individual fuel molecules suspended in the runners. Fuel is where the power is so it's imperative to learn everything you can about what it can do for you.

RPM Levels

Power and performance are sometimes restricted with an arbitrary engine speed limit. This forces you to fashion a powerband that

Factory-style fuel pumps like this Edelbrock race pump are often specified in lower sportsman classes primarily because they are inexpensive and they stop pumping when the engine quits in a crash.

RACE ENGINE PLANNING

Racing engines are often a collection of calculated compromises based on rules or operational requirements dictated by the engine's specific racing application. (Courtesy Automotive Specialists)

best suits operational requirements within the allowable range of engine speed. You are forced to target torque application according to tire size and gearing as they relate to track surface and length and how tightly the corners restrict vehicle momentum.

This limitation often accompanies a spec engine, which makes the racer's job easier. But non-spec engines may be further limited by compression ratio, airflow, or mechanical specifics such as a dual-plane intake manifold or 2-barrel carburetor. These applications are often trickier to design than unlimited engines. Thoughtful contemplation of all the factors and time spent with a PC engine simulator may help pinpoint selections and adjustments you can control to build the most effective package.

Performance Objectives

From the standpoint of specific goals it's usually instructive to list your operational requirements in terms of what the engine is expected to accomplish and how it is supposed to do it. Some parameters to consider include maximum and minimum engine speed and the dynamic operating range of the application. It's often helpful to examine similar engine packages including other brands with a critical eye.

Identify the things they are doing well and things that don't seem right. A broad range of factors affects the choices, but not everything is applicable to your application. Evaluate how much time the car spends in any particular gear and how that relates to torque and power positioning in the overall RPM range of the engine. Gearing and tire requirements, track type, and length influence the dynamic operating range including such things as RPM drop on shifts and projected engine loading in endurance or high-RPM, high-cycle environments. Each of these may have its own unique cooling and oiling quirks too.

Drag racing has a fixed-length track with varying track conditions including traction and atmospheric variables. A road race car encounters completely different track and environmental conditions at almost every race. These elements may prompt you to evaluate the value of torque versus high-speed power and the RPM where you want the torque and power to apply.

Compiling all the critical factors affecting a particular application helps develop a mature package that is better suited to your needs. Make a list including as much as you can learn about competitors' combinations and what the rules permit. Evaluate individual elements on their own merit and their contribution to the car's performance.

Say, for example, other racers are running headers that are too large for the RPM and exhaust volume being generated in the optimum torque range. If header size is not restricted you may improve performance by running an optimum header size based on torque peak requirements. That's only one example, but advanced engine building requires that you evaluate the contribution and compatibility of every single component, including doing the math that governs how these parts interact and perform (see my book *Performance Automotive Engine Math* for applicable formulas).

As previously stated, numerous factors affect the operational requirements of the engine. The effective operating range incorporates minimum and maximum anticipated engine speed, torque peak and power peak positioning, and functional operating conditions. That might include high engine speeds, sprint or endurance conditions, high cyclic loading, anticipated torque requirements for maximum loading, gearing and shift points, and the RPM drop on each shift.

The importance of torque curve shaping and positioning relative to gear selection in the transmission and final drive is discussed later in the book. This is of course reflective of track type and length, projected racing conditions, and shift frequency. To accommodate these concerns it is critical to match induction and exhaust components for torque optimization. When you really examine it, there are so many interrelated factors affecting competition engine design it can seem overwhelming. That's where careful planning makes the winning difference.

Once you have defined your operational requirements and objectives you can make preliminary judgments about basic engine architecture and the essential concerns that govern all competition engine builds. The following essentials affect parts selection: machine work, prep work, and assembly practices. It's best to make a list up front and revise it often as you develop and groom your package. Work in pencil as you will undoubtedly make frequent revisions.

An alternative is to put the information into a spread sheet so you can change and update it as required. Many of these entries give pause to review and alter previous entries as you cultivate the best possible combination for your racing application. Accordingly, many of the PC engine

Engine Simulation Programs

If you are interested in looking deeper into race engine technology you can take advantage of more sophisticated tools that allow you to actually model and test your engine-building ideas on a home computer. Engine-simulation software for home PCs has been available for more than 20 years, and it has steadily improved. Current programs are quite robust and surprisingly affordable.

Top engine simulators provide a wealth of information based on the accuracy of the information you input prior to running a simulation. They give you unparalleled freedom to design and test endless engine combinations without spending a dime on dyno time.

Advanced computer skills are not required to operate these programs. They are compatible with contemporary 32-bit operating systems up to and including Windows Vista and Windows 7. Most current home computers have the memory and processing speed to run them easily, although some advanced simulations may take a few minutes. If you bought your computer within the last decade you should have no trouble running these simulations. They walk you through all the steps and they provide excellent support and documentation, and in some cases online updates. For the most part, you fill in the blanks with appropriate specs and/or choose components from extensive parts menus. It's very easy and surprisingly instructive (see Source Guide for a basic list).

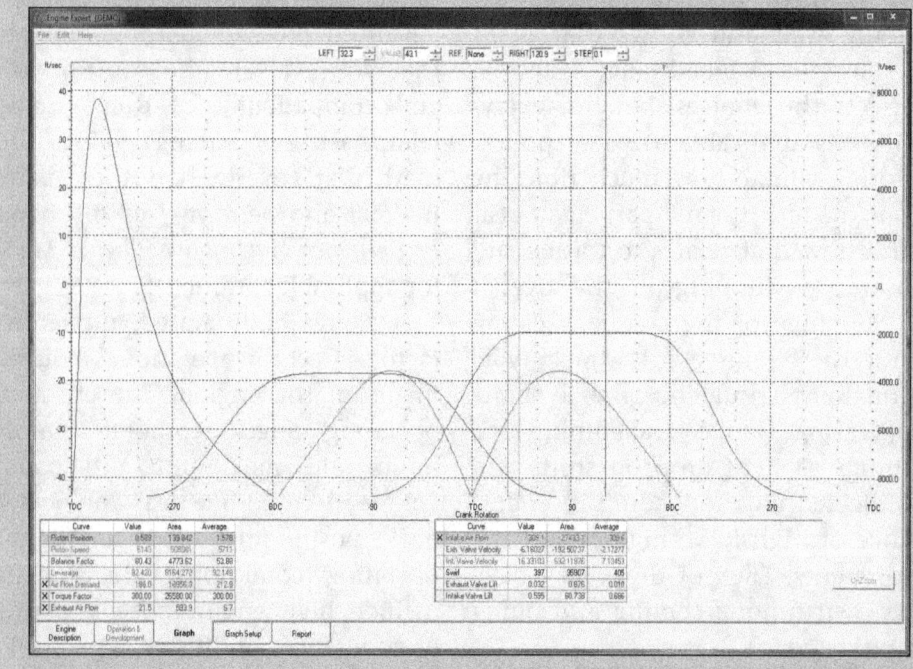

High-end engine simulation software programs such as Audie Technology's Engine Expert provide detailed mathematical analysis of in-cylinder events to help model and test potential engine combinations.

simulation programs help you do a better job of pre-planning and testing engine ideas. (See sidebar, "Engine Simulation Programs" on page 16).

Unlocking Hidden Power

On the assumption that all cylinders fire consistently (see Chapter 13) I now direct our attention to details that foster uneven power production in any grouping of cylinders called an engine. For the purpose of discussion I also assume a V-8 engine, which remains the predominant powerplant used in most domestic racing series. Upon further reflection what you really have is eight individual engines (cylinders) linked by a common crankshaft and cylinder case (block assembly). These engines are all racing toward the finish line in formation.

Your job as an engine builder is to promote a dead heat where every cylinder is a winner despite whatever performance shortcomings individual cylinders may exhibit. None of these engines are perfectly identical and once they are linked as a group, numerous factors conspire to upset the balance of power from one engine (individual cylinder) to the next. In almost every case, some cylinders are hauling ass while others lag behind. Savvy engine builders concentrate on modifications to bring those stragglers up to speed.

More specifically a single cylinder can be tuned for maximum power relative to a given displacement and VE. Since all engines (single cylinder or more) perform best when VE is optimized you can mathematically select an engine speed range where you want maximum torque and horsepower to occur. VE is a function of the total flow path through the engine and thoughtful optimization of flow path components (i.e., shapes and dimensions) promotes maximum output. Proper sizing of inlet and exhaust passages relative to piston position and valve timing are fundamental to these efforts.

For any given displacement there exists an ideal set of flow path dimensions (cross-sectional area and length) that produce maximum torque relative to a particular (desired) engine speed. These dimensions are known to control the ideal mean flow velocity (MFV) that accompanies peak torque production. Adjustments to these dimensions allow you to shape and position (RPM range or powerband) the torque curve for best performance in any given application. It is known to the discipline that an ideal MFV of 240 to 260 ft/sec accompanies peak torque.

Engineers have long recognized that this optimum flow path velocity is affected by cylinder displacement, compression ratio, and valve timing relative to piston position, which is controlled by stroke and rod length (rod/stroke ratio). Mean flow velocity is largely governed by flow path cross section on the inlet and exhaust flow paths. A larger cross section requires more engine speed (RPM) to achieve MFV and position a torque peak. A smaller cross section shifts the torque peak to a lower engine speed. Decades ago, widely noted engine authority Jim McFarland defined a mathematical equation for calculating the ideal cross-sectional area to achieve MFV at any given engine speed.

Flow is discussed in Chapters 9 and 14. For now just recognize the existence of an optimum flow velocity and the critical sizing of flow path dimensions to adjust the location (RPM) of the torque peak within the operational powerband. Optimize these elements in each individual cylinder and you achieve maximum torque production with the ability to adjust its position in the RPM range for maximum efficiency.

Now link that cylinder to another cylinder, or worse yet, seven other cylinders, and you encounter the potential for mass chaos in the system. Inlet flow paths (in most cases) are now linked via a common source (the plenum) and the exhaust paths are linked (in most cases) by a

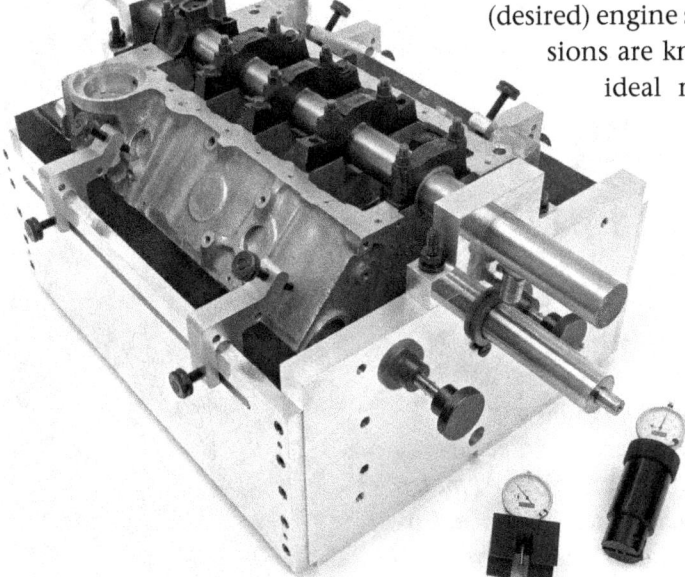

Regardless of the final application or level of rules restriction, precision machine work is always required to ensure optimum component relationships within every engine. (Courtesy BHJ Products)

CHAPTER 1

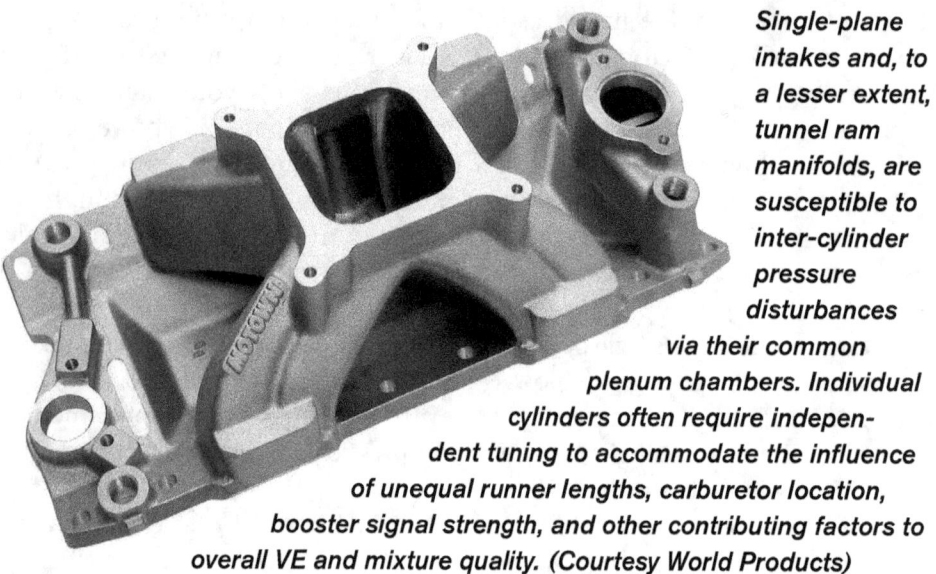

Single-plane intakes and, to a lesser extent, tunnel ram manifolds, are susceptible to inter-cylinder pressure disturbances via their common plenum chambers. Individual cylinders often require independent tuning to accommodate the influence of unequal runner lengths, carburetor location, booster signal strength, and other contributing factors to overall VE and mixture quality. (Courtesy World Products)

collector. While convenient for the purpose of packaging and fuel distribution this arrangement fosters influential dynamic relationships between cylinders to the extent that unequal power production can occur even when components have been properly matched to accommodate appropriate wave tuning.

Powerful wave dynamics and pressure changes communicate between cylinders via the inlet and exhaust flow paths. The consequence is often inconsistent fuel delivery and/or the promotion of poor mixture quality, which leads to inefficient combustion and unequal power delivery governed by the specific dynamics influencing each cylinder. This is often characterized by varying air/fuel ratios between cylinders, unequal exhaust gas temperatures (EGTs), poor combustion efficiency, and the potential for detonation in one or more cylinders.

A single cylinder can be tuned for maximum efficiency by optimizing intake and exhaust flow paths according to displacement and engine speed and by providing complementary ignition and valve event timing. Now contemplate how to tune all eight cylinders for maximum and equal output even as some individual cylinders exert undue influence on their neighbors via pressure "cross talk" within the plenum.

In effect individual cylinders must be tuned separately, which also presents an opportunity to tune specific cylinders for different torque peaks that can effectively broaden an engine's net torque production. In this context, it means that individual cylinders may incorporate differing components such as cam lobe timing, rocker ratios, inlet and exhaust dimensions, and other component variations that become useful tuning elements in concert with normal jetting and timing adjustments.

Exhaust headers designed specifically for an engine's final application are crucial for optimum performance. Primary tube length and diameter, cross-sectional area, and corresponding collector dimensions must all match correctly to ensure superior performance. Do not assume that the primary dimensions should always be the same for every cylinder.

How Cylinders Influence Each Other

Multiple cylinders connected via a common crankshaft and inlet and exhaust systems are influenced by assorted dynamics transferred through the flow paths and mechanical connections that link them together. Crankshaft radial deflection caused by cylinders connected via common crank throws can affect piston motion in companion cylinders. This can lead to incorrect ignition timing in the affected cylinders or even in cylinders at the far end of the crankshaft due to net torsional crank deflection.

Valve event timing is similarly affected by camshaft twist due to high valvespring pressures, which contribute their own net loss to the torque equation. The resulting inconsistent valve events may transfer harmful pressure waves to other cylinders via the common intake plenum. These disturbances can interfere with the

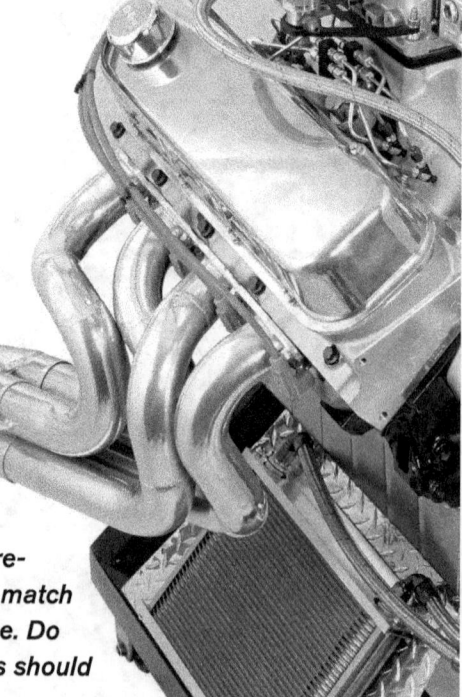

RACE ENGINE PLANNING

Precision adjustments are a fundamental part of the tuning process, but savvy builders also recognize that individual cylinders can be tuned with other methods such as varying lash and rocker ratios.

flow dynamics of adjacent ports in the manifold resulting in inconsistent flow rates and continuous variations in air/fuel ratio from cylinder to cylinder. This can also be affected by residual exhaust gas contamination that may transfer between cylinders during camshaft overlap periods.

Steps to counteract or alleviate these problems are required once they are recognized. Thus it becomes useful to examine the most common problem areas and suggested basic remedies. Each of the primary contributors to VE can be adjusted individually and/or collectively to improve efficiency and overall net torque. These include intake manifold dimensions, cylinder heads, camshaft, rocker arms, exhaust headers, and ignition timing, all of which may be affected by dimensional or mechanical inconsistencies contributed by deflection or distortion in the reciprocating assembly.

For further insight into planning and developing a competitive package see Chapter 2 on governing torque and horsepower and how they interact. You hear a lot about hitting on the right combination, but it really shouldn't be a hit-or-miss proposition. Every component in a race engine must be selected and massaged for optimum compatibility with other parts and the net contribution they all make to producing maximum torque and horsepower in the most useful range for the final application.

You must think critically about each engine component both individually and collectively. In the end, the most successful engines are highly evolved according to very specific component matching and operational requirements that include counteracting or limiting the effects of unwanted mechanical and/or pressure wave influences that upset the balance of power within an engine. The fundamentals of gas exchange control the process, but you can influence the action in many different ways to ensure that each and every individual cylinder contributes appropriately to net torque and power production in the specific engine speed range most suitable for your particular application.

Doing the Math

Mathematical principles define the final output and success of every racing engine. Like it or not, you must cultivate a thorough and near-second-nature understanding of the math that governs the operation of every competition engine. It is important to develop the ability to visualize how the math applies to all of the critical component relationships within the engine and how the sizing and configuration of certain core components defines the shape and positioning of the torque curve and the final power curve of the engine.

Machinists and engine builders are well versed in the dimensional relationships of competition engines and these are crucial to the durability and power output of every engine. It is also important to grasp the fundamentals that govern the dynamics of cylinder filling and emptying and the final combustion process. The mathematics that apply to engine airflow and the optimization of fuel mixture quality have a profound influence on the power curve and how the engine builder shapes it to meet the very specific requirements of various racing applications.

For more information on the mathematical fundamentals of high-performance engines and the basic formulas that apply, See my book *Performance Automotive Engine Math*.

CHAPTER 2

TORQUE AND HORSEPOWER

Competition engines are built and designed to make maximum torque and horsepower, but what exactly does that mean? Torque is the heart of the matter. Defined as a twisting force it represents the potential to perform work. Engine torque is the force potential or turning moment applied to the crankshaft flange or flywheel when combustion pressure is transferred to the crank throws via the connecting rods. When the flywheel turns, torque is measurable by the resistance to rotation. Once the flywheel is turning, torque is applied over a period of time and horsepower can be calculated, horsepower thus being a dependent variable of torque.

$$HP = \frac{\text{torque} \times \text{RPM}}{5{,}252}$$

Torque is the actual measure of an engine's ability to do work. Horsepower is the rate at which the work is performed. Torque accelerates the mass of a race car; horsepower is the function of torque that supports speed by maintaining the application of torque over time. Engine builders recognize the ability of good engines to produce torque rapidly over a specified range of engine speed (RPM). They call it "transient torque," or the rate at which a loaded engine can accelerate through a given range of engine speed. The greater the transient torque the faster the engine is able to accelerate under load.

All engines generate a torque curve, which peaks at some point in the RPM range. This peak represents the most efficient point in the engine's operating range and is closely aligned with the VE curve. Available tuning techniques enable us to position the peak at the most favorable spot in the powerband and to reshape the curve around it for maximum performance benefit.

All engines generate a torque signature based on displacement, engine speed, VE, and flow path dynamics, and not surprisingly, influenced by specific architecture, i.e., I-4, I-6, V-6, V-8, V-10, V-12, etc., each of which applies different attributes to cylinder filling, mean net torque, and overall engine smoothness. Every combination generates a torque peak or "sweet spot" where its particular tuning dynamics achieve maximum VE. In the case of competition engines, this often exceeds 100-percent VE, sometimes by a considerable margin. The old adage that an engine is an air pump is assuredly true, but also think of it as an air processor. Power is

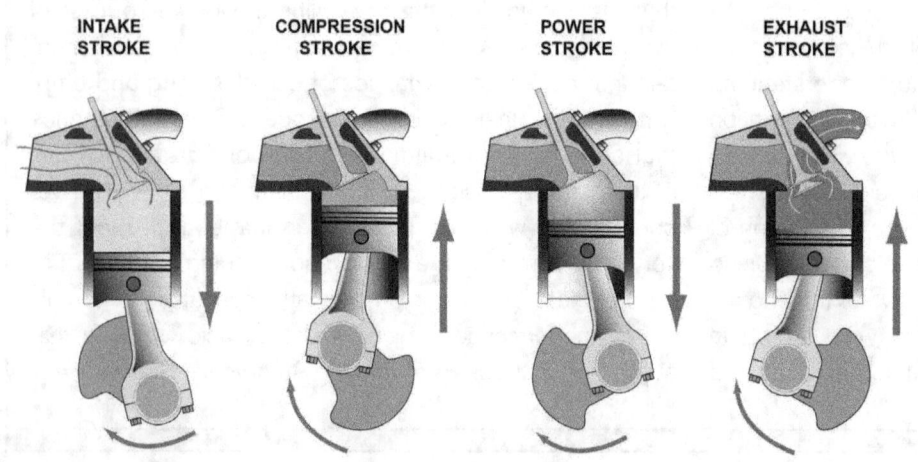

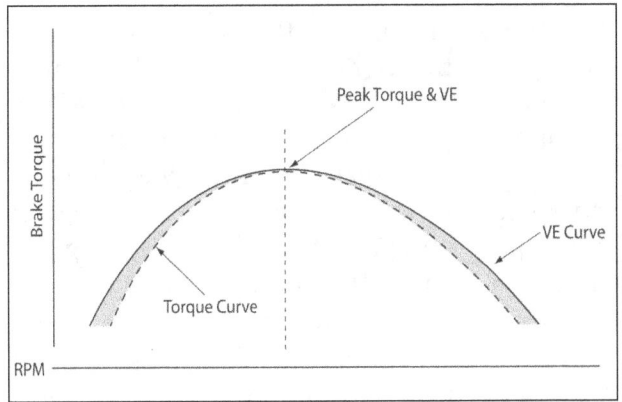

Note how the torque curve trails the VE curve below and above the torque peak due to flow issues and poor mixture quality at lower engine speeds while there is insufficient cylinder filling time above the torque peak due to increased engine speed.

governed by the amount of air and fuel the engine can process over time and the brake specific fuel consumption (BSFC) generated by the efficiency of the specific component mix. It's relatively easy to supply enough fuel, but it is considerably more difficult to maximize airflow without the aid of a power adder.

For any given collection of parts, an engine achieves a torque peak influenced predominantly by intake and exhaust tuning relative to its size or displacement and engine speed. Through attentive manipulation of these and contributing component hardware the torque curve can be shaped and positioned to suit the engine's final application. This is a principal focus of all competent engine builders and it begins with the pursuit of VE relative to the engine's static air capacity. The air mass component depends largely on available air density and the VE a specific component mix is capable of generating. VE is primarily governed by inlet and exhaust flow path dynamics, combustion chamber efficiency, valve timing, and elements of the bottom end and valvetrain, which dictate final RPM capability.

The shape of the torque curve closely mimics the VE curve at peak torque. This is the point of maximum engine efficiency and it typically reflects the lowest WOT brake specific fuel consumption numbers. Below the peak torque trails the VE curve due to reduced combustion efficiency caused by inadequate intake flow velocity, air/fuel separation issues, and poor mixture quality. Above the torque peak, torque and VE decline due to insufficient time for cylinder filling caused by rising engine speed (RPM).

There are methods to address the VE inefficiency on either side of the torque peak and inflate the overall torque curve. This refers to the "area under the curve" and seeks to expand the torque curve in all directions. Horsepower, being a function of torque, follows faithfully. More importantly, a broader torque curve often produces greater acceleration even with a slight reduction in peak torque because it applies more torque over a broader range. If the ideal mix of engine components targets an engine speed range most beneficial to the application, superior performance is the result.

Complementing these performance gains with appropriately matched gearing and tire combinations ultimately leads to faster cars and better racing, all based on the effective production and utilization of torque. This works well even for engines operating well above the torque peak because the upper end of the torque curve expands accordingly, thus contributing more horsepower to the car's performance.

Single 4-barrel Cup engines rank among the most powerful carbureted engines because every component is carefully optimized to complement the operational requirements of the application.

Volumetric Efficiency

The cornerstone of power building is volumetric efficiency. The more air an engine is able to process, the greater its power potential. VE is determined according to an engine's static air capacity or displacement. A displacement of 400 ci represents 100-percent air capacity for an engine of that size. At any given engine speed a percentage of that volume is being processed into torque depending on a host of variables that conspire to limit airflow. Without these pesky restrictions atmospheric pressure can easily fill the cylinders 100 percent every two crankshaft revolutions.

In practice this is difficult to achieve because airflow is restricted by a throttling device (carburetor, throttle body, or other), imperfect intake manifolding, intake ports, valves, and all the attending flow restrictions and pressure dynamics present in a running engine. Hence, VE in a production engine rarely exceeds 80 to 85 percent.

As previously mentioned, VE is reduced below the torque peak due mainly to insufficient airflow and poor mixture quality. Above the torque peak, VE is limited by inadequate time to fill the cylinder due to RPM. One of the engine builder's primary goals is to exceed the static air capacity of the engine and optimize combustion efficiency once fuel is introduced to the process. Savvy engine builders skillfully manipulate the component composition to accomplish this by broadening the torque curve and positioning it to best suit the intended application.

In specifying components to meet VE requirements you target intake ports, dimensional qualities of intake manifolds and exhaust headers, carburetor size, rod-to-stroke ratios, valve timing, and static compression ratio. The specific component matrix is adjusted to suit the application's operational requirements. Oval track and road racing engines typically call for a component mix producing a broad torque curve over a wide range of RPM. This affords the engine builder an opportunity to tune the intake and exhaust systems separately to effectively broaden the powerband. Conversely, drag racing applications seek a higher and narrower powerband in which intake and exhaust tuning are more closely aligned.

Identifying and targeting the required powerband is one of the engine builder's first steps. Since VE and engine speed are closely aligned it is critical to target VE modifications to the desired engine speed. If a drag racing engine leaves the starting line at 7,000 rpm and cycles between there and 9,000 rpm through the gears, its VE at 5,000 rpm is largely irrelevant. And of course an engine delivering power between 4,500 and 7,200 rpm needs broader tuning efficiency from its parts combination. Hence, airflow management within the targeted engine speed range becomes a central challenge in matching or exceeding an engine's potential VE capacity.

Understanding BSFC

Combustion efficiency is typically indicated by brake specific fuel consumption or BSFC. This expresses fuel usage in pounds per horsepower hour. Brake specific fuel consumption is frequently misunderstood. Many people mistakenly believe that it is an indicator of rich or lean fuel mixtures, but it is actually a measure of efficiency that indicates how well the engine uses the fuel it burns. More specifically, it is the rate in pounds of fuel per horsepower per hour that a given engine consumes to make power. There is a range of optimum efficiency for most engines, and BSFC defines that range.

As you may have already surmised, the term "brake" precedes it because BSFC is usually measured with an engine running on a dyno. BSFC figures are typically quoted for WOT conditions, but it is also a measurable quantity that relates to fuel economy at part-throttle operation. In the performance world, it is used to judge the efficiency contribution of various engine combinations and to predict certain requirements such as fuel injector flow rate.

A particular cylinder head may make more power with less fuel, and that's an indicator of higher efficiency, most likely due to improved

Many of the most powerful racing engines are still equipped with carburetors because carbs are surprisingly efficient in applications with narrow powerbands that do not require frequent throttle changes over a broad RPM range.

> ### Brake Specific Fuel Consumption
>
> BSFC = observed HP ÷ observed fuel flow in pounds/hour
> or
> Mass Fuel Flow = BSFC x anticipated HP
>
> The following BSFC figures are typical of most modern performance and racing engines:
>
> | | |
> |---|---|
> | .48 to .55 | Stock and medium performance engines |
> | .45 to .50 | Performance engines with good heads |
> | .38 to .45 | Most racing engines |
> | .35 to .38 | Pro/Stock-style engines |
> | .55 to .65 | Supercharged or turbocharged engines |

cylinder filling and a more efficient combustion chamber that extracts more energy from a given fuel mass. Guidelines for evaluating BSFC are well established and are frequently used to predict engine performance. One-half pound of fuel per horsepower per hour (.50 BSFC) is the default norm for most calculations.

Herein lies part of the problem with thinking of BSFC numbers as indicators of mixture ratios. At .37 BSFC a Pro/Stock engine may be thought to be running too lean when, in fact, it is operating at the highest level of efficiency. In contrast, supercharged engines run richer mixtures to complement boost pressure and discourage detonation. They absolutely run richer; not because they are inefficient, but to complement specific combustion characteristics inherent to boosted applications, not the least of which is charge cooling and the need for more fuel to augment the greater volume of air being supplied by the supercharging device.

When evaluating BSFC numbers, lower is almost always better (even when supercharged) where a .60 is still more efficient than a .65, as long as the combination supports safe combustion without detonation or overheating. However, any engine still needs to run at the air/fuel ratio that produces best power. That's usually about 13:1 in naturally aspirated engines and 11:6 to 12:1 in supercharged applications. You can't just run an engine lean and expect to get a low BSFC number.

Tune for maximum torque and let the BSFC indicate how efficiently you generate that torque. At an indicated BSFC of .50 an engine burns .5 pounds of fuel per horsepower per hour (lb/hr). If the engine makes 500 hp, that's 250 lbs/hr. If you're building racing engines, your BSFC should be way better, something on the order of .38 to .42.

Where Power Comes From

Extremely powerful racing engines generally require a short stroke and large bore to provide adequate breathing capability at high RPM and to ensure durability in a high-load, high-RPM environment. The engine's breathing potential increases with the square of the bore diameter, due to the corresponding increase in applicable valve size and port area. Greater piston area is also available to multiply combustion pressure.

This is a well-recognized path to power, but there are caveats. Larger bores present more piston area, requiring more time for the flame to make its way across the combustion space, and presenting more cooling surface area, which tends to absorb and reduce combustion temperatures and produce less cylinder pressure. Therefore, increased compression ratios are typically necessary to boost flame speed and maintain desirable combustion temperatures and pressure. Much smaller combustion spaces and/or chambers and steeper valve angles are often specified for this reason.

Large bore diameters and piston domes (where applicable) often wreak havoc with valve-to-piston clearance, particularly when running a narrow lobe center cam. Nonetheless, large-bore, short-stroke combinations with longer rods are mostly favored among professional engine builders who also agree that real power comes from the cylinder heads, intake manifold, and camshaft—all of which are air-processing components closely tied to airflow and thus VE. In a broad sense, total trapped air mass relative to displacement times RPM equals power. It's why a big engine makes more torque at lower engine speeds while a smaller engine has to rev higher to make the same torque (more power strokes per unit of time).

Once we acknowledge the importance of these components relative to airflow requirements we are then obliged to contemplate their companion role in the pre-combustion

CHAPTER 2

In any naturally aspirated application, cylinder heads are the primary key to power production. Complementary intake and exhaust flow paths are required to extract the most power from any given cylinder head, but in general, the better the head, the more power is made.

Forced-induction engines are a different story. Most of the fundamentals of torque and power production still apply, albeit with appropriate attention to the elementary rules of gas exchange in a boosted environment. With appropriate tuning, the results are usually spectacular.

mixture conditioning that ultimately produces maximum cylinder pressure (mean effective pressure, or MEP). This role is typically more sensitive in wet flow systems (carbureted or TBI) where fuel is introduced upstream of the intake valve as opposed to dry systems or port fuel injection systems where fuel is sprayed directly at the valve and is less adversely influenced by individual or collective flow path deficiencies. All multi-cylinder engines make a different amount of power in each cylinder, largely due to differences in airflow and fuel mixture quality. Port injection solves a multitude of mixture quality problems, justifying its wide deployment on production vehicles to improve economy, emissions, and power.

In the future, direct injection systems may replace port injection for even greater efficiency. While the tide is slowly turning in many circles, most racing applications still employ wet flow intake systems and their inadequacies must be addressed in any racing or high-performance application.

These basic issues apply to unlimited racing engines as well as average Saturday night bracket racers running single 4-barrel carburetors. If you ask knowledgeable engine builders and tuners, electronic fuel injection (EFI) has its place, particularly on engines with a broad operating range and frequent throttle activity, but for full-time WOT racing, it's often hard to beat a well-sorted carburetor.

What Influences Power?

The importance of shaping and positioning the powerband to match the intended racing application cannot be overstated. Assuming appropriate fuel mixture quality (octane, droplet size, burn rate, and energy content) power is typically produced and (in many cases) limited by various attending factors including but not limited to the following.

- Inlet and Exhaust Tuning
- Airflow and Cylinder Filling (VE)
- Mixture Quality
- Fuel Separation
- Quench and Turbulence
- Combustion Efficiency/Burn Rate
- Valve Timing (Intake Closing Event)
- Spark Timing
- Compression Ratio
- Pumping Losses (Negative Torque)
- Frictional Losses

These are mostly tuning and air/fuel processing components independent of, and yet co-conspirators with, standard competition engine building concerns such as piston configuration, ring seal, valvetrain geometry, bearing clearances, block material, and other factors that comprise a typical engine build.

CHAPTER 3

CYLINDER BLOCKS

Cylinder block selection is mostly application specific and is often limited by racing series rules. The requirements of your specific application may influence your choices based on block material, bore spacing, main cap material and configuration, cam location, and machinability. Selection might be limited to a two-bolt main stock production block or it may be unlimited depending on your particular competition environment. Whatever the case, it is useful to establish a starting point by identifying what your competitors are using and rating it based on positive and negative attributes relative to the necessities of torque and powerband placement.

You can build surprisingly good power in a production block, but how much is left on the table and how long it will live is another story. Much of what is discussed here revolves around block selection and preparation and why a machinist performs certain procedures. Many good engine builders do not perform their own machine work and therefore depend heavily on the competency of their chosen machinist. However, you should fully understand the machining procedures they require and how to check the machinist's work during preliminary mock-up assemblies.

You need a dial bore gauge for checking piston fitment along with main and rod journal housing bore diameters prior to checking bearing clearances. You also need a precision straightedge for checking deck surfaces and main bore alignment and a host of other measuring tools necessary to the task. You can take the machinist's word for some things unless you have your own precision equipment. This might include lifter bore indexing, cam and crank centerline parallelism, bore finish, and so

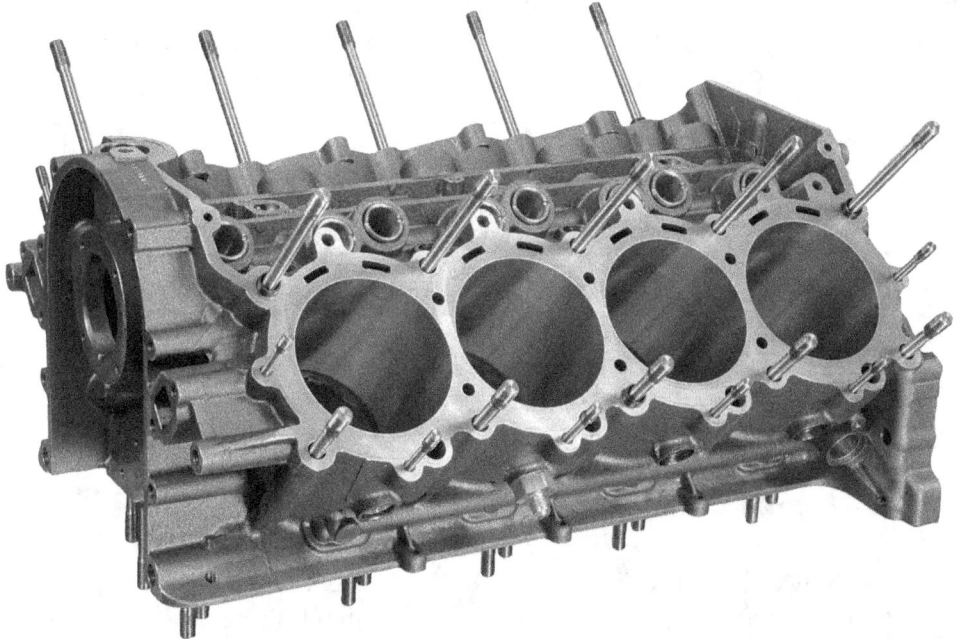

Chevrolet Sprint Cup R07 block. (Courtesy General Motors)

COMPETITION ENGINE BUILDING: ADVANCED ENGINE DESIGN & ASSEMBLY TECHNIQUES 25

CHAPTER 3

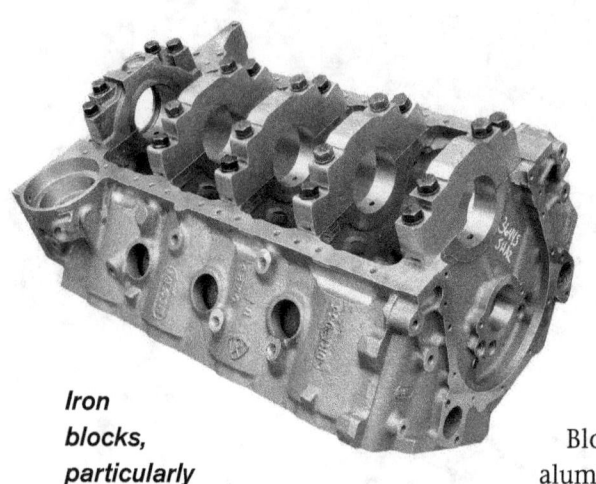

Iron blocks, particularly those manufactured with harder CGI remain the primary choice for most high-end competition engine builds.

on. You can be a top-notch engine builder without being a machinist, but it definitely requires a good working relationship with a competent machinist you can place your trust in.

Grooming the Short Block

People say there's not much power to be gained in the short block. If that's true, then why spend so much time massaging the block and prepping all the internals? If the engine is essentially a fuel and air processing device, it is clear that the camshaft, induction system, cylinder heads, and exhaust system pretty much dictate power levels and where torque is positioned in the engine's effective operating range. Think of the short block as the delivery device that contains, harnesses, and transmits power to the drivetrain.

As such it is subject to all the abuse the cylinder heads and companion power producers can dish out. It has to be tough to take the punishment. When properly prepared, it can effectively enhance power production by minimizing friction and ensuring the precise operation of all the contributing components. A well-prepared short block is every bit a player as every other component in your engine's power arsenal. The first place to start is with a well-prepared cylinder block.

Block Type

Block material is limited to iron or aluminum alloy, but there are many other factors to consider. If weight is not critical, many builders still favor iron blocks for their superior dimensional stability. The gap has narrowed in recent years as OEM production science has influenced block design and aftermarket manufacturers have eliminated most of the problems previously associated with aluminum cylinder blocks. Current aluminum blocks are far more dimensionally stable than their predecessors and are no longer considered a detriment to maximum power production.

The remaining drawback is cost. Aluminum blocks are significantly more expensive and they are often passed over unless weight is critical. This applies to overall engine and vehicle weight as well as the specific placement of mass in the chassis relative to handling and vehicle dynamics. The initial criterion for cylinder block selection incorporates most of the features of dedicated race blocks. Some things to consider include the following.

Bore Size and Bore Spacing

Bore size is a primary factor for any competition engine build because it dictates valve size and ultimately the breathing capability of the engine. Recall the primary goal of maximizing VE. Builders often favor the largest available bore consistent with the target displacement and attending factors such as bore spacing (the fixed distance between cylinder centerlines) and stroke length. Along with cylinder wall thickness, bore spacing is the limiting factor in determining maximum available bore size.

Most builders feel that the breathing gains from a larger bore outweigh any friction penalties that accrue from larger pistons with more skirt surface and potentially increased ring drag. A bigger bore

---

Cylinder Block Selection Criteria

- Bore size and bore spacing
- Main cap material
- Number of cap fasteners
- Cylinder wall thickness
- Deck thickness
- Camshaft position
- Material and machinability
- Priority main oiling
- Oil restrictor
- Siamesed cylinders
- Main bore size
- Main web structure

- Bay-to-bay breathing
- Blind bolt holes
- Fuel pump boss
- Rear main seal type
- Cylinder sleeves
- Lifter bore positioning
- Cooling jacket design
- Motor mount pads
- Oil filter
- Starter mount
- Clutch linkage boss
- Weight

also provides more piston area for combustion pressure to work against, but it also creates a greater distance for the flame front to travel and more surface area to cool the flame.

Cost also becomes a factor since a change in bore spacing to increase bore size requires a dimensionally compatible crankshaft, cylinder heads with properly spaced combustion chambers, and complementary intake manifold, camshaft, and exhaust headers.

Main Cap Material

Main cap choices include iron or billet steel in either two-bolt or four-bolt versions. Two-bolt blocks are generally avoided unless class rules require them, but many sportsman classes use them successfully, particularly when the main bolts are replaced with studs. The decisive factor is the size and limited strength of the two-bolt iron caps versus the higher cylinder pressures and elevated engine speeds associated with many contemporary sportsman classes. As a rule, only use a two-bolt production block if the prevailing rules require it. Four-bolt blocks with iron main caps are preferred for general competition. Most of them handle 500 to 600 hp without distress and their durability is typi-

Most dedicated race blocks are equipped with splayed four-bolt caps made from billet material such as 1020 or 1045 steel alloy. The splayed bolt arrangement anchors the outer bolts into the beefiest part of the main webs. Lower-tier four-bolt blocks typically have main caps manufactured from ductile iron.

cally acceptable except perhaps in supercharged or nitrous applications with ultra-high cylinder pressures or extreme engine speed.

These power levels can easily be exceeded, but you run the risk of reduced durability, particularly in applications that require extended operation. With the exception of moderate performance applications, main cap studs are preferred over bolts. Studs provide superior clamping force and they help spread the load more effectively, particularly in four-bolt applications where the outer bolts are splayed outward to transmit loading across more of the main web structure. Dedicated race blocks usually employ four-bolt caps on all five main bearings as opposed to the center three found

Aluminum blocks have enjoyed considerable favor in the recent decade thanks in part to the influence of high-performance and race-prepped factory-style blocks based on contemporary production engines.

Dart Big M Chevy blocks come with either ductile iron four-bolt caps (Sportsman version) or billet steel four-bolt main caps. Main cap bolts are suitable for most applications but are often replaced with optional studs.

on most production blocks. If a two-bolt block is your only choice, stud kits are available, and billet steel main cap conversion kits are available to refit the block if the prevailing rules permit it.

Maximum-performance efforts anticipating high cylinder pressures, extreme engine speed, and high cyclic loading should always use fully machined 1045 billet steel, splayed main caps, and studs. Where possible they should be pinned with ring dowels to maintain accurate positioning and prevent main cap movement under high loads. This is a durability issue that can also affect power. If the main caps are moving, bearing clearances and crankshaft stability are affected. In extreme circumstances the crankshaft may

CHAPTER 3

This Dart block's thicker cylinder walls stabilize the cylinders and promote superior ring seal under high cylinder pressures and elevated engine speed.

deflect enough to bite a bearing with potentially disastrous results.

This can also introduce additional instability into precise crank and rod relationships, which affect piston stability and ultimately ring seal. Crankshafts are subjected to extreme forces that can easily disrupt this chain of precision relationships. For maximum efficiency the cylinder block must contain the crank in a dimensionally stable platform that maintains all critical component relationships under all operating conditions, including standing up to the hammering effects of detonation and thrust loading on gear changes.

Cylinder Wall Thickness

High RPM and extreme cylinder pressure impart staggering loads to the cylinder walls, particularly on the thrust surfaces. Uniform cylinder walls of appropriate thickness are critical to the dimensional stability of cylinder bores. Dedicated race cylinder blocks like those produced by Dart and World Products are manufactured to incorporate the necessary cylinder wall thickness and appropriate heat transfer to the cooling system. Most other blocks should be sonic tested to determine cylinder wall thickness (see "Sonic Checking" below), except perhaps for OEM race program blocks that already come with a sonic check sheet.

Production blocks must be thoroughly checked for adequate wall thickness. This is particularly important on late-model blocks that incorporate modern thin-wall castings. While a hot street/strip engine is normally okay with a minimum of .125-inch wall thickness, most sportsman racing classes should not accept anything less than .140 inch. Dedicated race blocks offer .250 inch or more and are usually accompanied by a manufacturer's sonic check sheet so the builder gets an accurate picture of the cylinder block's dimensional character.

Sonic Checking

Sonic checking is an ultrasonic procedure employed to verify a block's cylinder wall thickness. While most factory and aftermarket race blocks now come with a factory sonic check sheet, many builders prefer to verify the sheet and in the case of previously bored blocks it is wise to determine the thickness of the cylinder walls. Most race

Aftermarket Sportsman cylinder blocks like this Dart SHP block incorporate many of the most desirable features of more expensive full-race blocks. These blocks are an excellent choice for many budget-conscious racers seeking affordable alternatives for their racing efforts.

blocks now provide cylinders with at least .250- to .300-inch wall thickness and it is important to maintain as much of that as possible. Sonic checking is not a lengthy process and most shops regularly have their own sheets to record the numbers. The sonic checker device comes with calibration standards that are used to calibrate the system prior to use. They have a known thickness and are made in a curved shape to simulate the cylinder bores.

Some builders break up old blocks and keep some curved sections

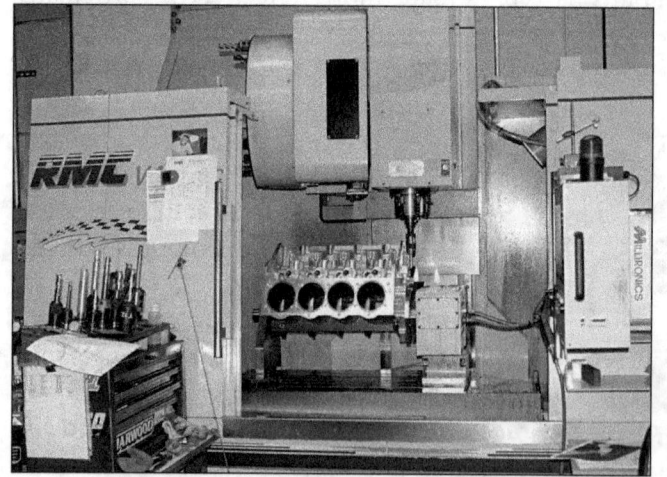

Modern race blocks are prepped on CNC machining centers like this at Dart Machinery. Modern casting techniques and CNC precision have made high-quality race blocks easily available to all racers.

---

28   COMPETITION ENGINE BUILDING: ADVANCED ENGINE DESIGN & ASSEMBLY TECHNIQUES

CYLINDER BLOCKS

General Characteristics of Cylinder Blocks

Characteristic	Race	Production	Characteristic	Race	Production
Gray iron castings	some	x	Beefier construction	x	
Compacted Graphite Iron (CGI)	x		Weight heavier		
Aluminum with liners	x	x	Fuel pump boss	some	x
Two-bolt mains	x		Oil filter pad	x	x
Four-bolt mains	x	x	Bushed lifter bores	x	
Splayed bolt main caps	x		Reinforced lifter bores	x	
Machined billet steel main caps	x		Liners or sleeves	some	some
Machined main webs	x	some	Blind head bolt holes	x	some
Dowel pin locators	x	some	Pin oilers	some	
Priority main oiling	x		Clearance for stroker cranks	some	
Raised cam bores	x		Main bore size selection	x	some
Larger cam bores available	most		Factory motor mount bosses	x	x
Isolated cam tunnel	some		Dry sump capable	x	x
Thicker cylinder walls	x	some	Dry sump only	x	
Thicker deck surfaces	x		Dual starter pads	x	
Siamesed cylinders	x	x	Revised coolant passages	x	
Accepts roller cam bearings	x		Threaded core plugs	x	

of cylinder walls to use as real-world calibration samples that can be easily measured for comparison. Once a unit is calibrated, gel is applied to the sensor and the sensor is held firmly against the cylinder wall at specified locations depending on the type of block.

Most builders prefer to check the cylinders at four equally spaced locations starting with the primary thrust surface and working their way around the bore 90 degrees at a time about 1½ to 2 inches down from the deck surface. Once these numbers are recorded, builders repeat the process roughly halfway down the bore. Some even record numbers at the bottom of the bore. When the process is complete the builder and/or machinist has an accurate roadmap of the block's cylinder wall thicknesses.

The primary or major thrust side is located opposite to the rotation of the engine. For clockwise rotation, stand in front of the engine and face toward it. The major thrust surface is the left side of each bank of cylinders (toward the passenger-side of the block for every cylinder). That's where the thickest readings should be—typically .300 inch or better, but no less than .250 inch. The minor thrust side is the opposite wall (the right side of all the cylinders as you face the front of the block).

If you have counter-clockwise rotation, or as in some cases are building a reverse-rotation engine,

NDT Systems is a major provider of sonic-checking equipment for automotive cylinder blocks. The units are easy to use and they provide very accurate results. (Courtesy NDT Systems, Inc.)

Sonic testing a race block's cylinder wall thickness at multiple points within each cylinder bore is the only accurate way to verify adequate cylinder wall thickness for any competition engine build. Here the engine builder is holding the sensor firmly against the cylinder wall to ensure an accurate reading. (Courtesy NDT Systems, Inc.)

the major thrust surfaces all shift to the opposite side. Non-thrust surfaces opposite the wrist pin axis in each bore (front and back side of each bore) are typically the thinnest and some builders accept walls as thin as .100 inch in this area. Obviously, the most thickness possible on the thrust side of the bores is best, but lateral thickness is also important to maintaining the structural stiffness of the cylinder block. A sub-standard wall for any lower-level sportsman class is anything under .140 inch. For most high-end stuff a minimum of about .180 to .200 inch is desired.

You may also discover, for example, that all the bores on one bank are thinner at the front, a problem most likely attributable to core shift during manufacturing. If the shift is not too severe, builders sometimes correct it by offset-boring that bank to shift all of the cylinders toward the thicker walls. Depending on the bore size and the degree of shift this often means an offset of .0005 to .012 inch, which helps save the block and doesn't significantly impact the cylinder bore to cylinder head/chamber relationship. Don't forget that you need to leave some room on the thin side for honing.

Small-bore shifts like this are not uncommon in racing circles and there is little or no impact on the rod-to-pin alignment in the piston. It's often said that the short block doesn't contribute much to the horsepower process, but high cylinder pressure with the cam and intake system won't do much good if the rings can't seal the cylinder.

Ring seal, strength, and durability are primary concerns when mapping cylinder wall thickness. Good ring seal can't be achieved if the cylinders are flexing under pressure, and at some point the cylinders will go out of round, crack, or simply collapse. Block-fill and grouting are often added to the water jackets to beef up the lower half of the cylinders, but this is a temporary fix and it doesn't particularly apply to most engines that need full-time coolant flow through the complete water jacket. Block-fill and grouting on drag-only applications are okay for the most part.

Deck Thickness

Race blocks and some production blocks have thicker deck surfaces to help stabilize the top of the cylinder bores. If rules permit, this type of block is desirable because it optimizes and retains the benefits of precision torque plate and hot honing techniques. Thick deck surfaces also promote more consistent head gasket sealing and they typically incorporate blind head bolt holes in reinforced bosses. This eliminates

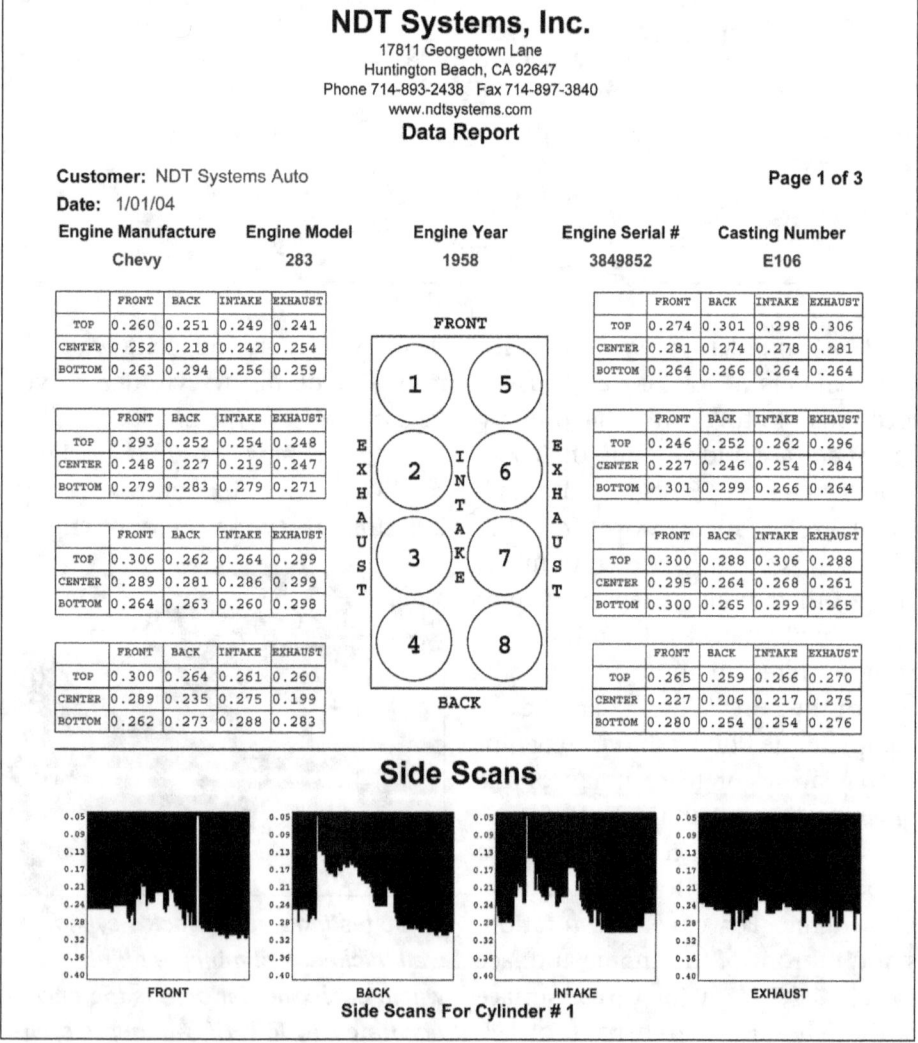

This NDT Systems cylinder data report for a 1958 283-ci Chevy V-8 illustrates the measured cylinder wall thickness data for the front, back, and major and minor thrust sides of all the cylinder walls. For this particular engine the major thrust surfaces are on the exhaust side for cylinders 5-6-7-8 and the intake side for cylinders 1-2-3-4. (Courtesy NDT Systems, Inc.)

CYLINDER BLOCKS

Thicker deck surfaces add considerable support to the top of the block, contributing stability to the cylinders while minimizing bore distortion and providing a superior gasket sealing surface. (Courtesy Dart)

This view through the open core plug on the side of this Dart SHP block reveals the solid structure between the siamesed cylinders. The siamesed structure stabilizes adjacent cylinders and provides superior rigidity.

BHJ's Cam-Crank Center Distance Gauge uses a large micrometer and precision machined cam and crank bore mandrels to verify the camshaft height dimension in relation to the crankshaft.

corrosion and leakage by keeping the head bolts or studs securely anchored in a more stable platform separated from the cooling jacket. It also prevents localized cracking around head bolt holes that otherwise have no solid foundation.

Siamesed Cylinders

A common practice in large-bore blocks that don't enjoy the luxury of wider bore spacing, siamesed cylinders incorporate an area of solid material between the cylinder bores that is normally open to water circulation. Siamesed cylinder blocks are currently used in many high-performance and racing applications. The siamesed structure further stabilizes the cylinder bores while providing desirable cylinder wall thickness. With proper preparation siamesed blocks are suitable for most competition environments.

Camshaft Position

Consistent with series rules, engine builders often favor large-diameter raised camshaft bores. A typical block of this configuration has the cam raised from its production centerline and the cam bores machined to accept larger 50-mm camshaft journals. This practice permits a larger, stiffer camshaft that is resistant to distortion from high valvespring pressures. It also encourages more aggressive camshaft profiles and shorter, stiffer pushrods to combat flexing at high RPM. Race blocks are also available with standard cam centerlines, but with additional material added so larger cam bores can be used with the standard cam height.

Material and Machinability

Production blocks are cast from standard gray iron, which has long proved to be reliable for passenger car and truck blocks. It is cost efficient because it is easier to manufacture and machine. Most desirable race blocks are now cast with compacted graphite iron (CGI) offering 50 to 75 percent more tensile strength than common gray iron. It has better thermal conductivity, superior high-temperature fatigue properties, and maintains dimensional integrity better than gray iron at the expense of being more difficult to machine.

The harder material tends to wear tooling and break taps more easily. It

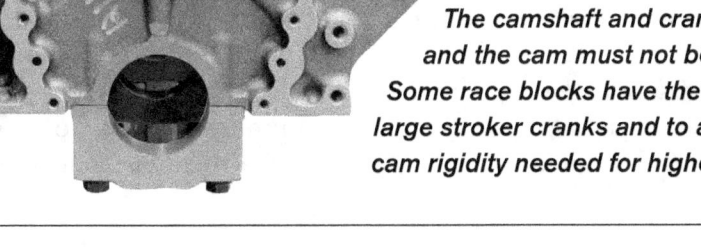

The camshaft and crankshaft centerline must be parallel with each other and the cam must not be skewed left or right from the crankshaft axis. Some race blocks have the cam height raised to provide more clearance for large stroker cranks and to allow for larger base circle cams, which add the cam rigidity needed for higher valvespring pressures.

CHAPTER 3

Top engine shops like Automotive Specialists leave no stone unturned to ensure maximum power and durability for engine customers. Here a MetaLax vibratory table from Bonal Industries is used to vibrate engine components outside their natural frequency to remove stress. (Courtesy Automotive Specialists)

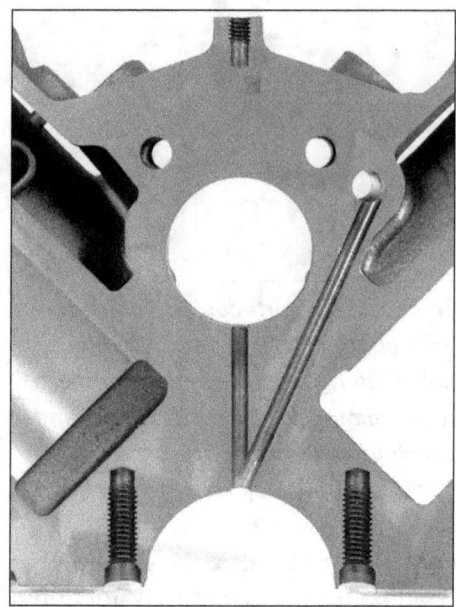

Priority main oiling routes oil from the main oil gallery straight to the main bearings and then the camshaft as shown on this Dart small-block. The camshaft and valvetrain are fed by the secondary vertical passage from the upper main bearing.

is also more sensitive to honing technique, but overall strength, stability, and superior finished qualities generally outweigh most machining issues for most serious engine builders.

CGI also offers weight-saving properties that allow block manufacturers to add material where necessary to provide optimum strength without incurring the increased weight penalty associated with strengthening efforts applied to common iron blocks.

Heat Treating and Stress Relieving

With the new generation of race-ready blocks, heat treating and stress relieving are often performed by the block manufacturer. Racers used to prefer used cylinder blocks that had already taken a set or the storied old block out behind the shop that was slowly being seasoned for future competition use. New factory race blocks or blocks from primary aftermarket suppliers like Dart Machinery and World Products have received proper treatment. The general procedure for stress relieving an iron block is to heat it to approximately 1,000 degrees F for several hours and then slowly cool it by a couple hundred degrees every hour until it returns to room temperature.

Cryogenic Treatment: While not as widespread, cryogenic treatments have gained popularity over the past decade. A cryogenic treatment is an additional stress-relieving process also that improves a block's wear characteristics. Because it is a follow-on treatment after traditional heat treating, it's an additional expense that some builders feel is unnecessary and some customers aren't willing to support. The cryogenic process is a deep cooling where the part is chilled to near absolute zero (-360 degrees F) for 24 to 36 hours using liquid nitrogen, then allowed to warm to room temperature.

Vibration Treatment: A more common method of stress relieving involves clamping the part to a vibrating steel table where it is vibrated at a lower frequency than the part's natural harmonic frequency. The subharmonic vibrations are applied for 20 to 30 minutes and the part is then checked to verify that the natural frequency has changed, indicating relief of inherent stress in the part. This process is performed on a special vibratory table manufactured by Meta-Lax.

Priority Main Oiling

All serious race blocks employ priority main oiling where full oil pressure is fed to the main bearings and rods prior to lubricating the camshaft, lifters, and valvetrain. This is critical to stabilizing the crankshaft in the main bearings and cushioning it against the ravages of high cylinder pressure, elevated engine speed, and the ever lurking potential for detonation.

World Products blocks are further refined from the original small-block Chevy design with revised oiling to the lifters as well. Lifter oil is rerouted to the center of the block where it is directed to the front and the rear along the lifter galleries. This oiling strategy eliminates standard small-block oil problems caused by compromised O-rings on the distributor shaft. World Products also drills

CYLINDER BLOCKS

Main bearing size is sometimes application specific. Durability engine builds typically call for larger stock-size mains while many naturally aspirated high-RPM, high-horsepower applications take advantage of smaller main bearings with bearing spacer inserts to reduce friction.

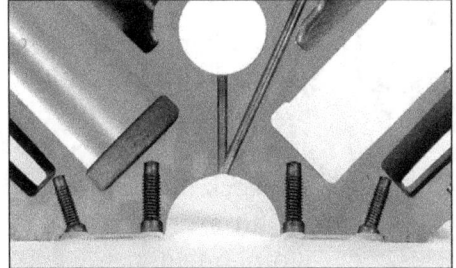

Cutaway view of a Dart high-performance race block shows the penetration of the main cap studs or bolts into the strongest part of the main webs.

its cam journal holes at the 5 o'clock position instead of 6 o'clock to introduce cam journal oiling slightly ahead of the point of maximum loading caused by high valvespring pressures.

Main Bore Size

Selection of main bore size is limited in most production engines, but given a choice, many builders are often drawn to smaller main bores to reduce bearing speed and frictional losses. Gen 1 Chevy small-blocks, for example, have a choice between 350 mains (2.45 inch) and 400 mains (2.65 inch), referring to the production main bearing sizes for those factory engines.

Once again the choice is application specific. High cylinder pressures found in supercharged or nitrous-assisted applications typically require the more robust size of larger mains. Likewise for circle track applications, like sprint cars, that hammer the bearings relentlessly with repeated applications of maximum-throttle. Drag racing applications with shorter exposure to extreme operating conditions can use smaller mains to reduce friction.

Many drag racing and oval racing applications run even smaller bearings using main bearing spacers. In selecting a main bore size it is critical to examine how hard your application is going to lean on it in terms of cyclic loading and RPM versus time, how much cylinder pressure you intend to create, how you lubricate the mains, and how much deflection you expect to occur in the crankshaft under load. It's very important that the cylinder bores and main bores remain dimensionally neutral except for predictable and controlled thermal expansion.

Everything builds on a dynamically stable crankshaft and a very rigid block with stable main bore housings that don't move around under high loads. Stability is often preferred over weight savings and frictional gains, but not in every case.

Main Web Structure

Blocks equipped with billet-steel main caps generally have beefier main web structures to ensure block rigidity. This is necessary and beneficial to operational stability. A wise engine builder once noted that a block has no moving parts, but that all the parts move within the block so it had better hold its shape. Block rigidity is extremely important, but getting there invites other problems depending on the design of the block.

Deep-skirted blocks such as current GM LS series engines encounter cylinder bay-to-bay breathing problems when outfitted with large stroker cranks. When the crank is captured farther up inside the block (as it is in these newer blocks), crankcase volume beneath the pistons is limited. Windage created by the rapidly reciprocating pistons can build excessive crankcase pressure. Without relief this creates additional pumping work against the bottom of the pistons, aggravates ring seal and oil control, and encourages seal leakage. Time spent contemplating cylinder bay dimensions and how best to control and relieve crankcase pressure will prove to be beneficial at the end of the day.

Filter, Starter and Accessory Mounts

Various applications may call for a revised starter location, so many race blocks are drilled for both right- and left-hand starters. Consider this requirement during block selection. Almost all blocks have an oil filter mount, but many race blocks do not incorporate a mechanical fuel pump boss, which may be necessary in some applications. Make certain that any block you choose incorporates all the necessary auxiliary features required for your specific application.

Block Inspection

All blocks (new and used) require meticulous examination to determine

CHAPTER 3

Precise cylinder bore alignment in relation to the crankshaft centerline is a fundamental step in basic cylinder block preparation. BHJ's block truing alignment fixture helps machinists position each deck exactly 90 degrees from the other and perfectly perpendicular to the crankshaft. (Courtesy BHJ Products)

whether you should invest time and money on expensive block preparation. New race blocks usually exhibit few problems, but they still require minor dimensional adjustments to perfect their critical structure.

Thoroughly clean any block with the most current hot tank process to remove scale, corrosion, and other objectionable material that might interfere with your examination. If the block does not come with a sonic test, perform one now to verify cylinder wall thickness (see "Sonic Checking" on page 28).

Examine the block for signs of core shift around the lifter bores and main webs. Crack checking is probably unnecessary on a new block, but used blocks should be carefully checked for cracks and other distressed areas that may leak or fail under load. Pay particular attention to the main webs and housing bores, deck surfaces, head bolt holes, lifter bores, cam bores, and the lower skirt area of each cylinder. Pressure checking is mandatory prior to performing machine work and crack repair is not a viable option for a competition engine so be prepared to scrap the block if a crack is detected.

This is also a good time to visually verify that all the oil galleries and fluid passages are unobstructed and flowing free. It is pretty easy to do with a simple garden hose and a restrictor to direct water pressure through all the holes in the block. Even if everything seems in order it's a good idea to chase all the internal passages with appropriately sized brushes to ensure that no debris contaminates the oiling passage. Some builders also polish the oil galleries using a long rod with a slot cut on the end to hold a piece of fine emery cloth. The rod is inserted into each oil gallery and spun with a drill. The best finish is obtained if you lubricate the emery cloth with WD-40.

Once you confirm the block is acceptable, it's time to verify its critical dimensions and note necessary adjustments. Everything is measured from the crankshaft centerline. Deck surfaces have to be the same height and absolutely parallel to the crank centerline. And they have to be exactly 90 degrees apart from each other. Check the distance from the crank centerline to the cam centerline and make certain that the cam

---

Block Measurements and Machining Operations

Basic Measurements
- Cylinder bore diameter
- Cylinder bore out-of-round
- Cylinder bore taper
- Cylinder bore alignment (to crank centerline)
- Cylinder wall thickness (sonic check)
- Deck height
- Deck surface alignment to crank centerline
- Main bore diameter and cap alignment
- Cam bore diameter and alignment
- Cam bore height
- Lifter bore alignment
- Basic machining operations
- Main bore align honing
- Cam bore align honing
- Cylinder boring
- Cylinder honing
- Block decking
- Lifter bore honing
- Lifter bore sleeving
- O-ringing deck surface (if required)
- Chamfering and deburring

BHJ's line boring fixture facilitates main bearing and cam bearing alignment using a standard vertical mill. This procedure corrects misalignment and makes the main bores and cam bores parallel while properly sizing the main housing bores. (Courtesy BHJ Products)

34 COMPETITION ENGINE BUILDING: ADVANCED ENGINE DESIGN & ASSEMBLY TECHNIQUES

CYLINDER BLOCKS

Shops already equipped with a line boring machine can use BHJ's cam tunnel alignment fixture to index the cam tunnel parallel to the crank centerline. (Courtesy BHJ Products)

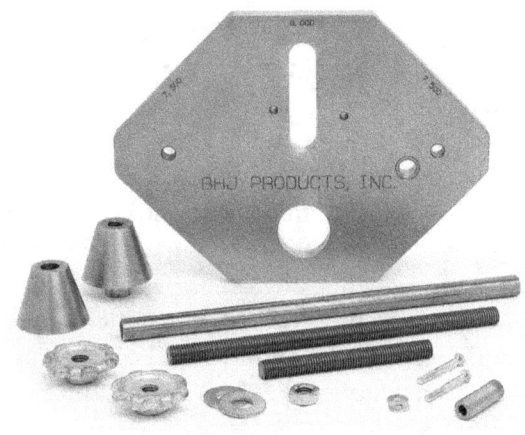

BHJ's Blok-Tru kit aligns deck surfaces to the crankshaft centerline. The precision index plate is machined with 45-degree angles for both deck surfaces. The basic kit is the necessary starting point for tailoring the Blok-Tru system to fit resurfacing machines supplied with a 2-inch-diameter support bar from the manufacturer. It consists of a precision-machined index plate, cam tunnel alignment cones, and cam tunnel clamping hardware. (Courtesy BHJ Products)

bores support the cam absolutely parallel to the main bores. It is essential that all dimensions are square and true. Check every main bore and every cam bore. Check everything twice. Align bore and/or hone the main bores to ensure perfect alignment.

BHJ's line-boring fixture enables accurate main bearing or cam bearing boring in a common vertical mill. This ensures that the crank and cam centerlines are perfectly parallel. These are normally pretty consistent on new race blocks, but you still have to check and recheck. Check the relationship of each cylinder bore to the crankshaft centerline carefully.

Lifter bores can present a major issue. If you're not going to bush them, make certain that each bore is perpendicular to the cam bore and perfectly aligned to the cam axis with no skew to the left or right. Lifter bores must be perfectly indexed to ensure optimum placement of flat-tappet and roller lifters on the camshaft lobes.

Although it's suggested to purposely mismatch some engine components to achieve specific tuning goals later on, everything in the block must be perfectly square, parallel, perpendicular, and/or correctly indexed for its intended purpose. These steps are critical to properly matching and supporting all the moving parts in the engine. Perfection is imperative. Strive for it relentlessly.

Additional block preparation details also include tighter tolerances and less core shift in aftermarket race blocks and Bow Tie and Super Duty blocks from the OEMs. Four-bolt blocks with beefier main webs and additional material for added rigidity often weigh more even when manufactured from compacted graphite iron (CGI). This is unnecessary for lower classes, and the engine package benefits more from having a lighter production-style block. Be prepared to make a judgment call regarding block rigidity versus weight as

The system also incorporates a deck height micrometer with an oversize, heavy-duty base, allowing the attached measuring spindle to easily reach from the edge of the deck surface out and down to the Blok-Tru Index Plate. Actual deck height is determined by adding the measured distance to the Blok-Tru center machined on the face of the plate.

it relates to your application. Some builders also stress-relieve blocks by vibrating them on a vibratory table.

Machine Shop Processes

Precision machine work is fundamental to engine building. Most race engines require some or all of the following procedures.

Squaring the Block

All cylinder block machining operations must align to a common reference point. The crank centerline is that point. Accurate machining begins with precise align honing of the main bore so that all other operations may reference from it. Most

builders don't have the luxury of high-dollar CNC machining centers to perform block preparation so they rely on the accuracy of their own particular machining equipment or BHJ's Blok-Tru kits (the industry standard) that work in conjunction with standard machining stations such as the Storm Vulcan Blockmaster series, Winona Van Norman units, and other overhead surfacing machines. According to BHJ, one or more of the following conditions are present in almost every block:

- Production equipment typically references off the oil pan rails and often fails to machine the bores exactly 90 degrees apart from each other and 45 degrees degrees from the block's vertical centerline. Minor variations go unnoticed on production engines, but are not tolerable on a race engine.
- Twisted blocks require the machinist to choose a reference point on the deck surface for setup, which leads to machining errors compounded by the original reference point.
- Deck clearances are often uneven between the upper and lower side of the piston tops because the deck surfaces are not 90 degrees to the cylinder bores.
- O-ring grooves are often cut unevenly on boring stands that reference off the oil pan rails.
- Poorly fitting intake manifolds caused by the deck surfaces not being machined exactly 90 degrees to each other and or parallel to the crank/centerline.
- Minor variations in cylinder head alignment causing ignition timing variations and the cylinder V not precisely 45 degrees on each side of the cam-crank centerline camshaft.

These conditions and others are corrected using BHJ's block truing equipment. The Blok-Tru Index Plate is precision machined with 45-degree angles on either side of the centerline. Once installed on the cam/crank centerline all of the angular dimensions can be machined to within 5 minutes of 1 degree. A special deck-height micrometer attached to a heavy-duty deck bar permits exact measurements from the deck surface to the Blok-Tru plate. This is then added to the known height of the fixture plate to determine the exact deck height.

The Bore-Tru kit is a blueprinting fixture that enables the engine machinist to accurately locate cylinder bores relative to the correct crankshaft journal location. It references from the rear main surface or the rear main thrust surface to position the cylinders at factory-specified bore centers. It also permits correction of the cylinder head dowel pin holes for precise cylinder head alignment. A precision deck plate attaches to a pair of universal alignment bars front and rear to precisely locate the bores relative to the crank centerline.

The accuracy of the Bore-Tru equipment depends on perfectly square deck surfaces, which are handled by the Blok-Tru equipment. Each component of the BHJ system complements the other, allowing any competent machinist to produce a precisely machined racing engine block.

Lifter Bores

Lifter bore truing is accomplished with a BHJ Lifter-Tru kit that facilitates the process on a standard Bridgeport machining center. To use the kit, attach the precision machined aluminum end plates to each end of the cylinder block for alignment via mandrels that pass through the main bore and the cam tunnel. The plates are shaped and positioned so the lifter bore axis (relative to the cam axis) is vertical when set up in the mill. Mount the precision cutting guide across the end plates directly over the lifter bore. It functions as the upper support while the mandrel passing through the cam tunnel serves as the lower guide so the cutter

BHJ's Lifter-Tru fixture kit allows machinists to properly index lifter bore position front-to-rear and up-and-down, as well as restore the correct lifter bore angle as referenced from the cam/crank centerline. Blocks without finished lifter bosses may also be machined with new lifter bores using optional cutters. The cylinder block is set up in the fixture at the prescribed angle while a piloted cutter is precisely guided from both above and below the lifter bore. This operation is typically performed in a vertical milling machine, but a valve seat and guide machine, or even a large drill press can be used effectively.

is supported above and below the lifter bore for precision placement.

The BHJ kit comes with cutters for standard lifter bore sizes including .8437-, .875-, and .904-inch diameters. It is possible to overbore the smaller GM lifter bores (.8437) to accept the larger Ford lifter (.875); Ford blocks can do likewise with the larger Chrysler lifter size (.904). Check with your cam supplier for compatibility and specific recommendations if you consider this kit.

You can also oversize the lifter bores to 1.000 inch to accept sleeves or bushings that can be accurately positioned and precision bored to any desired size. Again check with your block and cam manufacturer for the appropriate length and diameter bushing; this is primarily to ensure proper clearance for different styles of roller lifter tie bars. Once the bushings are installed, use the same BHJ kit to size them correctly.

Prior to installation check the bushings for the presence of lifter gallery oiling holes. If they are not present you must drill them yourself. Most bushings are supplied with or without oiling holes so you should be able to specify the hole size to your supplier and get bushings that are properly pre-drilled. Otherwise drill each bushing by referencing the oil gallery position from the top of the existing lifter bore.

A more common practice is to drill the bushings after installation using a long drill bit. The procedure offers precision hole placement using the oil galleries as a pilot fixture and it enables you to enlarge the lifter galleries at the same time if so desired. If you go this way, drilling the bushings first and truing the lifter bores last cleans up any burrs left by the gallery drilling.

Bushing installation is straightforward, but you have to work carefully. Bushings must not extend beyond the bottom of the lifter bore opening to the cam tunnel and they have to be installed in perfect alignment, particularly those incorporating slots for guided lifters, such as Jesel units.

Final lifter bore honing is accomplished with a BHJ or Sunnen honing kit that includes the appropriate stones and guide mandrels. A U-joint and shaft assembly is provided for honing with a 1/2-inch drill, but most builders prefer to finish the procedure while the block is still on the milling machine.

Alternative Lifter Oiling

Small-block Chevy engines running flat-tappet cams have a nasty habit of flattening cam lobes and wiping out the lifter faces. The problem typically occurs during the initial break-in procedure, but it can also happen in competition with very high spring tension and insufficient lubrication. The least expensive remedy involves grooving the lifter bores with a simple tool from Comp Cams. It incorporates a lifter-shaped grooving tool with an adjustable carbide cutter and a handle for drawing the tool through the lifter bore. The cutter is set to cut a groove (almost a scratch, really) .009- to .012-inch deep from the bottom of the lifter bore up to the oil gallery feed holes. The grooves should be cut on the right side (passenger side) of the block to ensure that each lobe is pre-oiled before it is subjected to maximum valvespring pressure.

For ultra-high-spring applications special flat-tappet lifters are also available with .010- to .15-inch EDM (electrical discharge machining) oiling holes drilled directly into the face of the lifter surface. These holes are connected to a feed hole in the side of the lifter that provides full-time oil pressure directly to the lifter/lobe

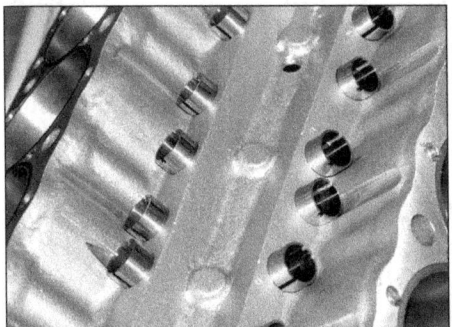

Bushed lifter bores are perfectly aligned to minimize friction and provide optimum cam-to-lifter alignment. They also permit the use of larger-diameter lifters for more aggressive camshafts.

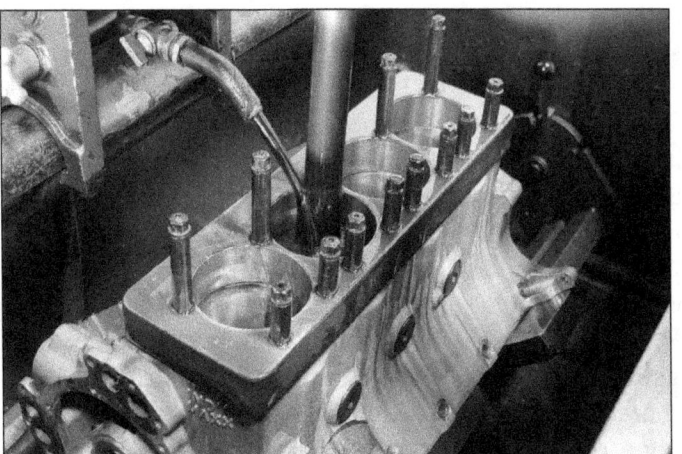

Torque plate honing is mandatory practice for all race blocks. It minimizes bore distortion when cylinder head clamping loads are applied and is particularly effective when combined with hot-honing techniques.

CHAPTER 3

The BHJ Blok-Tru setup corrects misaligned deck surfaces by registering off the crank centerline, establishing parallel decks and a true 45-degree angle to the cam/crank centerline.

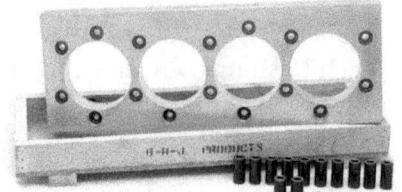

BHJ honing plates are the standard of the industry. The company offers a broad line of plates specifically designed for racing applications.

New race blocks are high-quality castings, but still require careful deburring and basic preparation prior to final assembly. This Dart Big M block illustrates the excellent casting quality available in modern aftermarket race blocks.

interface. This oiling strategy usually cures cam lobe distress under these conditions. Comp Cams offers these lifters for all popular domestic V-8s.

Align Honing

Now that the racing industry has largely shifted to dedicated race blocks, line boring the main cap housing bores is no longer prevalent. Align honing to ensure precision alignment is usually all that's required with most current engine builds. If align boring is necessary, the machinist generally machines the main bores to within .005 inch of the final desired housing bore dimension. Some machinists feel comfortable align boring to the actual final dimension, but most engine builders prefer to leave the last .0015 inch for align honing to gain a better finish on the housing bore. A 150-grit aluminum-carbide stone is typically used with billet or ductile iron caps while harder stones are reserved for cast-iron blocks.

Torque Plate Honing

Honing plates are available to fit more than 400 engine applications in all sizes, from single-cylinders to V-12s. BHJ is recognized as the worldwide authority in honing plate development and production today. Since the conception of the initial honing plate designs that were introduced by BHJ Products in early 1975, continued research and development has bred numerous design improvements that bring us to the models available today.

Head-bolt torque can dramatically distort cylinders and cylinders cannot be bored or honed accurately if cylinder dimensions change so significantly after assembly. Rings won't seal well, and scuffing is likely to occur if the engine overheats. Use of BHJ honing plates rectifies all of these problems, leading to more consistent tolerances, better sealing, and more power. They feature 1¾-inch-thick Meehanite cast-iron or cast aluminum, which gives maximum rigidity and resistance to permanent distortion and most closely simulate the stresses induced on the cylinder wall by the cylinder head when it is torqued in place.

In addition, these materials have essentially the same coefficient of expansion as cylinder heads, important to those honing at operating temperature. Cast-iron plates are Blanchard ground on both sides, flat and parallel within precision commercial tolerances. BHJ aluminum R Model plates are supplied with heat-treated steel inserts (T-washers) in all standard bolt holes. Plates are manufactured with a .090-inch to .095-inch-larger bore size than the largest standard engine bore diameter found in the applicable engine family in most applications, allowing the plate to accommodate .060-inch overbore. This maintains full gasket firing-ring compression, thus further enhancing bore stability. Special bore diameters are available upon request.

Head-bolt holes are precision machined to factory tolerances and special bolt-hole sizes are also available. Clearance holes for locating dowels are machined oversize to allow visual alignment before torquing. Indexed or "dialed-in" dowel holes are also available upon request.

CYLINDER BLOCKS

The R Model Honing Plate is the established standard for duplicating cylinder bore distortion and is a must for any high-performance engine application. The R Model incorporates all of the features of the standard version, plus is specially machined, and in most cases, supplied with DOM steel spacers and washers, to duplicate cylinder head height and facilitate the use of the OEM-length head bolts or aftermarket studs during the honing operation. Optional machining is also available for hot-honing.

In order to maintain the least possible block distortion when using the R Model Honing Plate, be sure to use the same type of cylinder head gasket and bolt or stud set as during final engine assembly. Some engines require that both cylinder banks be torqued to better simulate final assembly conditions during honing. Additionally, industry tradition dictates that the honing plate should be of a similar material as the heads being used in final assembly, thus a cast-iron honing plate is preferred when using cast-iron heads in final assembly and an aluminum plate should be used when aluminum heads are installed.

Hot Honing

Many engine builders acknowledge that hot honing cylinder blocks at a temperature closer to actual operating temperature provides superior results. Benefits include improved ring seal, reduced friction, and superior ring stability due to a more precise ring-to-cylinder-wall relationship. Most engine builders also acknowledge that hot honing is a messy, aggravating procedure that most of them avoid despite potential gains in performance.

It's easy to suggest that this is a high-end procedure best left to professional teams with dedicated engine facilities and that it probably doesn't make enough difference for more budget conscious sportsman efforts. But when should a known performance benefit ever be ignored? Hot honing requires a significant investment in equipment and certain modifications in honing technique, but it provides proven benefits that racers seeking maximum power and durability cannot and should not fail to consider. Even shops that do it regularly acknowledge that it is a pain in the ass, but they endure it because it is worth it.

Deburring Procedures

Most builders deburr the block to eliminate the source of casting flash that might break off in the engine under severe operating conditions. Millions of engines, particularly truck engines have logged tens of millions of miles with very few if any casting flash episodes. Still, never say never. Play it safe and deburr the block. You could be the one that it happens to on the final lap of the first race that you've led all season.

Deburring is also a safety procedure to keep you from cutting your hands to pieces during mock-up and final assembly. Deburring should be done everywhere on the block where a sharp edge exists or where casting residue protrudes from the surface. It also includes corners, nooks, and crannies where hidden stress risers may lead to localized cracking. That means deburring inside the crankcase as well as the lifter valley, timing cover area, bellhousing area, and all exterior surfaces.

When you are finished you should be able to work on any area of the block without cutting yourself. Devotees of the deburring art often smooth and polish all inner surfaces that are exposed to oil to encourage oil drainback and minimize the amount of oil clinging to any surface. Whether or not hot oil clings to or flows from a polished surface is still a matter of debate.

Special oil-shedding coatings are available for this now, but back in the day, most builders painted these inner surfaces to seal them. The preferred product was Glyptal, but in

Carefully inspecting and deburring the cylinder block is the first step in any competition engine build. The deburring process removes all sharp edges and casting flash. It also includes chamfering the freeze plug holes and breaking the leading edge of each cam bearing bore to facilitate the easy installation of the cam bearings.

Piston Pin Oiler Installation

Most dedicated race blocks for Sprint Cup racing, Formula 1, and other high-end applications are equipped with piston dome/pin oilers. Pin oilers provide direct full-time lubrication to the wrist pins to supplement the minimal amount of oil fed to the wrist pin bosses via passages leading from the oil rings. This is particularly important in dry sump applications where splash oiling of the cylinder walls is minimal due to reduced crankcase windage and the remote oil supply.

Tough as they are, wrist pins can bend along the longitudinal axis and they can temporarily deform into an egg shape within the pin bore at very high engines speeds. Pin deformation and bending under severe loading increases the need for full-time lubrication of the wrist pins. Pin oilers provide this lubrication and the oil serves a further purpose by carrying heat away from the piston crowns. You should consider adding pin oilers to your racing engine if you run very high engine speeds, severe loading, and/or high thermal loading such as found in high-output turbocharged applications.

Race block manufacturers offer the service of adding pin oilers to your block or you can do it yourself using a Mike Laws Research (MLR) pin oiler kit available from CV Products. These kits are available for big- and small-block Chevys and small-block Fords as detailed in the chart.

Each reusable kit includes the following components:

- Main bore housing drill fixtures (aluminum)
- 8 metering jets for one engine (extra jets also available separately)
- 1 drill tap with 8-32 thread
- 1 tap 8-32 thread
- 1 6-inch #28 drill

MLR kits allow you to drill and tap your block's main bore housings for screw-in pin oiler jets. Each main bearing feeds two opposite cylinders with pin oiler metering jets. To install the pin oilers the following installation sequence is recommended. Note: This sample installation is being performed on a Dart Machinery Big M Chevy big-block cylinder block.

Each kit contains two aluminum drill fixtures that install in the appropriate main housing bores to provide a drill bushing guide. Position the block on an engine stand with the main bore saddles facing up. Remove the main caps and set them aside. Install the appropriate aluminum drilling fixture into the main bore housing with the fixture pilot hole facing the appropriate cylinder.

Because there are so many variations in main bolt and stud locations, a compromise has been added to the fixtures in the form of elongated and enlarged mounting holes. This enables you to position each drill fixture so that you achieve the best alignment of the drill pilot hole and the desired point of impact for the oil jet. In some cases you may wish to further elongate the mounting holes to gain more freedom for properly positioning the fixture.

The drilling fixture must always align parallel to the main webs. MLR recommends positioning each fixture so that the drilled hole will be as close to the centerline of the housing bore as the mounting holes will allow.

Verify the cylinder number of the fixture and then bolt it securely in place using bolts or studs with spacers if necessary. Install the 6-inch #28 drill bit into your drill and insert it into the drill bushing in the alignment fixture. Carefully and slowly drill through the main webbing until the drill bit penetrates through to the base of the cylinder.

Do not rush this step. MLR advises that it is critical to remove the drill bit often to clean the flutes during this operation. Failure to do so may result in a stuck or

CV Products Part Number	Description
MLR400-010	Piston Dome Oiler Kit/SB GM 350 Main Journal/Dry Sump
MLR400-100	Piston Dome Oiler Fixture Kit/BB GM/454 Main Journal
MLR400-000	Piston Dome Oiler Kit/SB GM 283 Main Journal Size/Dry Sump
MLR400-210	Piston Dome Oiler Kit/SB Ford 351 Main Journal Size
MLR400-200	Piston Dome Oiler Kit/SB Ford 302 Main Journal Size
MLR311-000	Rear Four-Port Fitting for Spring Oilers

CYLINDER BLOCKS

broken drill bit accompanied by appropriate swearing. Do not use cutting fluid on cast-iron blocks as it tends to clog the flutes with metal.

After drilling the hole in the main webbing, remove the drilling fixture, turn it around, and re-install it so you can drill another hole in the opposite direction to feed another cylinder.

Remember that each main bore saddle feeds two separate cylinders.

When all the holes are drilled in the main bores, use a sharp X-Acto type blade or similar tool to lightly deburr the newly drilled holes.

Now you are ready to tap the drilled holes to accept the threaded metering jets. Begin the threading process with the 8-32 drill tap. This is a combination drill bit and tap called a "drap." The drill bit portion is used to align the tool in each hole so you can tap the hole to a depth of three or four revolutions. It is important that you do not tap any further with this tool as it is easily broken.

Once you have established several threads in each hole remove the tool and switch to the regular tap. The supplied 8-32 tap is used to finish threading each hole. Great care is required here. The metering jet depth is set by how far the threads extend into the drilled hole. MLR advises that six or seven revolutions are usually sufficient for proper positioning of the metering jets. This also depends on the type of block you are working with and the proximity of rotating components. Some trial and error is often required to accommodate specific block configurations.

The thread depth should be set so that each jet protrudes slightly into the cylinder area. This is typically not possible on cylinders number-1 and -8 due to the amount of available material in the main webbing area. Do not tap the threads all the way through into the cylinder area as this may allow the metering jets to eventually rotate farther into the cylinder area. Setting the thread depth as described here is essential for proper operation.

On some engines it may be necessary to slightly relieve the base of the cylinder to give the oil jet a clean shot at the piston pin. Prior to installing each metering jet, insert a 3/32-inch length of welding rod into each hole to determine where the oil stream contacts the piston/pin/rod assembly. This also allows you to discover and correct any obstructions that may interfere with the oil stream.

After you have set all the metering jet depths correctly, temporarily remove them so you can cut the feed passage from the man oil feed in each main bore saddle.

Use a black marker to draw a line between the main bearing feed hole and the new metering jet holes you just drilled in the main bore saddles. Then use a small-diameter circular cut-off wheel (.040- to .060-inch wide) in a small die grinder to cut a feed channel into the housing bore using the marked line as your guide.

The object here is to connect each main feed hole to the metering jet holes with a small channel so pressurized oil can feed the jets via the channels underneath the main bearings. The recommended channel depth for proper oil volume is .040 inch.

After cleaning the engine block and flushing all the feed holes thoroughly, the first step in your engine assembly process is installing the metering jets. A small amount of blue Loctite may be used if desired, but it isn't really necessary since each metering jet is fully captured by the end of threading on one end and the bearing insert covering it on the other end.

It is important to work patiently and deliberately. You need a new set of metering jets for each engine you modify. Replace the drill bit and the tap frequently for best results and to reduce the possibility of breakage. The aluminum fixture guides pretty much last forever if you take care of them. MLR advises customers to replace the drill bit for each new engine and the taps after every second engine. CV Products carries all of the required replacement tools and metering jet kits.

Once the metering jets are properly installed they provide trouble-free service with clean, filtered oil. Remember that the piston and pin are moving in and out of the oil stream during every stroke so there is ample opportunity to not only lube the pins, but to also extract heat from the piston top via the oil.

MLR advises that a 45-degree relief on the inner edge of the piston pin boss often helps the oil stream to maintain longer contact with the piston crown during each engine revolution. If you chose to do so remember that removing

Piston Pin Oiler Installation CONTINUED

material from the piston causes a balance issue unless the piston weight is corrected after the material is removed—not a problem when mocking up a new engine, but problematic on existing engines. Some big-block engine blocks running wet sump systems have an oil pump driveshaft interference problem, which can be remedied with MLR's 3/8-inch-long metering jet for cylinder number-8. Check for proper clearance during final assembly.

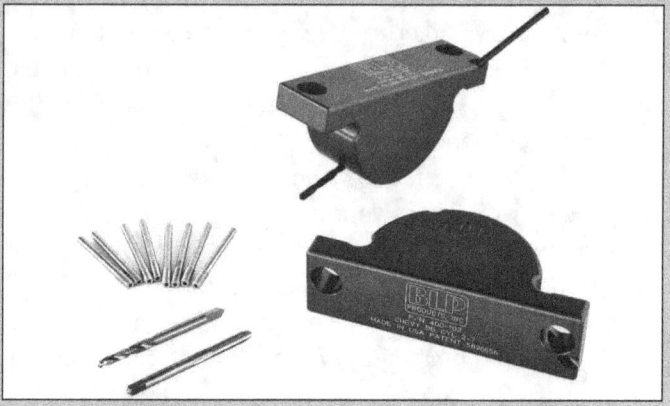

MLR performance pin oiler kits for small- and big-block Chevys use drill bushing guides that bolt into the main bearing housing bores to correctly position the drill for a direct shot at the piston pin.

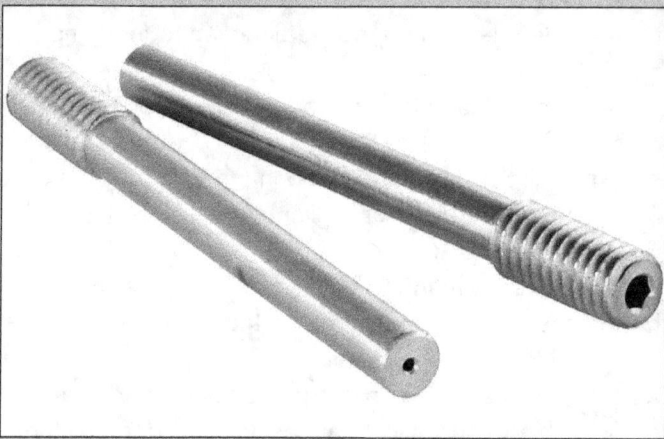

Threaded pin oiling jets are then screwed into the tapped holes in the housing bore to provide the correct feed orifice for oiling the piston pins and crowns.

Drill slowly and remove the drill bit frequently to clean out the metal shavings. You may need to remove and realign the assembly six or seven times to clear the drill of accumulated shavings.

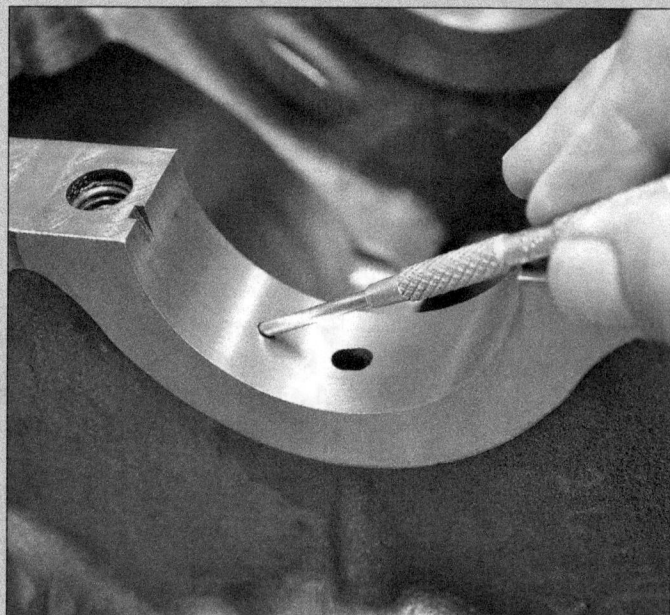

A magnetic machinist's pick works great for cleaing the shavings out of the hole. The bit is small and clogs quickly. Patience and care are required to drill a clean hole without breaking the bit.

CYLINDER BLOCKS

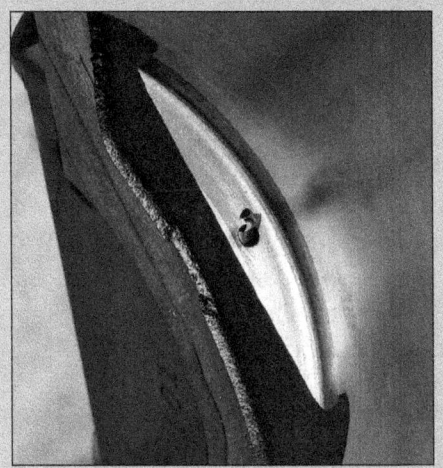

The drill bit must penetrate all the way through from the main saddle to the bottom of the cylinder as guided by the bushing in the drilling fixture. It emerges from the main web as shown here.

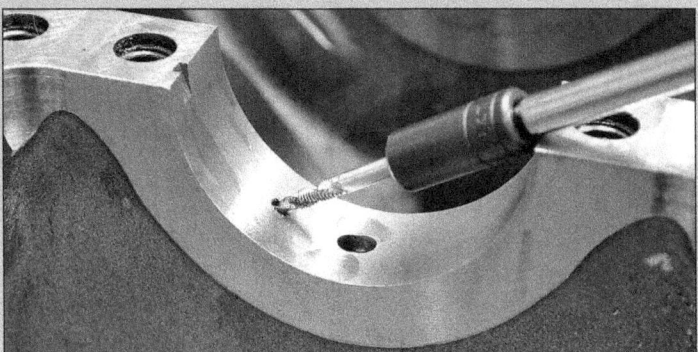

The kit's drap is inserted into the new hole to provide a guide for the starting tap. After three or four revolutions remove it and switch to a standard tap to finish tapping the hole.

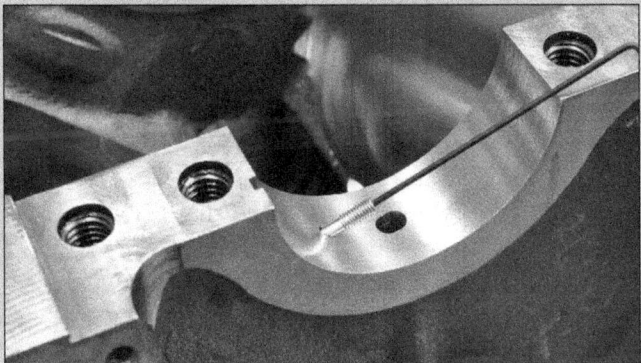

The pin oiler jet accepts a small Allen wrench to screw it into the freshly tapped hole.

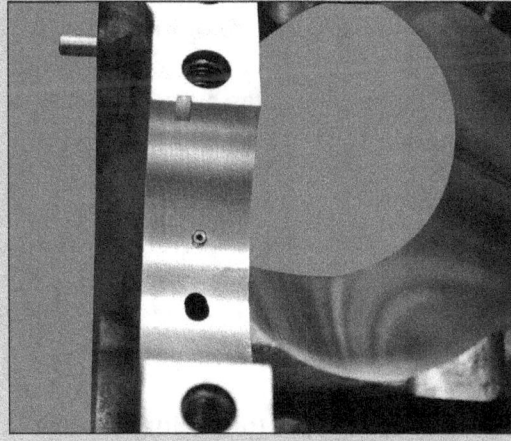

The pin oiler jet must screw in below the bearing saddle surface so as not to affect the bearing contact surface.

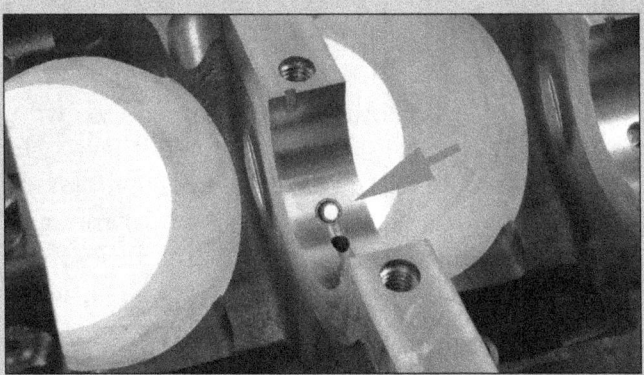

This Dart block prepped with a pin oiler kit shows the threaded hole for the pin oiler insert. A small rotary grinder is used to cut the feeder channels into the housing bore to direct pressurized oil to both pin oilers fed by this main bearing.

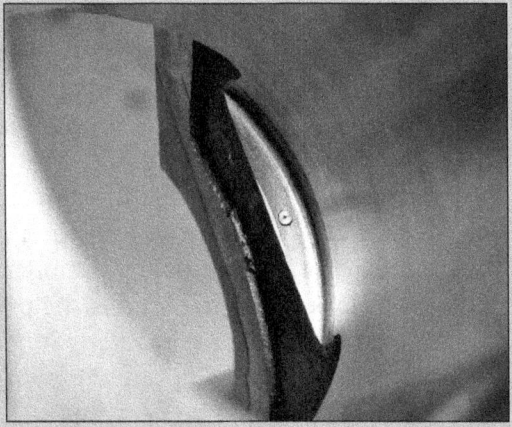

When properly installed the pin oil barely protrudes into the cylinder, if at all. If you accidentally tap too deeply the jet can be carefully shortened in a lathe. If this is required, be sure to deburr the new end and insert the appropriate drill bit to ensure that the jet opening is unobstructed.

reality, many builders simply used a spray bomb of blood-red electric motor varnish straight from a Krylon can. This provided a tough, smooth finish that sealed-in any residual dirt and promoted oil drainage.

The smoothing and polishing practice seems to have gained favor with a lot of builders who suggest that the paint might flake off. While there may be something to it, I can honestly say that in more than 40-plus years I've seen a lot of painted blocks and a lot of engine bearings and other components and I have never seen a failure traceable to paint chipping off an internal block surface. Not saying it couldn't happen, but it is unlikely if the paint was applied to a clean, well-prepared surface that had been hot tanked and prepped with lacquer thinner.

Threaded Hole Preparation

One very important aspect of competition engine assembly is preparation of the threaded holes for the fasteners that hold the engine together. The widespread practice of chasing all threads with a thread tap was generally okay back in the days prior to the extraordinary power levels engine builders achieve today.

A thread-chasing tap cuts metal wherever it encounters resistance. When this happens it alters the thread dimensions slightly, and over time it can diminish the capacity of the thread to properly hold and align the fastener. Proper thread preparation for new race blocks primarily involves careful inspection and cleaning.

If you're refurbishing a block during a rebuild it is best to thoroughly clean the block with a hot tank or other cleaning method. Next, inspect and prepare individual fastener holes as required. Clean each hole with bore- and thread-cleaning brushes and blow it out with compressed air. Finally, carefully run a thread roller tap into the hole to properly align the existing threads.

Piston Pin Oiling

Direct wristpin oiling is common enough now that engine speeds have increased and component mass has been trimmed to a minimum. Be aware that most cylinder blocks (including aftermarket race blocks) are not directly equipped to support pin oiling, but there are ways to incorporate it if desired.

Pin oiling is generally required for high RPM, severe loading, or endurance applications where pin and/or pin bore distortion may cause problems that can often be mitigated by additional pin lubrication. Pin oiling is also used to help cool the piston crown in severe-duty applications.

Cup engines run pin oilers and they're certainly a good idea on a sprint car or a Bonneville engine, but they are not often utilized on short-duration drag racing engines except perhaps in high-boost applications with high cylinder pressures and severe pin loading. Built-in pin oilers typically incorporate squirter assemblies mounted in the crankcase where they can direct a steady stream of lubricant against the bottom of the piston deck to remove heat from the piston and then splash oil on the pin.

Some factory performance engines actually have pin oilers (Honda S2000 for example) because they rev so high, but most domestic engines require custom fabrication. Many racers drill small holes from the main bore housings through the top of the main webs with precision placement to oil the piston pins. Mike Laws Performance (MLP) makes a kit to accomplish this on Chevy and Ford V-8s.

The MLP kits feature machined mandrels equipped with drill bushings that bolt into the main bearing housing bore to accurately position the drill bit. The drilled hole is then tapped and fitted with screw-in oil jets that are then captured underneath the main bearing. A hole is drilled in the bearing to feed the pin jet, or some builders grind a small slot from the housing bore oil-feed hole over to the location of the jet so that lubricant feeds to the pin oiler underneath the bearing.

Both methods seem to work equally well. Other racers have fashioned internal oiling manifolds or tapped into pan rail oil galleries and attached their own squirters. If you feel the need for pin oilers, be aware that to some small degree they contribute to windage problems due to the extra oil falling on the crankshaft. While direct pin oiling is important for durability issues, its primary goal is usually piston cooling. In that regard it is often more effective than the normal transfer of heat to the cylinder walls via the rings.

Special thread-chasing taps from ARP clean the threads in the block and other parts without cutting away more metal. This promotes proper thread engagement to ensure optimum fastener performance.

CHAPTER 4

CRANKSHAFTS

Like most parts in a competition engine crankshafts live a harrowing existence somewhat akin to having eight bullies beating you up over and over again. A high-end racing engine can produce a combustion pressure of about 1,400 to 1,500 psi. For example, if you apply that pressure to a 4.185-inch-diameter piston, as found in a Sprint Cup engine, it translates to a force exceeding 19,000 pounds against the rod journal for every cylinder. That's a staggeringly compressive load even under non-dynamic conditions. Racing crankshafts are pretty tough customers, but they do deflect under the intermittent torsional loading imparted by the engine's continuous firing sequence. This unseen dimensional elasticity (ductility) is necessary to absorb the dynamic forces at play. Dimensionally it is typically less than the existing clearance stack in the bearings, piston clearance, and ring pack clearances.

We're talking about forces imparted by the actual combustion process, but also must consider the reciprocating mass being flung back and forth in every cylinder. That includes not just the pistons, but the ring packs, wrist pins, pin retainers, the small end of the connecting rod, plus some amount of oil clinging to these parts. Whatever that weight may be in each cylinder, it is continuously being accelerated from zero velocity to maximum velocity and back to zero twice for every revolution of the crankshaft. And of course that is happening in each individual cylinder in an orderly sequence that tends to absorb minute variations.

In addition to combustion pressures, the crankshaft is also trying to maintain order among all these various masses being flung in all directions. Some pistons are coming (up to top dead center, TDC), others are going (down toward bottom dead center, BDC), and some are in transit, all with their own accelerations, velocities, and force vectors depending largely on the stroke, rod length, and engine speed. The reciprocating mass attached to each crankpin assembly must also be opposed by the crank throws to maintain balance.

If Atlas thought it was tough holding up the world, he wouldn't

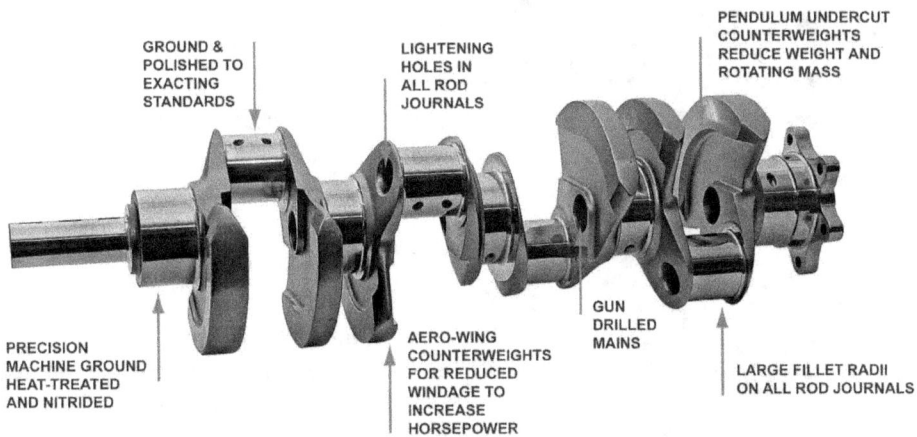

Racing crankshafts incorporate many of the essential features shown here to ensure maximum durability and top performance.

CHAPTER 4

be any happier trying to hang onto eight raging race pistons at maximum RPM. A 90-degree V-8 layout permits pretty complete balancing of the primary and secondary forces at play, but not so well that vibratory loading is totally eliminated. Depending on contributing factors such as component dimensions and mass, the rotating assembly goes in and out of tune at different engine speeds; it may be dead smooth at some RPM and not so smooth at others. To some degree or another, this affects crankshaft stability, ring seal, and bearing integrity and it is a primary reason that racing engines must be precisely balanced to ensure smooth predictable operation.

Crankshaft Types

Most racing applications use a steel forging or a billet steel crankshaft. Lower classes are often restricted to cast steel or OEM-type nodular iron cranks, which perform admirably in many sportsman classes, but are functionally unsuited for high-horsepower applications. These classes frequently place weight limits on crankshafts (such as a 50-pound minimum) to prevent the use of lighter high-dollar cranks. With a tensile strength of 65,000 to 80,000 psi, common castings are relatively brittle, but perfectly suited for general automotive use. OEM nodular iron cranks feature a tensile strength above 100,000 psi with better ductility and an elongation rating of about 3 percent. This is suitable for many heavy-duty truck applications and even some OEM performance engines. The elongation rating refers to the percentage of deformation the crank can endure repeatedly without failure. It is basically the difference between tensile strength (the force required to initiate stretching or deflection) and yield strength (the amount of force required to permanently stretch or deform the part). Cast cranks perform admirably in those sportsman classes that require them, particularly crankshafts such as Scat's 9000-series, which have a tensile strength equal to most basic

Whether to use twisted or non-twisted forgings is still debated. Many builders have good luck with both, but non-twisted forgings are commonly preferred for high-load applications running extreme engine speeds. (Courtesy Scat Enterprises)

The combination of a lightweight forged crankshaft, lightweight H-beam connecting rods, and forged pistons is a recipe for success in most racing applications.

TECH TIP — Crankshaft Selection Criteria

- Forged or Billet Material
- Stroke Length
- Main Journal Diameter
- Rod Journal Diameter
- Fillet Radius
- Number of Counterweights
- Heat Treatment
- Nitriding
- Cryogenic Treatment
- Crank Snout Size
- Windage Treatment
- Lightening Holes
- Crankshaft Weight
- Rear Main Seal Type
- Crank Flange Type
- Journal Surface Finish
- Straight Shot Oiling
- No Cross Drilling
- Balancing
- Material Properties
- Twist or Non-Twist Forging
- Mass Moment of Inertia
- Snout Keyway
- Dampener

forgings (105,000 psi) and an elongation rating (6 percent) nearly double that of most common castings. These cranks are quite comfortable in the 400- to 450-hp range in circle track racing applications and they often hold up very well even at the 500-hp level in high-performance street applications that only see part-time abuse.

Forged Cranks

Forged steel cranks come in two basic varieties: twisted and non-twisted, meaning whether the crank throws are forged in place all at one time or twisted into position during the manufacturing process. The forging process consists of heating a chunk of billet to 2,650 to 2,750 degrees F and then pounding it into shape with dies on massive 200-ton presses. Twisted cranks are forged in one piece and the throws are twisted into place all at once on huge automated machines. Twisted forgings are less expensive to manufacture, but the initial tooling investment is much higher even though overall maintenance costs less.

A non-twisted crank is forged with the throws in the correct position all at once and the tooling lasts longer because there is less overall displacement of metal. Depending on which manufacturer you talk to, the difference is negligible if the process is performed correctly. Debate over the relative merits of each type remains ongoing, but many manufacturers recommended a non-twisted structure as superior for competition use.

Most OEM performance cranks are twisted forgings and they are plenty strong for most applications. Note that the interruption of grain structure within the metal is greater in a twisted forging than a non-twisted forging. In a non-twisted forging, grain displacement is limited to roughly half the stroke length versus a similar displacement in a twisted forging plus a severe twist that further disrupts the internal grain structure. Hence, in theory, non-twisted forgings may be somewhat tougher and more able to resist crankshaft deflection under severe load.

Forged cranks are manufactured in a broad range of materials with varying degrees of strength depending on the alloy and the heat treatment involved. Factory-forged cranks are made from plain carbon steel, typically 1053 alloy and sometimes 1045. The tensile strength of these alloys is about 110,000 psi. While this doesn't seem that much better than a good cast crankshaft, the ductility of the forged crank is much better with nearly 25-percent-greater elongation factor prior to failure. The next strongest alloy is 5140 chromium steel, which is graded at 115,000-psi tensile strength. Beyond that, chromium and higher-carbon-content alloys such as 4140 are used for most high-performance forged crankshafts. These alloys are rated up to 125,000 psi. Top-of-the-line forged cranks for racing applications use 4340, a stronger and tougher alloy rated at 140,000 psi.

Forged cranks are more expensive than cast cranks and less expensive than billet cranks, but with the exception of absolute high-end applications requiring uncompromising strength (4340 billets), 4140 forged cranks are the primary choice for most sportsman racing applications. Additionally, most manufacturers today have cleverly designed their forgings to allow a range of different stroke lengths to be machined from the same basic forging. In many cases they can grind a particular stroke from an existing forging if it is within a specified range.

Other advantages of purchasing a forged crankshaft almost always include a generous radius on the journal fillets, which adds strength and resists cracking. This is no small matter as most crank manufacturers consider the design and machining

Drilled crankpins are the most effective way of reducing rotational inertia in a racing crankshaft without affecting the overall strength of individual crankpins. (Courtesy Scat Enterprises)

Billet cranks are preferred exclusively in Cup applications and that should tell you something. Wherever maximum strength and durability are required, a billet crank is almost always the superior choice. (Courtesy Scat Enterprises)

CHAPTER 4

Characteristics of Race Crankshafts

Material	Tensile Strength (psi)	Rating
Cast iron	70,000 to 80,000	OEM engines
Nodular Iron	95,000	OEM engines
Cast steel	105,000	Strongest casting
1010/1045/1053	100,000 to 110,000	High-carbon OEM forgings
5140 alloy	115,000	Sportsman racing
4140 alloy	120,000	Premium forging alloy
4340 alloy	140,000 to 145,000	Best performance alloy
EN-30B	160,000 to 165,000	Premium billet alloy
4330-M	160,000 to 165,000	Maximum strength alloy
300-M	160,000 to 165,000	Maximum strength alloy

of a proper fillet radius one of the most important features of a racing crankshaft. In particular they have begun to favor a non-circular contour or non-constant radius that is thought to impart greater strength to the transition from journal to throw. Most aftermarket forged racing cranks also have knife edging or bull nosing on the crank throws, a feature designed to help the crank throw cut through the swirling oil mass with reduced aerodynamic drag.

Billet Cranks

Billet cranks are CNC machined from a solid chunk of high-strength billet steel alloy. They are typically the strongest and stiffest units available and are the overwhelming choice for unlimited applications such as Top Fuel dragsters, Funny Cars, Pro/Stock and Pro/Modified, drag racers, Sprint Cup engines, and any form of unlimited competition that requires maximum strength and durability.

Among the major advantages of billet cranks is the ability to machine any desired combination of stroke and journal size while maintaining maximum strength. In contrast to a forging where the grain structure of the metal is stretched and deformed at high temperature, the grain structure of a billet crank remains unchanged with no residual stress from the forging process. The machining process interrupts the grain in both types, but it is seen as less intrusive in a billet. Further, billets permit very precise shaping and location of the crank throws to ensure maximum strength and precise balancing. Billets are typically manufactured from 4340 alloy or better.

If you subscribe to the notion that a piston, rod, and crankshaft all serve as shock absorbers it becomes a moot point. An unyielding crankshaft may be more prone to hammering bearings even as it provides more precise piston positioning. This is especially true under conditions of detonation where piston rattling and rocking may be severe. Since variable crank deflection can't be measured practically, all we can do is try to predict its consequence and act accordingly. It's a sound reason to tightly control piston ring side clearance, radial depth, and tension to very close tolerances. This ensures the best possible seal at the ring face and the ring land to minimize ring movement in the ring grooves when subjected to the hammering effects of detonation or high-speed flutter. Consider what happens

Note the generous fillet radius on this Scat rod journal. The radius spreads the load and removes a common point of stress fractures.

Gun-drilled mains are also used to lighten a racing crankshaft.

to ring seal when the ring is temporarily unloaded and how hard it is to regain that seal at elevated engine speeds. This is one reason piston rings have a slightly rounded face. They must maintain the seal even while the piston is rocking.

Strength Treatments

Various treatments are employed to toughen crankshafts for their severe-duty environment. They include heat treatments, hardening techniques, and severe-cold cryogenic treatments to stabilize the metal.

Heat Treatment

Interestingly, cast crankshafts generally don't require heat treatment because the manufacturing process hardens the metal during the machining process. That means cast cranks can be easily reground without loss of surface hardening. The same applies to OEM-style forge cranks if they have not been tuftrided or nitrided. In such cases the crank requires another heat treatment to restore the initial journal surface hardness. Forged cranks are actually softer initially and require specific heat treatments to make them suitable for competition use. Heat treating is applied to OEM forged cranks to improve their durability and resistance to wear.

Induction Hardening

Factory cranks are induction hardened—a process that generates rapid heat in the crank surface via a high-frequency alternating magnetic field. This procedure is quick and inexpensive and typically provides hardening penetration to a depth as much as .080 inch. Unfortunately it introduces stress to various parts of the crank because the heating and cooling process is restricted to the surface material and does not affect the rest of the crank material equally. The process is economical and useful for OEM applications, which generally never see the severe duty imposed by racing conditions.

Tuftriding

Tuftriding is a process developed specifically to avoid the uneven stresses caused by induction hardening. It is performed by immersing the crank in hot cyanide compounds, which creates a hard surface that is resistant to wear and fatigue. Tuftriding typically applies only a thin layer of hardening and it often introduces warping, which has to be dealt with in the final machining process.

Nitriding

The most common and favored heat treatment is nitriding—a chemical process in which the crank is heated in a special furnace and subjected to ammonia and nitrogen gas, which react with the carbon on the surface of the crank, hardening it to a depth specific to the length of time the crank is exposed to the hot gases.

Nitriding does not usually penetrate as deep as tuftriding, generally only about .010 to .013 inch or so, but it does not impart the localized stress caused by tuftriding. Its primary benefit is the improvement in impact and resistance to wear. Nitriding is a lower-temperature process that, unlike induction hardening, does not affect the core strength of the crank. According to Scat, it treats the crank evenly and imparts a surface tension that increases fatigue life by 18 to 20 percent. The process is more expensive and the cranks require re-nitriding if they are ever reground.

Many manufacturers still prefer to induction harden their cranks to control costs and it's not that these cranks are bad, the engine builder just needs to know this and contemplate the consequences if crank work is required later. Race engine builders weigh the relative merits of both and make their choice based on operating and endurance requirements and, in many cases, the allotted budget for any given engine project.

Cryogenics

Cryogenic treatment is another procedure used to improve strength and fatigue resistance. The cryogenic process chills the crank to –300 degrees F for a specified length of time, typically 24 to 36 hours. The crank is then set aside to slowly return to room temperature. This deep-freezing process relieves residual stresses in the metal, making the crank more resistant to breaking. Considered snake oil in the not too distant past, cryogenic treatments have come into favor and are now used by many top engine builders for maximum-effort engines.

Counterweights

There is wide belief among crankshaft manufacturers that standard two-plane V-8 cranks offer power and durability gains with the use of additional counterweights around the center main journal, particularly in long-stroke applications that have more flex due to less overlap between the throws and the mains. Center counterweights have previously not been used because they increase the difficulty and expense of manufacturing the crankshaft and because traditional six-counterweight cranks have a lower mass moment of inertia

(MMOI). More builders are recognizing the advantages of eight counterweights, particularly in long-stroke, higher-RPM applications.

Center counterweights reduce bending moment deflection at the center main bearing, which helps preserve overall crank stiffness and resistance to deflection along the crank axis. In this regard some short-stroke applications favor them because they make balancing more precise. Adding counterweights at the center throws also helps lessen the bending loads and reduces the overall size of the counterweights.

Shaped counterweights use various strategies to combat crankcase windage. This Scat crankshaft incorporates Aero-Wing counterweights, which are custom shaped to cut cleanly through the oil mass while the pendulum cut reduces weight and concentrates it in the most desirable location for optimum balance. (Courtesy Scat Enterprises)

A billet crank begins with a solid billet of material weighing several hundred pounds. The setup and programming time for this procedure is lengthy and expensive. (Courtesy Scat Enterprises)

The machining process for a billet crank is long and precise, but the result is a superior crankshaft with uninterrupted grain structure and maximum strength. (Courtesy Scat Enterprises)

This is frequently applied to shorter-stroke cranks intended for very high RPM operation.

From a durability and power standpoint center counterweights may be more desirable than a low MMOI except perhaps in a drag racing engine with short-event duration and a requirement for very rapid transient acceleration. Designers also concern themselves with the hardness and ductility of cranks. The movement is shifting toward harder and stiffer cranks to maintain dimensional integrity for improved power production, but a crank must still be able to give a little without cracking. This is called ductility. Cranks need some measure of ductility to absorb extreme loads without failure, but they also need high tensile strength to provide consistent bearing loads. This is currently an area of ongoing investigation among crankshaft designers.

Counterweights are necessary to offset the forces of the reciprocating components as the crankshaft spins. They are a necessary and effective balancing component, but they also present various problems with regard to crankcase windage. Crankshaft manufacturers all have their own preferred methods of shaping counterweights to reduce parasitic drag. The most common approach is to either radius or knife-edge the leading and trailing edges of the counterweights so they cut through oil more easily. This practice is generally more effective when accompanied by new oil-shedding coatings that enhance the overall effect.

Counterweights can also be undercut and/or narrowed on one or both sides to reduce mass and frontal area as presented to the swirling oil mass. Material is removed from the sides and the leading and trailing edges closest to the center of the crank, leaving a concentration of mass toward the outer radius of the counterweight for optimum balancing effect. Heavy metal or slugs of tungsten/nickel/copper alloy are often used to provide additional mass in cases where it is required to achieve proper balance. They are also used to reduce the frontal area of a counterweight, allowing the removal of considerable material from the leading and trailing edge while maintaining adequate mass with the heavy metal inserts. Heavy metal inserts must always be installed perpendicular to the direction of rotation by pressing them into appropriately bored holes in the counterweights.

A popular feature of racing crankshafts is gun drilling the mains, which effectively lightens the crank, but has little effect on the rotating inertia of the crankshaft because material removed from the center of the crank represents almost no leverage or moment arm. The rear flange can also be machined in a star pattern to eliminate material and further reduce weight without compromising the crankshaft-to-flywheel interface.

Operating Conditions

Like all objects, crankshafts are subject to the physical effects of mass and inertia. Crankshafts are constantly accelerating and decelerating. We are mostly concerned with the accelerating side and attending factors that contribute to deflection, inertia, resistance to transient torque, and the engine's ability to accelerate through a given RPM range. These factors include crankshaft weight, stroke length, and the distribution of mass within the crank and companion components such as rods and pistons.

For a fixed mass (rod, piston, and attending components), a heavy crankshaft absorbs more torque and accelerates less rapidly. More torque is required to overcome its inertia or resistance to acceleration. Lighter cranks are desirable for this reason, but they may trade away durability and performance if reduced structure results in greater crank deflection, reduced stability, and the resulting effects on durability, ring seal, and in some cases, event timing. The problem intensifies with stroke length; hence efforts are made to concentrate crankshaft mass closer to the crank axis to reduce the moment of inertia or resistance to change in acceleration.

Savvy machinists keep balance weight as close to the axis as possible. When removing weight for balancing purposes, they try to take weight from as far out as possible without actually drilling into the outer face of the crank throws, which can exacerbate windage problems at high engine speeds. Many cranks have the crankpins drilled. This is generally the most effective way to lighten a crankshaft unless you get into expensive counterweight machining. Drilling the crank pins removes weight at the farthest possible point from the center of the crank, thus reducing the rotating inertia.

Crankshaft Oiling

Pressurized oil is delivered to the main bearings via the main oil galleries in the cylinder block. Once oil enters the main journals it flows through drilled passages to the rod journals to lubricate the connecting rod bearings. This oiling system is used in virtually every production automobile because it is the most efficient way to lubricate the rotating assembly.

Cross Drilling

Many years ago racers decided that cross-drilling an additional hole straight through the mains provided better lubrication to the bearings, likely a result of trying to fix an oiling problem or some other problem caused by improper clearances and bearings that were not originally designed for the stress of a racing environment. In some cases the through holes were drilled in both the mains and the rod journals. This did no real harm to engines that never ran elevated engine speeds. But racers soon learned that at very high

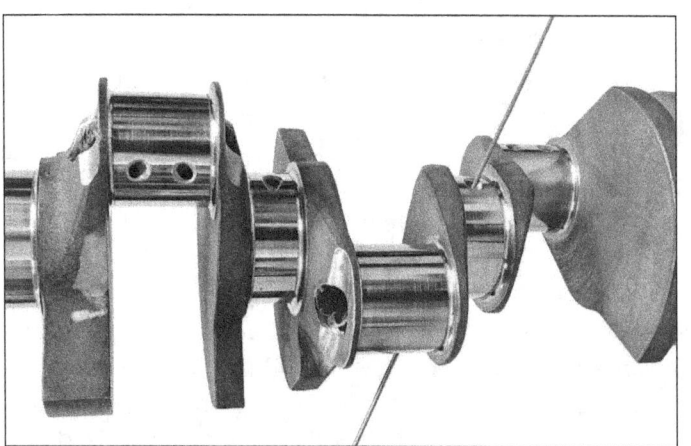

All top-of-the-line racing crankshafts utilize "straight-shot oiling" in which the rods are oiled via a straight, uninterrupted passage from the mains.

engine speeds, a cross-drilled crank centrifuged the oil out of the main journal, preventing it from flowing freely to the rod journals.

Smaller-Diameter Rod Bearings

In any properly designed oiling system, cross-drilling is unnecessary, particularly now that most race blocks feature priority main oiling. You won't see any high-end racing teams in NASCAR or professional drag racing using cross-drilled crankshafts. One important consideration regarding cross-drilling is rod journal size. Many of today's race engines have reduced bearing diameter and width. While this does good things for bearing speed and friction reduction, it increases bearing loading and makes adequate rod journal lubrication more important than ever.

Cup teams have developed this to a high degree and they know what they can and can't do. They run a 1.889-inch-diameter Honda rod bearing, which requires a specially designed crankshaft to ensure proper oiling. The smaller journals reduce bearing surface area and friction, but unit loading is increased. This tends to raise oil temperatures and promote bearing fatigue, but it becomes an acceptable trade-off because the engines only have to last about 600 to 700 miles before a rebuild and the teams have tweaked oiling system efficiency to support the use of smaller journals. One area that they do not compromise on is the fillet radius between the bearing journal and the crank throws.

Smaller-Diameter Main Bearings

While there is power to be gained from these procedures, mistakes are unforgiving. Main journal diameter is a primary factor of crankshaft torsional stiffness and thus influences a crank's resistance to bending and deflection under load. In other types of racing (like sprint cars and late-model dirt racers), builders prefer larger mains for greater durability because these engines make a lot of torque and they are expected to last for 1,000 laps or more without requiring a rebuild. Smaller mains have been tried mostly without success because they permit unacceptable crankshaft deflection under high loading.

Smaller mains reduce bearing speed and friction, but the stability and durability penalties are frequently unacceptable except in cases with exceptionally short strokes and minimal reciprocating mass—typically short-deck, small-displacement drag racing engines that turn a lot of RPM with lightweight reciprocating components and short event duration. Builders contemplating these types of engines often seek engineering expertise from crankshaft manufacturers to ensure the most compatible package.

Rod Journal Oiling

Of particular note are recent changes in oiling strategy for the delivery of oil to the rod journals. Engineers have long recognized the critical function of the hydrodynamic wedge of oil that prevents metal-to-metal contact in a fluid bearing design. They also recognize that the hydrodynamic wedge offers its greatest load-carrying ability at the center of the bearing journal interface as the wedge functionally tapers toward the sides of the bearing due to oil leakage. This is one reason appropriate rod side clearance is so important.

More recently, crank designers have turned their attention to the methodology of oiling the rod journals, particularly as it applies to the common engine builder practice of grinding chamfers on the oil holes to help distribute the oil to the bearing. This practice has always seemed logical, but there are several caveats.

The common rod journal oiling strategy is called "straight-shot oiling." Each main journal feeds an adjacent rod journal via a straight passage from the main at a position of minimum load (upper) to the rod journal at a position of maximum compressive loading. Virtually every performance crank is drilled this way because it minimizes oil starvation caused by centrifugal force at high engine speeds and it provides optimum oil feed to support the hydrodynamic wedge at the point of highest load on the journal.

Still, two potential problems remain. First, the angled passage from the main naturally creates an elliptical opening at the rod journal. This opening is often further enlarged by the chamfering many engine builders perform.

Second, the chamfer is ground in the direction of rotation to help feed the oil onto the journal, but some designers now see this as an interruption or potential point of

Conventional practice incorporates oiling holes in the rod journals that are chamfered to ease the flow of oil onto the bearing.

hydrodynamic wedge collapse directly in the center of the bearing where the wedge carries the greatest load. Also, with the reduced bearing width favored by most builders there is further potential to weaken the wedge at the point of highest loading. This line of thought was first introduced by Cosworth in the 1960s and its application remains controversial.

Some engineers propose drilling vertical journal holes centered in the path of each rod bearing so the resulting opening is perfectly circular. Each rod bearing on the journal is then fed via an angled passage from its adjacent main bearing. The smaller (cross-sectional opening) vertical holes concentrate oil delivery in the center of each rod bearing where the wedge forms its highest pressure and the smaller circular oiling hole minimizes disruption to the wedge. A second method of accomplishing this uses drilled horizontal passages from the main journal through the crank pin overlap. The horizontal passages are connected by vertical passages and ultimately lead to the perpendicular oil holes in the journal.

While complicated and more expensive, it is seen as advantageous because each pair of rod journals can be fed from only one main bearing. Thus the rod journals in a V-8 can be oiled from mains 1, 3, and 5 while mains 2 and 4 are left to enjoy the full benefit of priority oiling without having to also feed a pair of rod journals. According to some research, mains 2 and 4 in Chevy V-8s are more highly loaded because they have the thrust bearing at the rear instead of on the center main. Thus the application of direct oil pressure and reduced leakage ensures optimum lubrication of the most highly loaded mains.

Summary

These are some things to consider if you are experiencing or anticipating bearing issues. Consult your crank manufacturer for specifics and consider yourself in good company if they are willing to discuss the relative merits of these emerging views. By all means, provide the crankshaft manufacturer with every possible detail about your application and its operational requirements. The more details they have, the more closely they can match a crankshaft to your specific requirements.

Engine Balancing

Engine balancing is often thought of as a "black art" practiced by wily machine shop wizards, but it's not really all that mysterious. Thousands of highly competent engine shops do it every day and rarely experience balance-related engine problems. Balancing has become even more precise with today's modern computer-controlled equipment. Balancing components within 2 grams used to be commonplace in performance circles, but not anymore. Many balance shops claim to balance within 1/2 gram or less for maximum precision and engine smoothness, but this is largely sales hype. While everything in modern performance engines is lighter and potentially more fragile, particularly in a high-speed environment, balancing components to within 2 grams is still perfectly acceptable even on the stoutest racing engines.

Calculating Balance Weight

The primary difficulty with engine balancing is that some of the parts go round and round while others go up and down. Getting them to do it harmoniously requires precision balancing to within 2 grams. Adjustable bob weights are used to simulate the weight of the parts during balancing. Rotating weight includes the big end of the connecting rod, rod bolts, and rod bearings plus a small amount (2 to 3 grams) to simulate the oil between the crank journals and bearings. Reciprocating weight includes the small end of the rod, the piston, piston pins, piston rings and retainers if they are used, and a few grams for the oil that clings to the various moving parts. Once all of the component weights

This forged Scat crank displays aero-shaped counterweights, heavy metal inserts for balancing, radiused journal fillets, and chamfered rod journal oiling holes.

are equalized, the bob weights are calculated. A normal bob weight includes 100 percent of the rotating weight and 50 percent of the reciprocating weight. The crankshaft is electronically balanced with the bob weights attached and normal balance is easily achieved.

Overbalancing

High-RPM engines are frequently overbalanced to improve high-speed balance with less regard to low-speed smoothness. The intent is to further smooth the engine's state of balance in its intended operating range. Crank manufacturers view this with skepticism and most of them recommend the standard balance percentages. In theory, when an assembly is overbalanced, the trick is to balance it so that any critical imbalance falls outside of the intended operating range (either above or below it). To accomplish this, the bob weights are adjusted from the calculated norm. Instead of adding 50 percent of the reciprocating weight, the percentage is often increased to something in the 52- to 54-percent range.

If any of this is truly a black art it may be in actually determining the correct percentage of overbalance. Many builders claim to know from experience, but new combinations often require an educated guess and most builders don't seem inclined to reveal their preferred overbalance percentages or the strategy they employ to determine them. The most common approach attempts to err on the conservative side, say 51 to 52 percent. If the engine's performance and smoothness improves within its primary operating range, builders may overbalance it a bit more on the next go around.

- Normal Balance = 100-percent rotating weight plus 50-percent reciprocating weight
- Overbalance = 100-percent rotating weight plus desired percentage of increase in reciprocating weight (52 percent)

The overbalance percentage may cause dramatic vibrations outside of the engine's normal operating range, but it is considered a minor concern since you don't run it here for any length of time. Opinions vary regarding these balancing techniques. Many engine builders swear by the traditional 100-percent rotating and 50-percent reciprocating while some even prefer a small degree of underbalance, say 48 to 49 percent of reciprocating weight while others believe that an overbalance in the 52- to 53-percent range is highly advantageous for power and durability.

Overbalancing is a competition engine practice and not something normally done to a street or street/strip engine that operates over a broader RPM range. For race engines it is thought to have the potential to save parts and improve performance by reducing vibrations that might be harmful to ring seal, valvetrain dynamics, and other factors that affect power within a specific powerband. Also note that not all engine builders and crank manufacturers believe that it is necessary. If you feel the need to consider it, consult your crankshaft manufacturer first to get a recommendation.

Crankshaft Dampening

Another area considered a black art by many is the strange world of dampeners or, more correctly, torsional absorbers. The previously mentioned crankshaft deflections and bending moments cause vibration in the crankshaft. A crankshaft may be viewed in much the same manner as a torsion bar in that it has a specific mass and a spring rate that resonates at some particular frequency as determined by the engine's continuous firing sequence and influenced by crankshaft material, torsional stiffness, length, stroke, reciprocating mass, and contributing moments of inertia from flywheels, clutches, and even rotating assemblies driven off the crank such as water pumps, alternators, and dry sump pumps.

A resonate frequency is recognized as the frequency change with engine speed and the amplitude or degree of excitation varies accordingly. Hence the engine may run very smoothly at some speeds and shake at others depending on the influence of the various contributors. The frequency is the number of vibration cycles per second, as in 600 cycles per second, or 600 hertz. When a frequency is multiplied by an "order," it incorporates the number of times the excitation is produced (e.g., four power strokes per revolution in a V-8 engine). This represents a fourth-order excitation from which the frequency can be calculated. In a drag racing engine running at 9,000 rpm, the frequency of this fourth-order excitation calculates as follows.

$$\frac{\text{Order} \times \text{RPM}}{60}$$

$$\frac{4 \times 9{,}000}{60} = 600 \text{ hertz}$$

The process of controlling this vibration is called attenuation and refers in this case to the torsional absorber. Absorber is the correct

CRANKSHAFTS

Crankshaft Inspection and Prep

1. Inspect for visual problems such as an oiling hole that has been compromised by lightening holes in the throws
2. Check thrust flange distance to crank gear distance for proper dimension
3. Check thrust face to center of throws distance to ensure proper position of piston in bores
4. Verify stroke
5. Verify journal size
6. Check throw index

Many crank manufacturers recommend the smallest and lightest dampener available. This BHJ S.F.I. 18.1 unit for a big-block Chevy fits the description. Elastomer-type dampeners are preferred because of their durability and superior high-frequency damping qualities. And because they are capable of damping all types of vibrations: torsional, axial, and radial.

nomenclature since an absorber is designed to cancel out a specific frequency or order by oscillating in opposition to the vibration. For the purpose of this discussion I stick to convention and call it a dampener.

All racing engines need a dampener to control vibration. One exception is a sprint car engine, which operates without a flywheel. A flywheel is normally part of the absorption stack and operates in conjunction with the dampener to control vibrations. The lack of one in a sprint car changes the frequencies of the crankshaft and (in conjunction with the damping effect of the crank-driven water pump) allows them to operate safely, even in very high horsepower with frequent throttling under very high loading.

CHAPTER 5

PISTON TECHNOLOGY

Racing pistons are manufactured from aluminum forgings. Certainly plenty of racing occurs with cast and hypereutectic pistons, but only where class rules forbid aluminum forgings. This book deals with high-level racing engines, so this discussion primarily pertains to forged racing pistons. With the exception of clearances and certain performance features, cast and hypereutectic pistons can be prepped the same way, so much of what is discussed here still applies.

The primary aluminum alloy for piston forgings is 2618 although 4032 is often used when greater control of thermal expansion is required (see "Piston Alloys" on page 59). The downside is a reduction in strength due to higher silicon content. Choosing a piston for a racing engine requires careful evaluation of the final application in terms of engine speed and the sustained piston motion, velocity, and loading that occurs. Hence a brief discussion of piston speed is warranted.

Piston Speed

Piston speed (velocity) refers to the average or mean speed of the piston as it moves up and down in the cylinder bore during each crankshaft revolution. Since the piston actually comes to a complete stop at the top of the stroke (TDC) and at the bottom of the stroke (BDC), its speed and acceleration at any given point is always changing. The piston is always accelerating from or decelerating to zero speed.

The official formula for mean piston speed yields an average speed based on two times the stroke (up and down for one revolution), times the engine speed (RPM), divided by 12 to convert to feet per minute (fpm). To simplify the formula, you can divide the numerator and the denominator by 2:

With a fixed block deck height and stroke length, the rod length becomes the variable that dictates the pin height dimension and thus the relative location of the ring pack. Piston designers target specific ring locations according to the application, hence rod length must often be adjusted to achieve the best balance between ring placement, pin height, and the performance benefits of a specific rod length.

PISTON TECHNOLOGY

Piston Speed$_{fpm}$ = stroke x RPM ÷ 6

For example, piston speed for a 350 Chevy with a 3.48-inch stroke at 7,000 rpm is calculated like this:

Piston Speed$_{fpm}$ = 3.48 x 7,000 ÷ 6
Piston Speed$_{fpm}$ = 4,060

Accepted mean velocity for most racing pistons is about 4,500 fpm, but many racing engines routinely exceed that with mean speeds of 5,500 fpm or higher. Interestingly, many Formula 1 engines with an engine speed of 18,000 rpm typically have a mean piston speed below 5,000 fpm primarily due to their very short stroke. In contrast a Cup engine exceeding 9,000 rpm may have a piston speed approaching 5,500 fpm.

Mean piston speed has long been used as a predictor of component durability under severe service. It is a good rule of thumb and it is even more instructive if you calculate maximum piston speed (MPS), since one of the axioms of engine performance dictates that power comes from engine speed. The more power strokes per minute, the more power available to do work.

You can get a very close approximation of MPS (ignoring rod center to center length and rod angularity) with the following formula:

Multiply the stroke times pi and divide by 12 to get feet per revolution. Then multiply by the maximum engine speed to get the maximum feet per minute.

MPS$_{fpm}$ = (stroke x π ÷ 12) x RPM

This speed occurs about mid stroke where the connecting rod is 90 degrees to the crankpin and the crank angle is approximately 75 degrees. Before that point the piston is accelerating; after it the piston is decelerating. When the piston is exactly at either TDC or BDC it is stopped and there is no acceleration.

Continuing our example of a 350 Chevy with a 3.48-inch stroke, let's find its maximum piston speed at 7,000 rpm.

MPS$_{fpm}$ = (3.48 x 3.14 ÷ 12) x 7,000
MPS$_{fpm}$ = (10.92 ÷ 12) x 7,000
MPS$_{fpm}$ = .91 x 7,000
MPS$_{fpm}$ = 6,370 fpm

Acceleration

One of the most important considerations is the instantaneous piston acceleration and the staggering loads placed on the piston pin bore, piston pin, connecting rod, and rod bolts when the piston reverses at TDC. These are the most highly stressed components in the engine. Since an engine's ability to make power is closely tied to the RPM it can turn, every effort is made to lighten valvetrain components to combat valve float. But the real limit often turns out to be piston mass and piston acceleration.

A typical 350 Chevy piston weighs 1.3 to 1.6 pounds. Special racing pistons weigh less, but imagine trying to accelerate one to over 6,800 fpm (350 Chevy at 7,500 rpm) maximum piston speed at mid-stroke and then slam it to a dead stop and reverse direction in about 1¾ inches (stroke ÷ 2).

At TDC the piston is headed for the moon and the rod has to stop it and yank it back the other way. That's enough to pull the piston pin right out of the piston, and it does on occasion. It also exerts similar loads on the rod bolts and rod cap. Acceleration (and thus g-force) is greatest just after TDC on the exhaust stroke (because there is no compression to cushion the piston).

The commonly used formula for calculating the maximum acceleration (MA) of a piston is:

MA = [(rpm^2 x stroke ÷ 2,189) x (stroke ÷ 2 ÷ rod length) + 1]

For example, the maximum acceleration of a 350 Chevy piston at 7,500 rpm using the stock stroke of 3.48 inches and the stock rod length of 5.7 inches is calculated like this:

MA = [(7,500^2 x 3.48) ÷ 2,189] x [(3.48 ÷ 2 ÷ 5.7) + 1]
MA = 7,500 x 3.48 x 1.3052
MA = 89,424.39 x 1.3052
MA = 116,716.71 ft/sec^2

That's insane acceleration for a 450- to 600-gram object that is not a cannon projectile. Because they are captured by the ring grooves, the piston rings are along for the ride, slamming up and down within the ring grooves trying desperately to maintain a seal with the cylinder wall. Is it any wonder that they experience ring flutter at very high engine speeds? Hence, the practice of using the tightest ring grooves possible without seizure and the thinnest and lightest rings that have minimal inertia.

If you apply this math to a Formula 1 engine you'll find that the instantaneous acceleration is far beyond the normally accepted limit of 150,000 ft/sec^2. How do they do it? The pistons are changing direction more than 150 times per second. It seems far beyond the physical limitation of the components involved, but then Formula 1 uses some very light and very strong exotic materials.

CHAPTER 5

With the advent of shallower combustion chambers, flat-top pistons are often a favored choice among engine builders seeking higher compression ratios and optimum flame travel.

An exception to the flat-top revolution is this Honda S2000 piston designed for a pent-roof combustion chamber in the Honda four-valve-per-cylinder head.

Piston Speed Issues

As discussed earlier, piston speed is an issue for component durability as it relates to engine speed and g-loading. But there is another factor of near equal importance. Note that even NASCAR and Formula 1 engines don't like to exceed an MPS of 5,000 feet per minute. The reason is oil control.

In most engines, the pistons and rings are lubricated by oil splash being thrown off the spinning crank and rods. NASCAR and Formula 1 engines have an additional source provided by pin oilers, which spray a small jet of oil at the bottom of the piston to lubricate the piston pin and cool the piston crown. But most engines rely only on splash. This becomes a potential problem when you dry sump an engine to remove all oil from the pan. In many cases efforts are also made to isolate the cam tunnel to eliminate cam and lifter oil from dripping on the crankshaft. All of these things combine to reduce the amount of oil being splashed on the cylinder walls. Why is this important? At elevated engine RPM and the attending high piston speeds, reduced cylinder oiling makes it difficult to maintain a consistent hydrodynamic oil film between the piston and the cylinder wall. When MPS exceeds 5,500 rpm, inconsistent lubrication causes the piston to scuff and, worst-case scenario, friction-weld itself to the cylinder wall. This typically results in cylinder wall scoring and ultimately engine failure. The greater the piston speed, the bigger this problem can be, especially when other oiling system modifications combine to reduce cylinder wall oiling. When piston speed is too high, the minimal fog of lubricant in the crankcase has no time to attach itself to the cylinder wall.

Selection Factors

Piston selection incorporates numerous factors including alloy type, expansion characteristics, skirt design, deck and dome configuration, pin type, and ring design and placement.

Piston Alloys

Virtually all pistons are made from either 2618 or 4032 aluminum. These alloys differ primarily in their material content and thermal and fatigue properties, which dictate their suitability for different applications. A 2618 piston has almost no silicon content. It expands approximately 15 percent more than a piston manufactured from 4032 alloy, but it yields higher strength at racing temperatures, particularly above 500 degrees F. Therefore, more race pistons are manufactured from 2618 than from 4032, which is more

Basic piston top choices include flat tops, dished, and various domed shapes designed to increase the compression ratio.

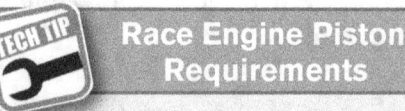

Race Engine Piston Requirements

- Stability in the bore
- Minimize piston rocking
- Consistent thermal expansion
- Piston ring support

PISTON TECHNOLOGY

Alloy Comparison

	4032	2618
Nominal Density	2.68 g/cc, .097 lb/in^3	2.81 g/cc, .100 lb/in^3
Ultimate Tensile Strength	380 MPa, 55,000 psi	440 MPa, 64,000 psi
Tensile Strength, Yield	315 MPa, 46,000 psi	370 MPa, 54,000 psi
Modulus of Elasticity	79 GPa, 11400 psi	74 GPa, 10,400 psi
Fatigue Endurance Limit	110 MPa, 16,000 psi	125 MPa, 18,000 psi

Courtesy JE Pistons

popular for street engines that utilize less cold clearance and require minimal startup noise. 2618 is the material of choice for Cup engines, Formula 1, and most high-end applications. Unless piston choice is limited to cast or hypereutectic pistons, the application will almost certainly be machined from one of the various proprietary 2618 forgings utilized by the major piston manufacturers.

Coefficient of Thermal Expansion

2618 alloy expands roughly 15 percent more than 4032 alloy, hence its initial piston-to-wall clearance is 15 percent greater. Both alloys have approximately the same clearance at operating temperature with 2618 expanding approximately a half a thousandth (.0005-inch) more at 375 degrees F on a 4-inch-diameter piston. Pistons made from 4032 alloy are typically used for street/strip applications while most race applications use 2618 alloy for its superior tensile strength, fatigue resistance, and lower modulus of elasticity.

Piston Top Selection

Choice of piston top configuration is application specific and dependent on the compression ratio and combustion chamber configuration. High compression is still a staple of engine efficiency and big horsepower, but contemporary racing engines achieve it in different ways. In many cases large piston domes no longer prevail. Flat-top pistons and some gentle dome configurations are much more prevalent. They are designed specifically to work with modern cylinder heads that have shallower, highly efficient combustion chambers.

These combinations can still achieve high compression ratios and they are much more efficient due to improved mixture motion and combustion characteristics. Also, smaller combustion chambers help to build static compression and they generally provide shorter flame travel, which lessens the initial timing requirement and reduces negative work against the piston as it approaches TDC.

Piston Skirt Design

Piston skirts stabilize the piston in the bore. If the ring pack alone were capable of maintaining stability and optimum ring seal throughout all the various direction and pressure changes and the overall range of engine speed, you could remove the skirts altogether and eliminate a major friction source. Unfortunately that's not possible, particularly with the current trend to lower tension rings.

Skirts are necessary to provide stability to the piston's secondary motion, which is rocking in the bore caused by thrust loading, friction characteristics, piston center-of-gravity, pin location, and offset and temperature variations. The piston designer's goal is to optimize stability and minimize frictional losses at the same time. This is accomplished by optimizing the skirt contact area based on the application. Shortening the skirt length reduces friction, but it may also tend to compromise stability. More effort is generally expended in shaping the surface contact area to minimize friction while maintaining stability.

Most pistons still incorporate a cam grind or elliptical shape to the skirt area as a means of controlling contact area. The same goes for the barrel profile, which also influences contact area. The barrel shape tapers inward, reducing the piston's diameter as it approaches the bottom of the oil ring groove. This reduces the amount of skirt material exposed to cylinder wall contact. Critical factors are oil film viscosity, the thickness

Modern race pistons typically employ inboard pin bosses to shorten and stiffen the piston pin and to reduce weight. Depending on the application different types of skirt struts are used to add strength and stability to the piston.

CHAPTER 5

of the oil film, the degree of cylinder wall lubrication brought about by the engine's particular crankcase and rotating assembly characteristics, and the presence or absence of pin oilers.

All of this is dependent on the engine speed range, stroke length, and rod angularity. Piston salesmen are well versed in the latest trends and procedures so don't fool yourself into thinking you know more than they do. Quite likely, you don't, but it's a shared experience. Piston salesmen and designers are constantly evaluating feedback from racers to accumulate an enormous body of knowledge that covers a broad spectrum of applications.

Piston-to-wall clearance at the skirt is normally measured at the gauge point 1/2 inch up from the bottom of the skirt, but some manufacturers have very specific measurement points that you should use if they are provided.

To some degree the clearance needs to be greater on larger cylinder bores to allow for increased expansion on larger pistons. Because of their greater thermal expansion characteristics, 2618 pistons require more clearance than 4032 pistons.

> **TECH TIP**
>
> ### Basic Piston-to-Wall Clearance
>
> | | Bore Range (inches) | 2618 Clearance (inch) | 4032 Clearance (inch) |
> |---|---|---|---|
> | Sport Compact | 2.500 to 3.999 | .0030 to .0040 | .0020 to .0025 |
> | SB applications | 4.000 to 4.200 | .0035 to .0045 | .0020 to .0025 |
> | BB applications | 4.200 to 4.600 | .0040 to .0050 | .0030 to .0035 |
>
> *Courtesy JE Pistons*

> **TECH TIP**
>
> ### Piston-to-Wall Clearance per Applications
>
> | Application | Clearance (inch) |
> |---|---|
> | Drag Race | + .0005 to .0010 |
> | Forced Induction or Nitrous | + .0010 to .0015 |
> | Circle Track or Road Race | + .0005 to .0010 |
> | Marine Applications | + .0010 to .0020 |
> | Filled Block | + .0010 to .0020 |
>
> *Courtesy JE Pistons*

The rule of thumb is approximately .0012 inch per inch of bore diameter.

Many applications require additional clearance to accommodate extreme pressure and thermal loads and/or extreme engine speed. These are arbitrary guidelines and you should always determine the optimum clearance by consulting with a piston salesman and machinist.

Deck Clearance and Piston-to-Head Clearance

The deck clearance is defined as the distance between the piston top and the deck surface of the cylinder block when the piston is stopped at TDC. Deck clearance is one component of the piston-to-head clearance

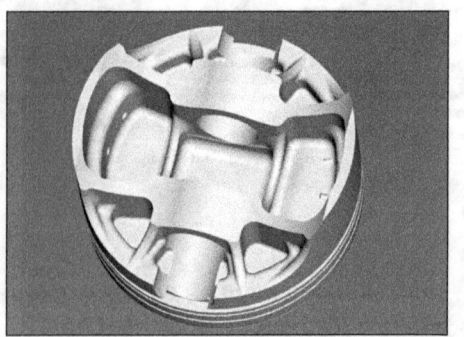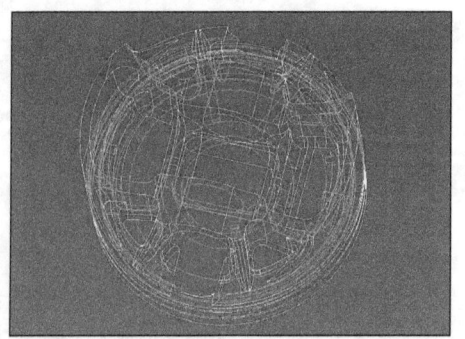

Piston engineering and design software helps piston designers model and evaluate various piston designs to suit specific operational requirements. The rendering on the left illustrates the use of reinforcement struts around the inboard pin bosses. The wire-frame model on the right shows the basic engineering design prior to surface rendering. (Courtesy Ross Pistons)

Contact reduction grooves are machined into the top ring land. They minimize piston-to-wall contact on piston rock-over. The accumulator groove is machined between the top and second ring grooves. It helps relieve excess combustion pressure below the top ring, which can unseat the ring.

PISTON TECHNOLOGY

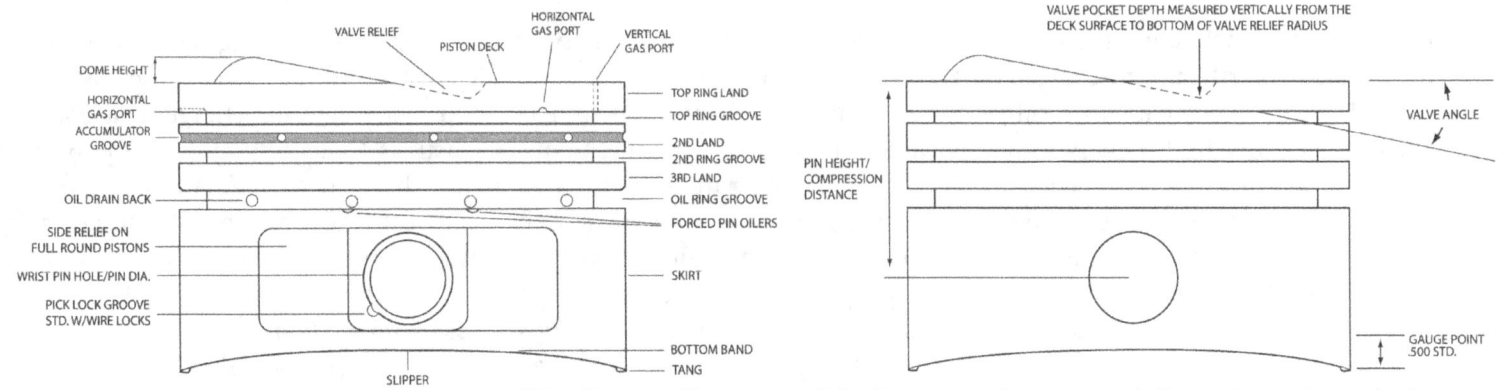

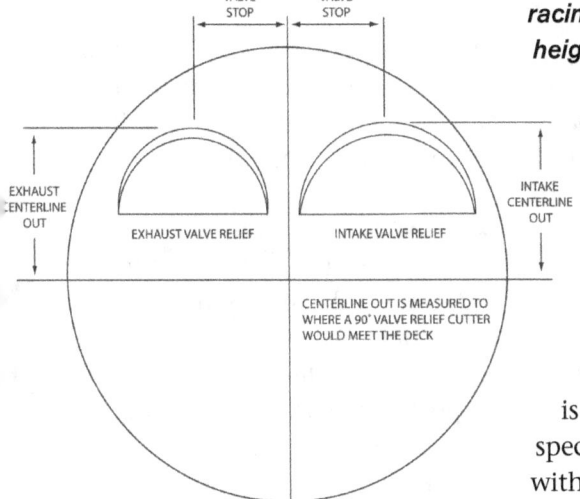

This diagram illustrates all the important features and dimensions of a typical racing piston. Note in particular the valve angle and pin height or compression height, which varies according to rod length.

dimension that seeks to accomplish the minimal clearance possible without sustained piston-to-cylinder head contact. The purpose is to promote maximum quench effect (or squish) in a wedge-type chamber that physically forces the fuel mixture closer to the spark plug, where it is more prone to combust properly. The resulting turbulence enhances mixture quality and frequently permits a reduction in spark timing to reduce negative work against the piston prior to TDC. Power is typically increased and brake-specific fuel consumption is improved with less chance of detonation.

Deck clearance can be manipulated by altering the piston pin location relative to the fixed rod and stroke dimensions or by selective piston top machining in some cases. Many times, off-the-shelf pistons from major manufacturers can be used with considerable comfort as they incorporate common compression height dimensions that are usually compatible with available block deck height dimensions.

Many builders take a minimum cut off the block deck surface to square it with the crank centerline and then order custom pistons with pin placement specifically positioned to accommodate the piston-to-head clearance they intend to achieve with the proper combination of deck height and gasket thickness.

Wrist Pin Height

Choosing a pin location involves considerably more than simply fitting the whole reciprocating package into the available space. The position of the wrist pin in the piston must accommodate many critical dimensions. Most racing engines use longer than stock connecting rods, which help reduce piston weight while having positive effects on torque positioning and combustion efficiency. The higher the pin position, the shorter the piston and there is a resulting reduction in piston mass. This frequently requires the ring pack to be located higher on the piston.

In naturally aspirated applications, builders appreciate this because they like to move the ring pack to lighten the reciprocating assembly, improve piston stability, and minimize unburned gases in the crevice volume above the top ring. However, longer rods in a supercharged application are often more problematic because boosted applications need to

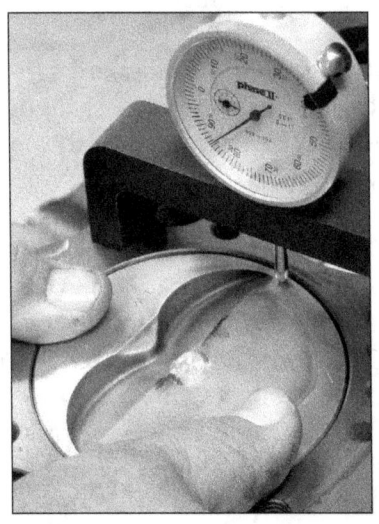

Accurate deck height measurement is essential for computing the compression ratio. With or without a ring installed during mockup, the best location to check deck height is near the edge of the piston along the pin axis. This eliminates any effect from piston rocking.

move the ring pack down the piston to position it farther from excessive heat. Longer rods make this difficult to accomplish. In many cases a shorter rod can be specified for boosted applications because boost pressure reduces the need for the critical rod/stroke tuning relationships required for efficient naturally aspirated operation.

When long rods force the pin higher in the piston they require careful checking for interference between the top of the rod and the underside of the piston top. You need a minimum of .050-inch clearance between the rod and the piston at this point. In many cases the pin bore also interferes with the oil ring groove and a support rail must be added to stabilize the oil ring. There is a practical limit to how high the ring pack can be moved, typically no closer to the top than .200 inch, although many short-duration drag racing engines run it higher.

One important factor is the depth and location of the valve relief pockets relative to the proximity and depth of the top ring groove. This presents a potential structural weakness at the closest point and higher potential for burn-through or irreparable damage from detonation. All major piston manufacturers are very familiar with these requirements and salesmen normally keep customers out of trouble even though many may wish to go there. In many cases they can select an alternate forging and machine it to accommodate your requirements. If, in the case of naturally aspirated applications, you are using rod length to help position a torque curve, the sales people can get you as close as possible to your desired dimensions while making sure you don't exceed limits that lead to early failures.

Piston Coatings

Piston coatings are now commonplace. Several types are used on pistons depending on the desired results. Various thermal barrier coatings are frequently applied to piston tops. They help hold heat in the combustion chamber to increase cylinder pressure while reducing the amount of heat transfered into the piston. Benefits also include reduced oil temperature and piston expansion.

Contact Reduction or Anti-Detonation Grooves

These grooves are designed to limit piston-to-cylinder-wall contact at elevated temperatures and high RPM. They are machined into the top ring land to protect the top ring by theoretically disrupting detonation pressure waves. Engine builders are split regarding their value, particularly since many pistons already incorporate a small degree of vertical taper on the top ring land to guard against contact between the piston and cylinder wall. The general consensus is that they don't add power and that once detonation occurs, ring seal is lost and bigger problems usually ensue.

Accumulator Groove

A V-shaped or U-shaped groove is machined into the second ring land to collect excess blow-by between the top and second ring. This groove collects excess residual combustion gases to help control top ring flutter while maintaining ring seal.

Cam and Barrel Shape

Every piston requires the correct cam and barrel skirt shape for the application and the anticipated engine speed. Different cam and barrel profiles are utilized for maximum performance. Piston manufacturers have a range of cam and barrel profiles that apply depending on the specific forging and the final application. When the skirt shape has been optimized it promotes:

- Tighter clearances
- Improved ring seal
- Increased power
- Improved durability

Piston skirt cam shapes are generally divided into two types: high-cam and low-cam profiles. Both are slightly elliptical but the high-cam shape is more pronounced. Both styles produce similar fictional losses, but the high-cam profile permits tighter cold-piston-to-wall clearances. Both cam profiles tend to resume their round shape once they come up to temperature. A piston sales rep can help you decide which is best for your application.

 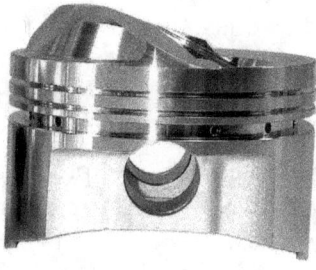

Extra-tall domed pistons are still required for certain applications with large combustion chambers in order to achieve higher compression ratios.

These pistons require close attention to detail regarding valve-to-piston clearance, valve shrouding, and a generous fire slot to ensure efficient flame travel.

Piston Taper

In addition to a barrel shape or taper below the oil ring groove, pistons also taper inward above the oil ring to accommodate thermal expansion and prevent piston-to-wall contact upon piston rock. The difference in diameter of the top ring land compared to that of the oil ring land often is .025 to .040 inch.

Vertical Gas Ports

Vertical gas ports are a series (8 to 12) of vertical holes drilled around the perimeter of the piston deck at a radius that coincides with the back of the top piston ring groove. These holes direct combustion gas pressure to the back side of the top compression ring to force the ring out against the cylinder wall for improved sealing. These ports are typically used for short-duration drag racing applications and are designed to work with a tight ring groove side clearance of about 0.001 inch.

Lateral Gas Ports

Lateral gas ports perform the same function as vertical gas ports except they are half-round slots drilled horizontally into the top ring land at the top of the ring groove. Like vertical gas ports, they are essential for sealing low-tension compression rings. Lateral gas ports are more commonly used in longer-duration and endurance circle track and road racing applications. They offer similar ring sealing ability, but tend to acquire less carbon buildup than the vertical ports over time.

Valve Reliefs

Piston-to-valve clearance is one of the most critical clearances in a racing engine. The intake valve comes closest to the piston at approximately 10 degrees ATDC and the exhaust valve is closest at about 10 degrees BTDC. Many racing pistons are now manufactured with valve reliefs that already incorporate the correct valve angle and accommodate the necessary depth, but you must check every single one of them personally, particularly if you are practicing individual cylinder tuning via different cam profiles and/or rocker ratio in alternate cylinders.

Minimum clearance should be .100 inch on the intake valve and .120 inch on the exhaust valve and this should be increased by .020 to .030 inch if you run aluminum rods. Engine builders frequently fudge this a bit, but it is a dangerous course.

The radial clearance on each valve should be at least .050 inch and the valve relief pocket must be machined at the proper angle and perfectly perpendicular to the valve axis.

Asymmetrical Pistons

JE Piston's asymmetrical pistons have gained favor with many import engine builders. A recent development pioneered by JE, asymmetrical pistons, are manufactured with smaller, narrower skirts on the minor-thrust side. This configuration retains the standard design intent skirt for the major-thrust surface as required by the specific application.

The skirt on the minor-thrust side is reduced in size (width) to help minimize friction while still supporting piston stability within the bore. This also reduces overall piston weight. To date this piston design is only being applied in import engines with smaller, lighter pistons.

Valve-to-Piston Clearance

Some engine builders like to push the valve-to-piston clearance pretty tight, but there are guidelines that most builders use to keep themselves out of trouble. For steel and titanium rods with minimal stretch, .060 to .080 inch is the generally accepted minimum clearance. To some degree this also depends on the camshaft and valvetrain and the engine's operational speed range. With lower engine speeds, some builders may fudge the intake clearance a little below .060 inch while maintaining the exhaust valve clearance at .100 to .120 inch. Two times the intake clearance is the generally accepted rule of thumb.

Higher-speed engines require even more precise fitment to ensure safe operation. This is particularly important in order to provide a safety factor in case of missed shifts or other conditions where an over-rev may occur. The intake valve comes closest to hitting the piston at approximately 10 degrees ATDC and the exhaust valve comes closest at about 10 degrees BTDC. Note that from this point the intake valve is actually chasing the piston down the bore as it opens, thus from the closest point, the clearance is always increasing.

Theoretically the intake valve should never hit the piston as long as you have adequate clearance at this point. While not good for power production, some small degree of pushrod and rocker arm flex at this point actually works in your favor in terms of valve-to-piston clearance.

On the exhaust side the piston is bearing down on the exhaust valve as it closes. It is imperative that contact be avoided at all cost. Additional exhaust valve clearance is required to accommodate thermal growth of the valve due to high exhaust temperatures. It is also important that the valve reliefs in the pistons are geometrically parallel with the faces of the valves. This can sometimes minimize damage if slight contact does occur.

The radial valve relief clearance around each valve should be no less than .050 to .060 inch. Exhaust valve piston-to-valve contact is typically exacerbated by high engine speeds where the valvesprings have trouble keeping the lifters in contact with the cam lobes, causing some degree of lofting or float. Loss of lifter control frequently causes exhaust-valve-to-piston collisions due to thermal lengthening of the valve and the more critical dynamic relationship of the piston chasing the valve as it closes (see Chapter 11).

Race Piston Terminology

Understanding the many factors of race piston design is fundamental to making the correct choices to suit the intended racing application.

Contact Reduction or Anti-Detonation Grooves

These are grooves machined into the top ring land to protect the top ring by theoretically disrupting detonation pressure waves. They are designed to limit piston-to-cylinder-wall contact at elevated temperatures and high RPM. Engine builders are split regarding their value, particularly since many pistons already incorporated a small degree of vertical taper on the top ring land to guard against this contact. The general consensus is that they don't add power and that once detonation occurs, ring seal is lost and bigger problems usually ensue.

Accumulator Groove

This is a V- or U-shaped groove machined into the second ring land to collect excess blow-by between the top and second ring. This groove collects excess residual combustion gases to help control top ring flutter while maintaining ring seal.

Constant Pressure (CP) Groove

This is a channel or groove on the lower part of the top land that equalizes pressure to the back of the top ring groove. When used with lateral gas ports, the CP groove reduces carbon buildup in the gas ports and prevents the top land from pinching the top ring if the land contacts the cylinder bore.

Flat-top pistons have become much more prevalent because they minimize the loss of combustion heat to the surface area. They also promote superior flame travel when paired with shallow combustion chambers.

High-performance dished pistons are desirable in supercharged and turbocharged applications where the static compression ratio must be limited to ensure a safe and effective compression ratio under boosted conditions.

Contoured piston tops cut specifically to match a known combustion chamber shape and size are commonly used in specific racing applications. Manufacturers such as Ross Pistons can digitize your chambers for an exact match.

This close-up of a typical gas port arrangement illustrates size and placement of vertical gas port holes drilled to direct combustion pressure to the back side of the top compression ring. Gas ports are beneficial when using low-tension rings with reduced radial width. They use combustion pressure to provide superior ring seal on the combustion stroke while providing reduced friction on the other strokes.

PISTON TECHNOLOGY

Cam and Barrel Shape

Every piston requires the correct cam and barrel skirt shape for the application and the anticipated engine speed. Different cam and barrel profiles are utilized for maximum performance. Piston manufacturers have a range of cam and barrel profiles that apply depending on the specific forging and the final application. When the skirt shape has been optimized it promotes tighter clearances, greater stability, improved ring seal, increased power, and improved durability.

Advanced piston coatings have become the norm in many racing circles. This piston features a thermal heat barrier on the crown and a friction-reduction coating on the skirts.

Vertical Gas Ports

Vertical gas ports are a series (8 to 12) of vertical holes drilled around the perimeter of the piston deck at a radius that coincides with the back of the top piston ring groove. These holes direct combustion gas pressure to the back side of the top compression ring to force the ring out against the cylinder wall for improved sealing. These ports are typically used for short-duration drag racing applications and are designed to work with a tight ring groove side clearance of about .001 inch.

Lateral Gas Ports

These ports are meant to perform the same function as vertical gas ports except they are half-round slots drilled horizontally into the top ring land at the top of the ring groove. Like vertical gas ports, the intent is to enhance the sealing of low-tension rings. Lateral gas ports are more commonly used in longer duration and endurance circle track and road racing applications. They do not offer the same ring sealing ability as vertical ports and they tend to negatively affect top ring sealing unless everything is perfectly aligned.

Rings

Piston rings have one of the toughest jobs in a competition engine. They are subjected to various conflicting forces while constantly being slammed back and forth up to 150 times per second or more. Consider for a moment the primary goals of the piston rings in a modern racing engine.

- Seal combustion pressure within the combustion space
- Maintain compression ratio
- Prevent oil contamination of the fuel charge
- Transfer heat from the piston to the cylinder wall
- Resist ring flutter and chatter (vertical displacement) to maintain optimum seal

These are formidable goals for thin metal rings that are subjected to the massive forces of combustion. To better understand the ring's function, let's examine each ring in the cylinder kit separately.

Top Ring

The top ring's sole function is to maintain the compression ratio and seal the combustion space against

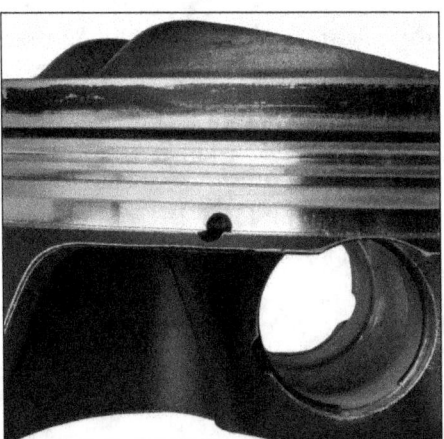

These views of a modified Dodge Cup piston show vertical gas ports, precisely shaped dome and valve reliefs, and careful blending of all sharp edges. Note the combustion residue above the top ring, but none below it. The left view shows the forced pin oiling slot inside the pin bore.

Calculating Piston Position

For the purpose of accurate camshaft selection, it is important to know the piston position where the maximum pressure drop is created in the cylinder. If you recall our core mission of maximizing VE, it's easy to grasp the critical relationship between crank angle, piston position, and the timing of valve action relative to piston position. The basic "slider crank" mechanism describes the mechanical relationships between the piston and crankshaft angle relative to rod length. For a given rod length, the piston achieves maximum velocity at some point during the stroke. This point (crank angle) varies according to rod length since stroke length is fixed. You may have heard that a longer rod supposedly makes more power, but that's not necessarily true.

As a rule, changes in rod length tend to move the power peak closer to or farther from the torque peak RPM depending on the change. When rod length is increased, the horsepower and torque peaks move closer together, but the peak values may not change significantly. Shortening the rod tends to separate the peaks more, which may or may not be beneficial depending on the application. A longer rod causes the piston to linger longer in the vicinity of TDC and the rate of acceleration and deceleration is diminished. To some small degree this provides a little more time for combustion pressure to rise higher before the power stroke. This is beneficial in high-RPM applications where combustion time is limited.

Contemporary engine simulation programs pay particular attention to rod length versus crank angle, and with good reason. The important thing to remember is the crank angle where the piston achieves maximum velocity and maximum pressure drop within the cylinder. The intake valve opening at this point should be sufficient to maximize flow. Simulations help you calculate and visualize this point.

While this function is controlled by the rate of cylinder volume exposure to atmospheric pressure via the inlet system, some highly successful championship engine builders still refer to it as "the suck." Since all of this can be calculated mathematically, cam designers use this information to optimize valve events to take advantage of piston motion for maximum cylinder filling effect. To calculate piston position in the bore relative to crank angle, keep in mind that the point of maximum velocity differs according to rod length. This point generally occurs when the rod centerline is 90 degrees to the crank pin, but the actual crank angle varies with rod length. Use the following formula to calculate piston position relative to crank angle for any given combination of stroke and rod length:

$$P = S(1 - \cos C) + (S \times S) \div L (\sin^2 \text{ of } C)$$

Where:
P = piston position relative to deck surface
S = stroke length
Cos C = cosine of angle C
L = rod length
$\sin^2$ = the sin squared of angle C
C = crank angle relative to cylinder centerline

This formula is valid for any given value of C. While longer rods are generally preferred for high-RPM operation with narrow powerbands where burn time is minimal, shorter rods have higher acceleration rates and less dwell time around TDC. Higher acceleration rates equate to quicker exposure to the pressure drop in the cylinder, which tends to separate the peaks and promote greater efficiency at lower engine speeds. The difference is often subtle, but savvy engine builders use these tools to accurately position the peaks they want relative to specific applications.

Moving the peaks closer together may bring more effective power to bear on a super speedway or a Bonneville engine, while separating the peaks may be more useful for a circle track or road racing engine where a broader powerband is more desirable. In either case, doing the math often helps illuminate the way.

many thousands of pounds of combustion pressure upon ignition. This is a formidable task. The ring is required to maintain bi-directional sealing under all conditions even as it is subjected to the rapid high pressure rise of normal combustion, which then dissipates quickly as pressure is applied to the piston during the expansion cycle (power stroke).

Comparatively speaking, the top ring gets a bit of a breather during the exhaust and intake strokes, but it still has to maintain its seal while subjected to rapidly varying changes in pressure, direction, and velocity. It has to hold compression on the compression stroke and then gets slammed back the other direction under maximum combustion pressure on the power stroke.

Throughout all of this the piston is rocking and vibrating in the bore while crankshaft oscillations attempt to impart a jerking motion to ring travel to the point where the rings don't know whether they are coming or going. And then the engine detonates and ring seal is totally lost.

Top rings are subjected to massive and near instantaneous forces just as they are attempting to change direction in a hostile environment of severe heat and pressure. Current trends toward thinner rings to reduce friction and resist ring flutter only exacerbate sealing problems; hence ring configuration and preparation are extremely critical. For years the traditional front-line application has been a high-strength ductile iron ring with a moly (molybdenum) inlaid face. Over time, this type of ring evolved to the current plasma moly facing that is sprayed onto the ring face at high temperature and velocity. This ring treatment is more resistant to the cracking and flaking that sometimes plagued inlaid rings under severe operating conditions.

Plasma-coated rings are preferred for many high-performance applications, but they are still susceptible to damage from high shock load conditions such as those found in nitrous-oxide and other power-adder applications. For these conditions, newer-style gas nitride ductile iron rings are usually a better choice. Gas nitriding is a specialized surface treatment used to harden the ring face for improved wear characteristics and resistance to detonation. Gas nitride rings are superior in every respect and have even found favor in many OEM applications. Standard steel rings are also a good choice for power-adder applications where severe duty is anticipated.

Racers in high-contamination environments such as dirt track or off-road racing often prefer chrome-faced top rings for their durability, but more recently many builders have switched to plasma-coated rings for their superior heat resistance under severe operating conditions. A new generation of thin vacuum-deposited chromium nitrite rings has reinvigorated chrome ring applications and many OEMs have now adopted them for their excellent wear characteristics. The general trend in racing rings points to thinner steel or stainless rings, many with exotic coatings such as tungsten or titanium nitride. These rings offer exceptional wear and sealing characteristics with enhanced friction reduction.

Coatings are applied using a positive vapor deposition process that has proved to be reliable and substantially beneficial in terms of power and durability although still quite expensive for all but well-funded applications. If any single ring type seems to be losing favor it is probably the L-shaped Dykes, or headland, ring with a 1/16-inch face and a .017- or .031-inch step on the back side to provide gas pressurization without requiring gas ports on the pistons.

Dykes rings require compatible piston ring grooves and they are generally harder to seat. They also exhibit higher wear characteristics due to gas pressurization behind the ring. They are in limited use, such as blown fuel drag racing applications where they are resistant to high pressures and excessive fuel wash in the cylinders.

Second Ring

Second compression rings are really misnamed since their primary function is to assist with oil control. Most ring manufacturers hold that the second ring is about 85 percent devoted to oil control and only 10 to 15 percent to compression sealing. Its main mission is to scrape oil missed by the oil ring to ensure

Where the pin bore encroaches on the oil ring groove, most applications use an oil ring support rail with a shorter inboard pin. The alternative is to use pin buttons with machined ring grooves that serve as oil ring supports. The buttons control pin placement and ring support, and they are much easier to assemble than the standard Spirolox or Truarc rings.

CHAPTER 5

Ring Gap Placement Guide

This ring gap placement guide is suitable for most racing applications. Note the specific placement according to the pin centerline and the front of the engine.

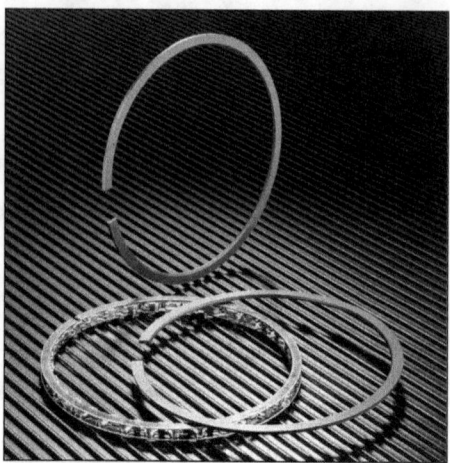

Basic racing ring applications typically incorporate a plasma moly compression ring and medium- to low-tension oil ring.

that it doesn't find its way to the combustion chamber to contaminate the fuel mixture. Since heat is not an issue with the second ring, a conventional cast-iron ring with a reverse bevel and tapered face is still employed with the primary task of scraping oil.

A recent improvement is the Napier-style ring, which features a hook or claw shape on the back side that serves as a reservoir for oil being scraped off the cylinder walls. Napier-style rings have found favor in both OEM and racing applications because they provide exceptional oil control and reduced friction. They also permit builders to open the second ring gap wider to promote more effective pressure relief between the top and second ring, thus easing the top ring's sealing effort.

Oil Ring

Most oil ring packages employ a three-piece unit with a primary expander ring supported by upper and lower scraper rails. Many of the performance gains associated with ring technology have come from oil ring weight and tension reduction. Low-tension oil rings have long been known to aid performance via friction reduction, but recent improvements have realized additional gains. Ring tension is the primary focus of these efforts.

Ring tension is mainly a function of the ring's radial depth in the ring groove. For decades oil rings have maintained the SAE standard of .199 inch, but recent development has reduced radial depth to .150 inch or less. With the piston ring groove machined to a corresponding depth and appropriate clearance, tension is reduced because the thinner ring is more flexible.

Conventional low-tension rings provide about 12 to 14 pounds of tension and low-tension rings in OEM performance engines like the Modular Ford or the GM LS series now operate with less than 10 pounds of radial tension. They offer exceptional oil control in a production environment and superior frictional qualities that dramatically impact fuel economy. By way of comparison, the best high-end Sprint Cup ring sets use a 1.5- to 2.0-mm oil ring with only 2.5 to 4 pounds of radial tension. These professional racing rings, such as Perfect Circle's U-Flex oil ring, are made in limited sizes for Cup requirements and require very precise CNC ring groove machining and dry sump lubrication supported by additional vacuum pump crankcase pressure evacuation to limit pressure below the rings.

Piston Ring Terminology

The following design elements apply to piston ring selection.

PISTON TECHNOLOGY

Axial Clearance
The clearance between the ring axial height and the height of the piston ring groove.

Axial Height
The vertical thickness or height of the piston ring in the axial direction.

Back Clearance
Clearance between the back or inside diameter of the ring and the back of the ring groove when the ring face is flush with the ring land.

End Gap
The clearance between the ends of the ring when compressed within the cylinder bore.

Free Gap
The end gap clearance when the ring is not compressed.

Inside Diameter
The inside diameter of the ring when compressed to the bore diameter.

Outside Diameter
The outside diameter of the ring when compressed to the bore diameter.

Radial Width
The width of the ring in the radial direction.

Ring Axial Sides
The top and bottom surfaces of the ring.

Ring Face
The front of the ring that contacts the cylinder wall.

Torsional Twist
The installed position of the ring, which imparts cross sealing due to a chamfered area on either side of the ring. This configuration makes the top ring cone slightly upward and the second ring come slightly downward.

Ring Installation

Now let's examine the currently favored techniques for piston ring preparation and installation. Savvy engine builders recognize the importance of proper cylinder wall preparation in terms of surface finish and efforts to control cylinder shape under load at operating temperature (see Chapter 3). Assuming optimum cylinder wall preparation for the purpose of this discussion, we can examine the role and preparation of rings as it applies to a racing environment.

Successful piston ring application begins with proper ring groove preparation. Because the ring seals on its face and against the ring land, precision-fit ring grooves are essential for proper piston ring operation. The tightest possible clearance between the ring and the ring groove is desirable for optimum ring control, but it is absolutely critical that the ring not stick in the groove. Ring clearance is necessary to allow for component expansion and to allow gas pressure to migrate behind the ring.

Many high-end builders prefer to purchase piston blanks and cut their own ring grooves to exacting specifications. This is found at the highest level of competition, but it is primarily a function of habit and does not constitute a slam against ring grooves cut by any of the major piston manufacturers, which also go to great lengths to cut very precise ring grooves.

Micro-Welding

Piston ring micro-welding occurs when aluminum from the bottom of the top compression ring groove transfers to the bottom of the top compression ring, causing it to stick in the groove. This causes ring rotation to cease and typically results in increased blow-by as the ring loses bore conformity and torsional twist. The primary cause is usually poor ring groove finish or the ring not being exactly perpendicular to the piston. It is more frequently seen near the ring gap since this is a potentially greater source of hot gas leakage, which contributes to the problem.

The condition is often exacerbated by improper ring groove clearance (too tight) and may be precipitated by excessive temperature, which affects the hardness of the piston material. Micro-welding typically begins during engine break-in, particularly with engines that run a vacuum in the crankcase.

One remedy is to perform the break-in with zero vacuum so the rings receive proper lubrication during the initial seating process. If done correctly this often avoids the problem. Many builders fail to even recognize that micro-welding has occurred even though the engine may lose power and blow-by increases dramatically with a significant loss in crankcase vacuum. They often attribute it to something else and never really solve the problem because they don't examine the rings carefully upon disassembly. Hard anodizing the top ring groove helps prevent it unless ring groove machining is poorly done. Builders have hard anodized ring grooves for years and more recently they have

Calculating Deck Height, Rod Length and

While deck height is commonly referred to as the depth of the piston top in the bore when the piston is at TDC, it also refers to the distance from the crankshaft centerline to the deck surface of the cylinder block. It influences all combinations of stroke, rod length, and pin height. A simple formula is used to calculate the combined dimensions for comparison with the cylinder block's fixed deck height dimension:

Assembled Deck Height =
block height − [(stroke ÷ 2) + rod length + pin height]

Where:
Block height = fixed deck height of the cylinder block
Stroke = crankshaft stroke length
Rod length = connecting rod center to center length
Pin height = pin centerline depth from piston top (compression height)

Since block height is fixed within a narrow window available for deck milling, the combination of stroke length, rod length, and pin height must add up to the same height with a small tolerance for desired deck height and piston-to-head clearance, which also incorporates gasket thickness. A common practice in performance circles is to zero-deck the block. The flat portion of the piston top is exactly even with the deck surface of the block. That means that the combination of one-half the stroke length plus rod length and pin height equals the fixed deck height of the block.

This forces the builder to select the appropriate compressed gasket thickness to control piston-to-head clearance. Not surprisingly, most performance head gaskets are .039− to .042-inch thick when compressed. The commonly accepted minimum piston-to-head clearance with steel connecting rods is .035 inch; hence, the built-in fudge factor on the head gaskets averages about .005 inch.

This calculation is often used to help determine the required piston pin height to accommodate a desired rod length and stroke combination, particularly when there is a concern that the selected rod length might push the pin location up into the ring package.

For example, let's use a typical 350-ci small-block Chevy V-8, which has a nominal factory block height of 9.020 inches. The factory stroke length is 3.48 inches, the stock connecting rod measures 5.7 inches, and the factory pin height is 1.560 inches. Plugging these variables into the formula results in the following assembled deck height (ADH):

ADH = 9.020 − [(3.48 ÷ 2) + 5.7 + 1.56]
ADH = 9.020 − (1.74 + 5.7 + 1.56)
ADH = 9.020 − 9.00 = .020 inch

Stock small-block Chevy pistons are indeed about .010- to .020 inch down the bore from the factory. This small amount of deck clearance allows for minor deck milling to recondition the deck surface for future rebuilds. Suppose you want to build this into a performance engine with longer connecting rods and new pistons. The .030-inch oversize flat-top piston from the Howards Cams catalog (PN HRC4567) accommodates a 6-inch connecting rod by virtue of a 1.268-inch pin height. It is also designed to work with either a 3.48- or 3.50-inch pin. Let's see how that works out.

Assembled Deck Height = block height − [(stroke ÷ 2) +
rod length + pin height]
(stroke ÷ 2) + rod length + pin height = ADH
1.74 + 6.00 + 1.268 = 9.008 inches

If the original block is indeed 9.020 inches from the crank centerline to the deck surface, you can cut the decks up to .012 inch to make them parallel and achieve a zero deck assembly. To use this particular piston with a 3.50-inch stroke, the assembly adds up to 9.018 inches, only .002 inch less than the nominal block height of 9.020 inches.

1.75 + 6.00 + 1.268 = 9.018 inches

If the block requires more than .002-inch milling to make the decks parallel, you may end up with some degree of negative deck (piston protruding from the bore).

Pin Height Combinations

Depending on the amount, you may need to juggle the gasket thickness or cut the piston tops slightly to achieve zero deck or the desired piston-to-head clearance and optimum amount of quench.

If the block had to be cut .010 inch to bring the decks in line with the crank centerline you would have .008-inch positive deck and only .031-inch clearance with a .039-inch gasket. There is some wiggle room here, but it requires careful attention.

When ordering custom pistons, you can specify a custom pin height to accommodate any dimensional discrepancies in the block. The piston manufacturer will tell you if your proposed combination interferes with the ring package and in the case of minor interference they can supply a support ring for the bottom ring to ensure stability.

Speed Pro's top-quality gas-nitrided HellFire series racing piston rings provide the essential combustion seal in the cylinders. These rings require much less special preparation than those of days gone by. Clearance checking, end gapping, and deburring are all that's required.

This small-bore, carbureted, small-block Chevy built for a roadster running at El Mirage incorporates large valve reliefs in the cylinder bores, high dome for compression, gas ports, fire slot, and highly polished surface. Looks nice, huh?

employed coated rings and ring lands, typically with phosphate dry lubricant.

Most manufacturers now offer top ring groove anodizing and specially coated rings specifically designed to combat micro-welding. All racing engines are susceptible to this problem and race piston manufacturers have done their part by specifically targeting the quality of their ring groove machining to achieve the smoothest possible surface finish with minimal peaks that can attach themselves to the rings. Engine builders look for it specifically upon teardown in order to take the necessary steps during assembly and initial fire-up to help prevent it. In addition to coatings, they often hand lap the rings to smooth the surface and they pay very close attention to ring clearance in the groove.

Here's the same El Mirage dry lakes roadster engine after a 175-mph spin in the dirt. The car snap spun so quickly the driver had no time to close the throttle, hence the immediate unavoidable transfer of assorted lakebed material to all cylinders.

CHAPTER 6

CONNECTING RODS

Stroke length aside, connecting rods are one of the basic tunable components in a competition engine. As rod length (center to center) varies, it affects piston motion such that it can be used as a primary tuning ingredient. By influencing piston acceleration and velocity it dictates the rate at which a differential is created between atmospheric pressure (above the carburetor) and cylinder pressure during the intake stroke. Accordingly, it impacts major contributors to the VE equation—intake and exhaust path cross sections, valve event timing, and optimum ignition point. Faster exposure to atmospheric pressure improves cylinder filling and thus VE, provided that intake tract dimensions and valve event timing are appropriately sized and synchronized.

It is important to recognize that piston acceleration and velocity are both zero at TDC and BDC. At all points in between, acceleration and velocity are dictated by rod length. For any given rod length, the piston achieves maximum velocity at a precise point in the stroke relative to the crank angle where the rod axis is 90 degrees to the crank throw (typically, but not limited to about 70 to 75 degrees of crank angle). This point represents the highest rate of pressure drop exposure in the cylinder and is closely tied to intake valve timing for optimum cylinder filling.

Proper rod-side clearance is essential to ensure adequate oil pressure and the integrity of the hydrodynamic oil wedge at the bearing. With too much clearance, oil bleed-down is excessive and the wedge begins to lose its effectiveness in supporting the crank in a film of oil. Too little clearance may result in undesirable contact between the crank face and the rod, and elevated oil temperature due to limited bleed-off from the bearings.

Rod Length as a Tuning Component

To some degree, longer rods effectively slow the arrival and departure rate of the piston at both TDC and BDC. This is often referred to as piston dwell time and any number of magazine dyno tests have been conducted to prove that it does not significantly alter peak power. But they are missing the point. The real value of rod length tuning is realized in shaping the powerband to suit application-specific performance requirements. As a rule, connecting rod length can be employed to tighten or spread the RPM range between peak power and peak torque. This is an important function in matching engine performance to the vehicle and its specific racing requirements.

An example would be using a longer rod (and compatible inlet dimensions) in a superspeedway or Bonneville application to shift peak torque closer to peak power so that more effective torque is applied within the specific RPM range of operation. With slower piston departure from TDC, higher combustion pressure is applied to the piston over more crankshaft degrees.

Many builders agree that the rod length should be 1.7 to 1.9 times the given stroke length. Because the longer rod slightly increases piston dwell time, it also provides more time for combustion pressure to build against the piston before it is applied to the power stroke; hence, more net torque is applied in the most desirable range for the application. It is also generally conceded that longer rods tend to make a bit more power in most high-speed applications while shorter rods tend to boost lower-end torque due to faster piston acceleration and the associated higher port energy.

A piston with a shorter rod arrives at TDC more briskly and doesn't hang around long before it departs swiftly. This is useful in some forms of racing. The piston achieves maximum velocity sooner and at less crank angle, which reduces cylinder volume exposure at the point of maximum pressure differential. Appropriate intake valve timing is required to ensure optimum efficiency under these conditions. Since the piston achieves maximum velocity sooner, the intake valve can be opened sooner to take advantage of the cylinder pressure differential. Less overall cylinder volume is exposed at this point, but the early initiation of flow chases the piston down the bore as volume exposure increases. This is commonly referred to as the piston tugging harder on the charge due to its increased acceleration.

Determining cam timing requirements for situations such as this one have become increasingly easier now that the average builder has access to powerful PC-based engine simulation software that illustrates any given crank angle to valve event timing. For example, the more aggressive action of a short rod combination implies the ability to consider slightly larger intake and exhaust dimensions (cross-sectional area) for the intake manifold and the headers without sacrificing vital port energy. PC modeling can help confirm this. In some cases you may be limited to a specific manifold and/or header combination whose fixed dimensions resonate about a particular rod length that can be identified through diligent PC simulation. Given the low cost of current simulation programs, there is no reasonable excuse for not modeling these concepts in advance on your PC.

Optimizing rod length further reveals tuning considerations that can improve combustion efficiency and reduce the amount of negative work performed on the piston prior to TDC. With a longer rod, the instant cylinder pressure rise approaching TDC is faster and greater and typically requires less total spark timing, depending on chamber efficiency. As spark timing is reduced, negative work (piston struggling against rising combustion pressure ahead of TDC) is diminished while increased

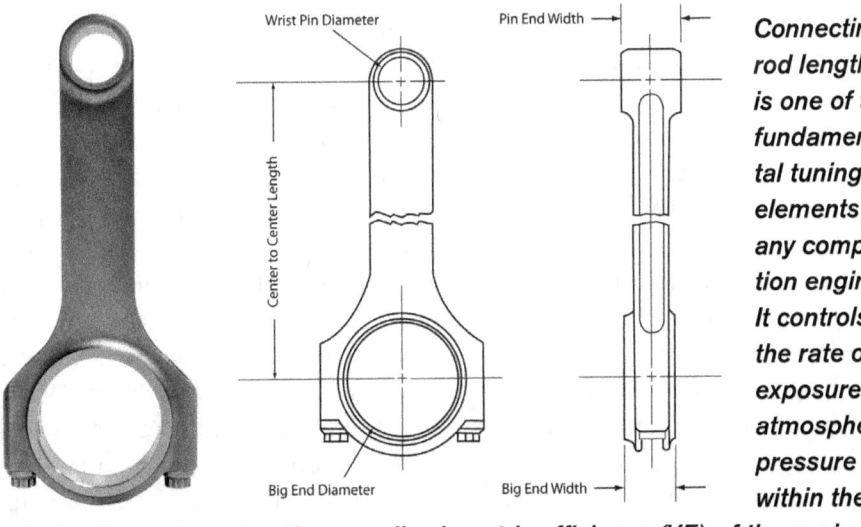

Connecting rod length is one of the fundamental tuning elements of any competition engine. It controls the rate of exposure to atmospheric pressure within the cylinder thus influencing the overall volumetric efficiency (VE) of the engine.

CHAPTER 6

This Scat H-beam rod uses high-strength, 12-point chrome-moly ARP bolts. Most racing rods use bolts only, no nut-and-bolt combinations. This reduces the big-end weight. Bolt tensile strength ranges as high as 220,000 psi.

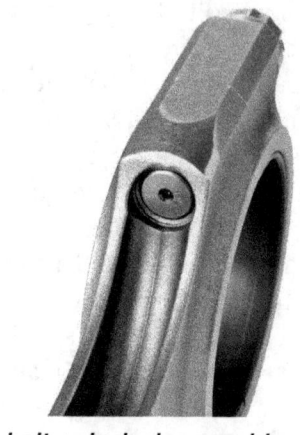

A bolt-only design provides a smoother transition from the rod beam. This eliminates potential stress risers typically found on the flats that normally seat the rod bolt heads.

A generous chamfer on the big-end journal housing is designed to accommodate the large fillet radii on most racing crankshafts. Note that the bearing insert incorporates a matching chamfer.

dwell time provides greater post-TDC pressure rise against the piston (positive work).

Rod length also impacts piston selection to the extent that it dictates pin height (compression height), and in many cases the final location of the ring package. This is an important consideration since different racing applications require different ring pack placement to accommodate attending combustion- and heat-related issues (see Chapter 5). Longer rods tend to reduce pin height and often require an oil ring support rail because the pin bore encroaches on the oil ring groove. This adds weight to the ring package, but most builders feel that the benefit of the longer rod and attending piston configuration outweigh any mass penalty, at least in those applications where a longer rod positively impacts power-band positioning.

In addition to creating more time for combustion pressure to rise and apply more torque to the crank, a longer rod speeds the burn rate due to enhanced charge density. Consequently the RPM separation between peak torque and peak power is reduced, effectively concentrating more torque in a narrower band, which benefits certain applications such as Bonneville, speedway oval, and drag racing engines that operate in a narrow RPM window with appropriately matched transmission and rear end gearing. Also, longer rods generally require appropriate intake manifold adjustments to accommodate slower piston motion around TDC. That frequently includes slightly smaller (cross-sectional area) intake runners to preserve port energy and in some cases advancing the cam to further enhance torque.

While retarding the cam for high-speed power is the traditionally accepted practice, it does not take into account the beneficial effects of specific rod length tuning in certain applications. Here again, PC modeling often illuminates unexpected paths to the most effective combination of valve timing and inlet- and exhaust-tract dimensions for a given rod length.

Finally, note that a longer rod and corresponding higher pin height is usually reflected in a shorter, lighter piston, which reduces reciprocating weight.

At the other end of the spectrum it's often advantageous for road racers and some circle track applications to investigate shorter rod lengths and the associated higher port energy, which may prove to be useful for selected applications that are restricted in terms of manifolding or camshaft timing and are seeking more torque off the corners. While the shorter rod exposes less initial cylinder volume to the pressure drop, it promotes increased port velocity to aid cylinder filling efficiency. This

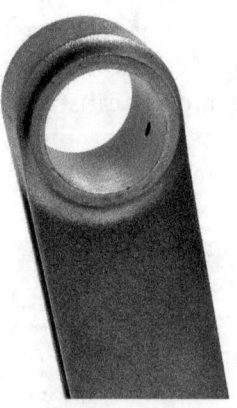

This example illustrates dual-pin oiling holes from each side of the rod beam. Some builders still drill a hole in the top, but this practice seems to have fallen out of favor.

calls for different valve timing than what is appropriate for a longer rod, particularly as it applies to the intake closing point. Because the instantaneous pressure rise is greater with a longer rod, it can effectively use a later closing intake to gain additional time for cylinder filling.

Conversely the shorter rod's higher port energy offers superior filling efficiency, but calls for earlier intake closing due to slower cylinder pressure rise and reduced dwell time at TDC. This tends to build torque earlier in the RPM range and moves the peaks farther apart. As a bonus, higher port energy often contributes to enhanced throttle response. Of course with shorter rods, the piston tends to outrun the flame front after about 30 degrees from TDC so it is important to choose a faster burning combustion chamber and appropriate fuel to accommodate it.

Connecting Rod Materials

Primary factors influencing connecting rod design are extreme inertia forces and cylinder pressure as defined by maximum engine speed, rotating assembly geometry, and weight. Increased engine speed, displacement, component mass, and firing pressure all dictate design characteristics incorporated in racing rods. These are further influenced by dynamic drivetrain loading such as wheelspin or freewheeling propellers (out of the water) in the case of marine applications. Still, connecting rod failures are less prevalent today than in the past. Reasons include superior materials, precise preparation and assembly, and improved control of contributing factors such as spark timing, detonation suppression, and over-rev protection. Mechanical issues such as piston pin stiffness, lubrication, and bearing clearances are also credited with reducing overall connecting rod stress.

Two materials dominate modern connecting rod production: aluminum and forged steel. Aluminum rods predominately populate the professional drag racing ranks where load and life cycles are relatively short and the weight savings are beneficial to transient torque acceleration across narrow powerbands. Their utility has broadened in recent years, but outside of drag racing, most racing applications still rely on steel or titanium rods. For the purpose of this discussion I concentrate on these basic types with brief attention to other materials.

Lower classes frequently specify factory-style forged rods, although in some cases compressed powdered metal is employed along with an OEM-based cracking technique that physically breaks the big end of the rod in half along a pre-scored line. This creates a unique match of irregular fracture surfaces that only mate correctly between the original cracked halves. It is a useful technique that ensures absolutely accurate rod cap alignment and resistance to movement. It is used successfully in fairly powerful production engines, but is not yet widely employed in competition engines although aftermarket rod manufacturers now offer cracked rod technology.

Using compressed powdered metal rods of this kind is typically safe up to around 500 hp in

High-strength fasteners have a ground necked-down area between the head and the threaded portion to provide the proper bolt stretch during final tightening.

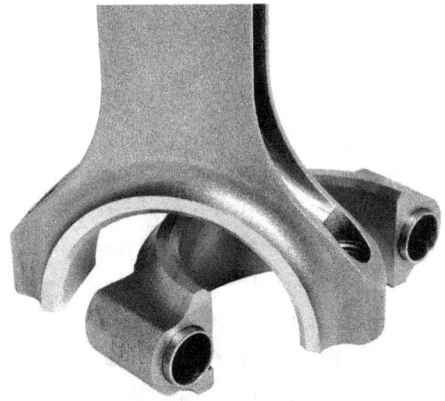

Precision-fitted dowel caps, as on this Scat H-beam rod, provide precise cap alignment and prevent cap walk under severe service or detonation.

Scat's innovative Ultra-Lite connecting rod incorporates a hole through the beam just above the big end. This provides a significant reduction in weight and engineers have determined that there is no compromise in strength.

production-based modified street engines, but most serious competition engines rely on aluminum or forged and billet steel aftermarket rods of varying configurations.

Aluminum Rods

Aluminum racing rods are forged from heat-treated 7075 T6 aluminum alloy, which has a tensile strength of 83,000 psi. They are approximately 65 percent lighter than steel rods, but only have about half the strength of steel. Unfortunately, a significant portion of the weight advantage is sacrificed because aluminum rods have to employ increased bulk to maintain strength. Accordingly, block modifications are often required to accommodate the larger physical size of most aluminum connecting rods.

In many cases the oil pan rails must be ground for rod clearance and care must be taken to ensure that the larger bulk does not contact the camshaft. Increased rod size takes up more space in the crankcase and affects crankcase windage differently. Aluminum rods require a pinned lower rod bearing to ensure proper rod bearing alignment and to guard against spinning the bearing.

These rods are primarily used for high-RPM drag racing applications where their lighter weight provides a benefit in transient acceleration. They offer superb damping qualities that are useful in resisting detonation, but their lifespan is relatively short due to the increased tendency to work harder from repeated stretching and compression. If you are going to run aluminum rods take note of the following requirements:

- Accommodate the increased stretch factor
- Modify the block for clearance
- Check for camshaft clearance
- Use the correct pinned bearings
- Handle carefully to avoid nicking the surface
- Fit pins precisely and provide adequate pin oiling
- Replace rods after 50 to 60 runs to guard against breakage
- Consider how the bulkier rod shape affects windage

Steel Rods

Steel rods are the most widely used due to their dimensional stability and exceptional long-term durability. Most steel connecting rods are manufactured from 4130 or 4340 alloy steel. Racing rods are commonly made from Mill Certified Aircraft Quality, vacuum carbon-arc deoxidized E4340 alloy, which has a tensile strength of up to 186,000 psi. Although normally calculated by dividing the maximum load by the original cross-sectional area of the component, tensile strength may be thought of as the amount of force required to pull a rod apart at the beam.

The onset of combustion pressure rise (negative work or torque) acts, to some degree, as a cushion for the piston as it approaches TDC, thus it helps to absorb the forces and g-loading that occurs when the piston reverses direction at TDC. This cushion prevents the piston from freewheeling through TDC and tends to soften the g-loading upon piston reversal because the piston is actually working against some amount of cylinder pressure at this point—another delicate balance that affects net torque.

All engines incorporate a measure of piston-to-cylinder-head clearance to accommodate rod stretch at TDC. The degree of stretch or elasticity is governed by engine speed, piston weight, rod ratio, and the characteristic of connecting rod materials known as the modulus of elasticity. Simply put, "modulus" describes a load factor indicating a known range of deformation characteristic to a given material whereby the deformed part returns to its original shape when the load is removed. Part failure typically occurs when the modulus is exceeded under repetitive loading. Either the rod stretches permanently causing piston-to-cylinder-head contact and subsequent failure, or the piston-to-head clearance is insufficient to accommodate the known modulus of the rod's parent material. In this case piston-to-head contact also ensues, usually with major carnage.

Steel rods stretch less than aluminum rods. Accordingly both types have a favored clearance range that accommodates known or (in some cases) anticipated stretch factors.

The commonly accepted minimum piston-to-head clearance for aluminum rods is about .055 inch depending on engine speed and associated component dynamics. The closer you shave it, the closer you flirt with component failure in the event of an over-rev or other unexpected abnormality. That doesn't mean that many builders don't fudge them close enough to produce witness marks on the piston tops where the pistons have been slightly kissing the head. If you see this you should regard it as a problem, not only because of inappropriate component contact, but because of the affect that is has on ring seal and the loss of cylinder pressure that may be occurring due to the ring unloading from the unexpected jarring.

Steel rods typically accept a piston-to-head clearance of about .035 inch, but this is often increased by

Characteristics of Long and Short Rods

Rod length characteristics can successfully be used as a tuning component for most race engines.

Long Rods

Pros
- Best for high-speed power.
- Increased piston dwell at TDC promotes smaller compression volume as combustion pressure begins to build. This maintains charge density longer and promotes a faster burn and higher cylinder pressure as the piston departs TDC. Excellent for high-speed torque and power.
- Less timing is required due to smaller initial combustion space. This reduces negative work against the piston as it approaches TDC.
- Reduces the chance of detonation and accommodates higher compression ratios.
- With a fixed block deck height, longer rods require shorter and usually lighter pistons. This supports safe and efficient high-RPM operation and provides positive benefits to balance and vibration characteristics.
- Works well with larger bores where increased piston surface area tends to cool the charge and reduce combustion pressure. Higher charge density and faster burn prevent this.
- Reduced rod angle applies less force to the thrust surface of the piston skirt, thus reducing friction and cylinder wall wear.
- Slower piston motion resists ring flutter at high engine speeds.
- Higher pin location promotes piston stability.

Cons
- Reduced cylinder filling. Low-speed VE is reduced due to slower piston motion in the vicinity of TDC. The piston achieves maximum velocity at a later point in the crank's rotation as dictated by the specific rod length. Cam timing must be adjusted to accommodate this.
- Sensitive to port size. Generally require smaller and longer inlet passages that may not be readily available from fixed-dimension manifolds.
- More sensitive to piston-to-valve clearance.

Short Rods

Pros
- Promotes higher intake and exhaust velocity at lower engine speeds. This tends to enhance mixture quality due to higher port speeds (less fuel falling out of suspension). As a result low-speed and mid-range torque are improved.
- More aggressive camshaft timing can be used with short rods.
- Less sensitivity to fuel quality (knock). Faster piston departure from TDC delays point of maximum cylinder pressure, which benefits boosted applications or those running nitrous oxide.
- Higher vacuum permits larger carbs and inlet passages without loss of port energy.
- Less sensitive to piston-to-valve clearance.
- Permits longer intake cycle with reduced tendency of reversion.

Cons
- Less dwell time at TDC reduces cylinder pressure and combustion temperature, particularly at higher engine speeds.
- Increased friction and cylinder wall stress due to higher rod angularity.
- Ports that are too small stall at higher RPM.
- Earlier timing is required to accommodate a larger dynamic combustion space, potentially increasing negative work against the rising piston ahead of TDC.
- Unless deck height is reduced, typically requires taller, heavier pistons that increase reciprocating weight.

.010 to .015 inch for high-RPM applications or those using lightweight cranks that are more prone to crank throw deflection both radially and along the direction of piston travel.

Characteristics of Rod Activity

In addition to rod stretch issues, builders also consider the material characteristics of rods in compression loading, particularly under conditions of detonation, which can fracture a rod that is too stiff or hammer the rod bearings repeatedly to the point of failure. While bearing failure typically occurs under compressive loading, most rod failures actually happen under tensile loading where the rod gets ripped apart upon piston reversal at TDC, particularly on the exhaust stroke where there is no opposing pressure to soften the transition. This is most often seen to occur about 1 to 1/2 inch down the beam from the pin. Or it fails at the hinge point where the beam expands to the big end. Rod bolt failures are rare unless improper torque and/or bolt stretch are applied.

More often than not the big end is still attached to the crankshaft with a tensile failure at the beam. Consider also that paired rods on a common crank throw have the opportunity to transfer the effects of detonation (via load sharing) in one cylinder to the adjacent rod, which may cause extreme stress or temporary lubrication problems that may spin a bearing or seize a rod.

There is also little doubt that rods absorb crankshaft radial deflection and some degree of vibratory distress under cyclic loading. It may not reveal itself on the dyno, but at the end of a long straightaway, after 250 laps, or just before the 5-mile marker on a long pull at Bonneville, rod stress may show itself. This belies the importance of proper crankshaft dampening and accurate balancing or (in many cases) overbalancing to smooth engine operation within the effective operating range (RPM) of the individual engine.

Another area of concern is the relationship between the rod and piston pin. Even the best rods can be undone by careless pin fitting or poor pin selection. While tighter pin clearances are desirable to prevent piston rattling on the pin, bending forces introduce pin distress that can destroy a piston or break a rod. Piston pin modulus must be sufficient to resist bending along the pin axis as well as radial distortion in the pin bore where the pin temporarily becomes egg shaped and bites the pin bore or the rod bushing, frequently with unpleasant consequences.

Excessive bending along the pin axis typically causes the pin to seize in the small end of the rod. Even if the condition is not severe enough to cause pin seizure, it introduces additional frictional drag and heat rise that may lead to pin failure over time. Numerous steps can be taken to address piston pin issues, particularly in high-speed, high-horsepower engines where pin distortion is more prevalent.

When selecting pistons, it is important to work closely with the piston supplier to secure the best pin configuration possible (see Chapter 5). The lightest possible pin is desirable, but not at the expense of pin distortion. Increased wall thickness is often used along with a tapered inside diameter that thickens toward the center of the pin and rides on inboard-style pin bosses that allow a shorter overall pin.

Piston manufacturers deal with this regularly and usually have a good solution if you can provide accurate information regarding stroke length, rod type and length, crankshaft and rod material, pin bushing material, and anticipated engine speed. In particular, manufacturers now offer diamond-like coatings and other coating procedures that significantly reduce pin bore galling. These coatings have a very low coefficient of friction (combined with proper pin bore honing) that can virtually eliminate wrist pin problems. This is particularly true in applications that employ block-mounted pin oilers to provide additional pin lubrication while also cooling the piston.

Rod-to-Piston Clearance

One dimension that may promote engine failure is the clearance between the top of the connecting rod and the underside of the piston top. This is particularly notable on racing pistons with a low compression height dictated by longer rod length. In this case the rod rides high in the piston and has a greater chance of interference with the bottom of the deck surface whose shape often mirrors the piston top to achieve a uniform thickness. The shape of the rod's small end and its thickness above the pin bore also influence this relationship.

To ensure adequate operating clearance it is necessary to check each rod and piston assembly carefully. Fortunately, most racing pistons use floating pins that make it easy to check this clearance prior to assembly. There are two places where the rod can interfere with the bottom of the piston. The first is the top of the rod interfering with the underside

CONNECTING RODS

of the piston deck. The second is the upper radius on either side of the rod pin bore where interference may occur with the radius of the piston pin boss to the piston deck.

To check these clearances, apply machinist's bluing to the bottom of the piston and the inner radius of the pin bosses.

Assemble the rod to the piston with the correct orientation and swing the rod to both sides until it contacts the inside of the skirt.

Slide the piston to the right and left and repeat in closer proximity to each pin boss.

Remove the pin and rod and check the bluing for witness marks that indicate contact. While performing this operation observe carefully with a bright light, as the clearance may be inadequate even though it does not physically indicate contact with the bluing. You need at least .050-inch minimum clearance, which can be verified by passing a large bent paper clip between the piston and rod. If you observe witness marks and/or not enough clearance with the paper clip, you may be able to gain clearance by grinding the bottom of the piston slightly.

Be sure to check piston deck thickness prior to performing this operation. If you observe interference at the pin bosses, you can often chamfer the small end of the rod to gain clearance. Many connecting rod manufacturers offer tapering of the small end to accommodate these issues.

Be sure to recheck the clearance after performing any of this work. If you modify the rod, make certain you recheck the small end weight for correct balance.

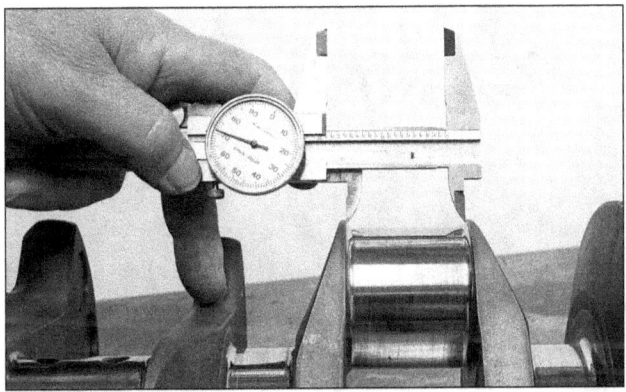

Measure between the rod journal side thrust surfaces to determine the available rod side clearance. Compare this dimension to the combined width of both rods.

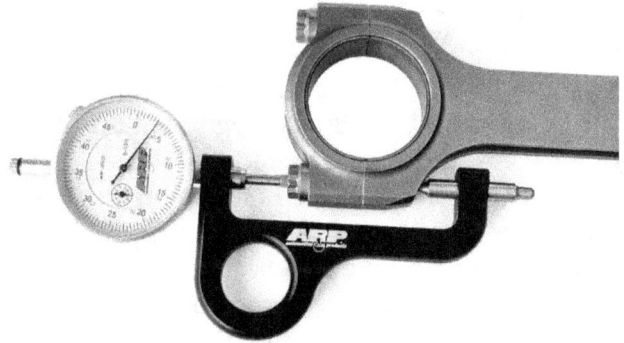

An ARP rod bolt stretch gauge is one of the most important tools in the engine builder's arsenal. Use it whenever resizing rods, setting up rods with new bolts, performing final rod assembly in the engine, and checking bolt condition upon engine teardown. The handy finger tab makes it easy to insert the tool between the crank throws during engine assembly.

Consistency is the key to torquing rod bolts. Stretching them to the proper spec is strongly influenced by the lubricant used. Some builders still use plain engine oil, but most use lubricants like ARP's Ultra-Torque, which is specially formulated to provide consistent loading and accurate stretch.

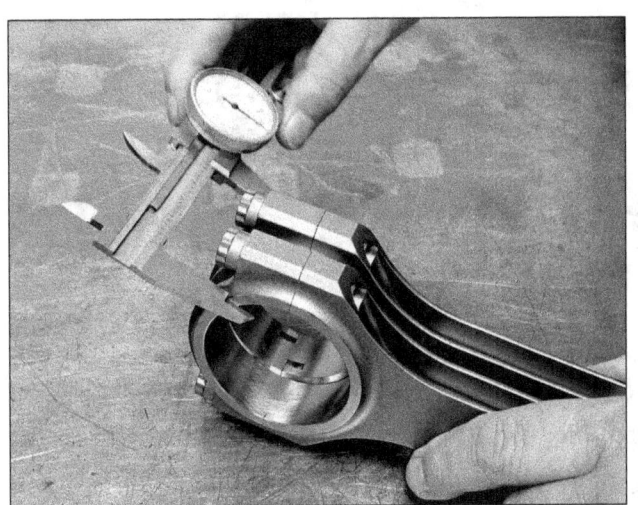

The combined measurement of both rods is compared to the measurement between the thrust surfaces on each side of the rod journal to determine the rod side-clearance. This can also be checked by inserting the applicable feeler gauge between the rods during mockup assembly.

CHAPTER 7

ENGINE BEARINGS

Virtually all modern engines use bearing shell inserts for the crankshaft, rods, and camshaft. Mains and rods use a split bearing with upper and lower half-shells. Cam bearings are mostly single-piece, ring-style inserts that are pressed in place with an interference fit in each housing bore. Most bearing inserts have a thick metal backing made of aluminum or steel to maintain their shape.

The inserts are coated with copper or Babbitt material, which usually consists of copper, tin, and antimony depending on the application. Bearing Babbitt is relatively soft. This allows it to embed small particles of dirt and debris and prevent them from damaging the journal surface. In a race engine, embedability is often sacrificed in favor of high-fatigue strength and the ability to carry higher loads—the idea being that race engines have highly filtered oil that is changed frequently.

Tri-metal bearings are the preferred bearing for all race applications except perhaps the extremely high-load environment of blown fuel and alcohol engines where short-duration applications require a softer Babbitt material to absorb shock loads. Tri-metal bearings consist of a hard steel shell to provide conformability and load-bearing capacity. The shells are then coated with copper, lead, and tin to provide the desired characteristics. The bearing shell surface is first treated with a copper micro-structure that incorporates minute pockets. This matrix is then covered with an overlay of a tin-copper mix or lead-indium.

Examine a bearing shell closely and note that it fits snugly in the housing bore with a noticeable amount of tension (called spread) and extends beyond the parting line of the bore. This small degree of tension and oversize on both shells provides bearing crush to increase the contact friction between the bearing back and the housing bore and help the bearing tang lock the bearing in place so it can't spin. This is called conformability.

In the case of aluminum rods, high thermal expansion causes the rod to relax its grip on the bearing

Lower main bearings must have full load-carrying capacity. Grooved bearings should never be used on the lower half of the bearing shell. Again, maintaining the load-carrying capacity of the hydrodynamic wedge via proper clearances and oil pressure is the primary goal. Rod bearings are not grooved because they are fully loaded all the way around.

even with adequate bearing crush. The solution is a dowel-pinned bearing. All aluminum rods come pre-fitted with a fixed dowel in the rod cap. All race bearing manufacturers make rod bearings with the dowel hole pre-drilled.

Characteristics of Engine Bearings

The physical characteristics of engine bearings vary with the application, but it is important to recognize and take advantage of the primary characteristics associated with all engine bearings.

Crush

This refers to the characteristic that forces or crushes the bearing into its housing bore. This is done to assist the bearing tang in preventing the bearing from spinning. Race engines with higher loads require bearings with more crush. Bearing manufacturers are very precise in their tolerances, making it incumbent upon the engine builder to check and adjust bearing crush. This is done primarily by precise machining of the bearing housing bores to exact specifications. In the range of journal sizes for most racing engines, the target bearing crush is typically about .015 to .016 inch for rod bearings and .019 inch for main bearings.

Eccentricity

Bearing inserts do not maintain uniform thickness throughout their circumference. They are thickest at the center of the bearing and taper toward the parting lines, creating a very slight eccentric oval shape. This is necessary to accommodate bore distortion under extremely high load conditions. While very slight, these minimal dimensional changes must be spot on to prevent undesirable engine damage.

Spread

Bearing shells also incorporate a slight degree of spread, which in effect spring loads or preloads each insert against the housing bore to lock it in place. Spread is incorporated as an assembly aid to hold the bearings in place during engine assembly. A small amount of effort is required to force the bearing inset into place during assembly.

Note how this Calico main bearing extends slightly beyond the housing bore. This is the bearing crush that helps the tang lock the bearing in the housing bore. Both bearing shells have a small amount of crush built into them. When torque is applied to the main cap bolts the shells crush against each other forcing them firmly against the housing bore.

Arrows indicate the oiling hole and groove in the upper main bearing shell and the locator tang used to position each half shell in the bearing housing bore. This Calico coated main bearing illustrates bearing spread or the spring effect that holds the bearings in place during assembly.

Roller cam bearings are used primarily to reduce friction and lower the total volume of engine oil flow. This lessens the load on the oil pump and helps to reduce windage in the crankcase.

Parting-Line Relief

Bearing inserts are slightly thinned beginning approximately .375 inch from each parting line to prevent the bearing from bulging inward and contacting the bearing journal when the bearing is crushed in its housing bore. This prevents unwanted contact when the big end distorts and tends to pinch the bearing upon piston reversal (at TDC). This is why you cannot measure bearing clearances in the vicinity of the parting lines.

Chamfer

Most race engine bearings are pre-chamfered on the edge facing the crank throw to accommodate large journal fillet radii. This does not excuse the competent engine builder from checking each insert in place to ensure that the chamfer provides adequate clearance.

Oiling Grooves

Most main bearings are grooved on the upper half only, leaving the full load-carrying capacity available on the ungrooved bottom half. It is important to remember that any groove or journal chamfer introduces an interruption in the hydrodynamic oil wedge causing a partial collapse. This is critical since the wedge's greatest load-carrying ability is near the center of the bearing and tapers off toward each side due to oil leakage from the bearing. Manufacturers do not recommend extending grooves into the lower bearing inserts. The oil groove in the upper insert provides the oil supply for the rod bearings. Also, the insert with the oil feed hole must go in the block and not in the main bearing cap.

Size

Engine bearings come in standard, undersize, or oversize depending on the journal size. Unlike street engines, most true racing engines rarely incorporate crankshafts with journals that have been turned down from standard size. Manufacturers do, however, provide special .001-inch-plus-one inserts that can be used to fine-tune clearances. Builders often use a standard shell on one side and a .001-over shell on the other to adjust the clearance by a few tenths.

Tang Depth

One important clearance that many builders overlook because they assume it is correct is bearing tang depth. If incorrect, it can prevent the bearing from properly seating in the housing bore and ultimately lead to insufficient clearance and probable engine damage. While this is normally not an issue with high-quality aftermarket racing connecting rods, it is nonetheless part of the essential "check everything twice" philosophy that top engine builders practice.

Coatings

Bearing coatings have become commonplace in many racing engines. They reduce friction and improve heat transfer, which generally permits tighter clearances, but they are not a cure-all for bearing issues. They possess better survivability characteristics that can help save a bearing during brief periods of low oil pressure. While they do support tighter clearances, they are not a substitute for the minimum safe clearance. All good engine builders know that being a little loose is better than being a little tight, especially when it helps you finish a race that might otherwise end prematurely due to engine failure.

Polishing

All bearing manufacturers recommend installing bearings without modifications other than perhaps increasing the chamfer if it is found to be insufficient. Some builders still insist on polishing their bearings with a variety of materials from newsprint to the more common Scotch-Brite pad.

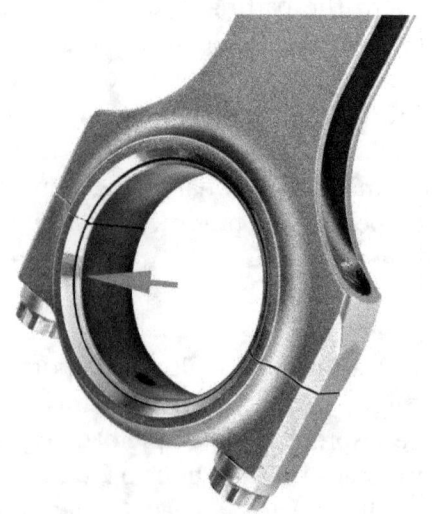

The bearing chamfer on rod bearings prevents contact with the fillet radius on the rod journal. Note how the bearing shell chamfer closely matches the chamfer on the connecting rod.

This bearing has been run in the adjacent Carrillo rod cap. Note the even surface contact pattern between the back of the bearing insert and the rod cap bore with no sign of movement.

ENGINE BEARINGS

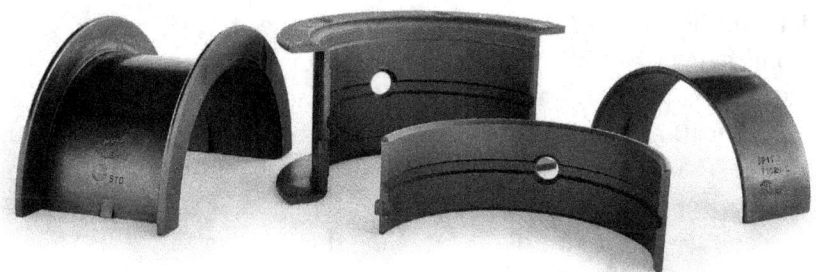

Coated bearings like these from Calico Coatings are favored because they reduce friction, permit tighter clearances, and increase survivability in the event of a temporary low oil pressure event.

Some suggest that the coating applied by the manufacturer comes off and wads up in small chunks. If that is the case it probably has more to do with insufficient clearance than a problem with the coating, which manufacturers have spent untold sums on perfecting. Interestingly, you won't see many builders polishing bearings with high-tech coatings, which seem to be more readily accepted.

Another trick practiced by some builders is polishing the backs of the bearings to theoretically improve the contact surface between the bearing and the housing bore. This may or may not provide some benefit, but it is undoubtedly less harmful than polishing the actual bearing surface where the coating is designed to help with initial fire-up and break-in.

Roller Cam Bearings

Many race engines incorporate roller cam bearings to reduce friction, but they are not necessary in every case. Standard cam bearings are employed in many successful race engines with great success. Roller bearings require a block designed or machined to accept them and their chief advantage is their high load-carrying ability with valvespring pressures that approach or exceed 1,000 pounds.

Because the rollers are splash oiled off the spinning crankshaft they do not require pressurized oiling. When the bearings are press fit in the block they cover the oil feed holes for the camshaft, reducing oil flow volume through the engine with less oil through the pump, hence less drag. That said, some builders shy away from rollers because of the havoc they wreak when they fail. In many cases they install larger diameter Babbitt bearings with good results. It all depends on the combination and how hard you stress the cam.

Clearances

Consistency is the cardinal rule of bearing clearances. Always set clearances the same way and with the same equipment. Engine bearings and the journals they run on are also temperature sensitive with regard to size. Clearances are used to accommodate thermal growth, but the components themselves should always be set at a consistent temperature for best results. If you're working in a cold shop, don't check clearances with bearings you just retrieved from a warm storage room.

The same goes for measuring equipment. Bearings, crankshafts,

---

Basic Bearing Rules

The following bearing rules apply to 99 percent of all racing and high-performance engine builds.

- Slightly looser clearances are always safer.
- Ambient temperature affects the accuracy of your micrometer and the size of the journals.
- Always use the same micrometer for both the journals and to preset the inside micrometer diameter.
- Always check your mic with a known standard prior to taking measurements.
- Changing rod bolts or moving from studs to bolts affects bearing clearance.
- Small changes in main bearing clearance can be made by adjusting main bolt torque.
- Most bearing clearance issues are caused by inconsistent housing bore diameters.
- Torque rod bolts to proper stretch before measuring the bearing or the housing bore.
- Never adjust rod bearing clearance by altering rod bolt torque.
- Always measure rod bearing clearances at 90 degrees from the cap parting line.
- Don't mix bearings from different manufacturers or different bearing families.
- Don't mix a half-shell coated bearing with a half-shell uncoated bearing.

COMPETITION ENGINE BUILDING: ADVANCED ENGINE DESIGN & ASSEMBLY TECHNIQUES

rods, and micrometers are manufactured from various steels that expand and contract differently according to temperature. Micrometers are designed to be used at a standardized temperature of 68 degrees F. For best results, all components and measuring equipment should be close to the same temperature.

Main Bearings

Main bearing preparation and installation must be preceded by proper housing bore dimensional preparation and careful deburring of the main caps and housing bored edges. No bearing should be fitted prior to checking for proper tang depth.

Rod Bearings

Quality racing rod bearings are very consistent in their manufacture. An issue with clearances is that it is almost always related to inconsistent journal sizes or housing bore diameters. All engine builders have preferences when it comes to checking rod bearing clearances. The procedure is critical because we are taking about tenths of a thousandth of an inch.

Many builders skip the procedure of measuring the rod housing bore diameters, but this is the first place where something can go wrong. Measuring the housing bores and writing them down is useful later when clearance issues crop up and you are trying to determine which bearings can be swapped to a different housing bore to achieve the proper clearance. Measuring and recording the housing bores is the mark of an experienced quality engine builder. Those figures may also be useful later if a bearing issue arises and you are trying to determine what caused it.

Many builders like to set their dial bore gauge to the rod journal size and read the clearance on the dial indicator. This is fine if the rod journals are consistent. Others prefer to set the dial bore gauge to a common journal diameter and calculate the clearances. This allows them to measure all the rod bearing inside diameters based on one setting.

With racing engines you can never take too much time or care so it's best to work slowly and measure each journal and bearing independently. Write the journal number and the clearance on the back of the bearing shell to avoid mixing them up. If the bearing shells are identical, also mark which one is the top half and which is the bottom half. It is not uncommon for a tight housing bore diameter and a slightly oversized rod journal to stack the tolerance beyond the target rod bearing clearance.

The common cure for clearance issues is most often the use of undersize or oversize bearings that are offered in +.001 or -.001 with an X-suffix on the part number. An example would be the Clevite series available in -9, -10, and -11 (or 10X) and -10, -20, and -21, which allow you to set precision clearances even on cranks that have been ground .010- and .020-inch undersize. These sizes can even be mixed with standard-size shells to home in on exact clearances. For example, you can combine one standard-size half-shell with a plus-one or minus-one half-shell to reach a specific clearance.

In theory, and most often in practice, mixing half-shells increases or decreases the clearance by .0005 inch. When you do this it is best to use the thicker bearing on the upper half of the rod where it can supply additional load-carrying capacity. Note also that bearings are purposely made thinner at the parting line to accommodate the pinch effect of the housing bore when the rod stretches as the piston reverses direction at TDC.

Never measure bearing clearances near the parting line. They are always off. Always measure them 90 degrees from the parting line and in line with the beam of the rod.

Bearing Failures

Bearing issues are a clear sign that something is dimensionally incorrect, overstressed, or exposed to excessive heat and/or dirty oil. Most bearing problems can be traced to improper machining, incorrect clearances, or sloppy assembly techniques. Evaluating bearings upon disassembly is an important step that many engine builders ignore completely, yet it can often tell them many things about the engine's performance even if the bearings look perfect.

You can pretty much divide bearing failures into two primary categories: assembly problems and operational problems. Dirt and foreign material can contaminate the bearing environment in either category, so it is critical to determine the source and to always practice squeaky-clean assembly techniques and engine maintenance practices.

Assembly Problems

The following are the primary causes of bearing problems initiated at the engine assembly stage.

- Incorrect clearances
- Improper bearing crush

ENGINE BEARINGS

- Inadequate lubrication
- Improper fillet radius chamfer
- Improper tang fitment
- Dirt behind the bearing insert

During assembly, small particles of dirt can inadvertently be captured between the bearing back and the housing bore. This debris (which is often hard to detect) resides behind the bearing, deforming it outward toward the crank journal where loss of clearance can initiate localized overheating and bearing flaking. In severe cases it causes contact distress that typically leads to early failure.

The cure is to closely inspect each housing bore and both sides of the bearing insert prior to installing it. Close examination of the bearing inserts and housing bores using a magnifying glass is a sign of a quality engine builder. Appropriate deburring with detailed inspection of the bearing tangs and their fitment is essential.

Even within the cleanest environment it is possible for dirt particles to contaminate the bearings during assembly. When small particles of dirt find their way between the bearing insert and the housing bore they initiate a local stress source and often deform the bearing with "high spots" that may contact the crank journal. Similar high spots also occur when dirt embeds itself on the bearing surface. This displaces insert material around the particle causing a buildup of material that may be greater than the available clearance. The results may scratch the journal or foster a condition where more and more material becomes displaced causing the bearing to begin flaking or coming apart.

The best cure is a cleaning regimen that includes thorough washing in hot water and detergents incorporating a strong degreasing agent.

Operational Problems

Checking bearings after a race or after a season of racing is a basic necessity. Under the best conditions with properly machined and lubricated parts, the bearings and the crank journals should experience little to no contact under all operating conditions except in circumstances such as severe overheating, pump failure, or debris in the oiling system. Frequent checks help identify problem areas and suggest the correct fix, which may not necessarily be the most convenient or the least expensive, but is probably absolutely necessary.

An out-of-round bore and/or excessive crush display similar characteristics. When the housing bore is out-of-round, bearings are excessively worn near the parting faces. According to Clevite this problem is often seen in rod bearings exposed to high RPM and high inertial loads where the rod bore becomes oblong, or because of misaligned rod and piston combinations, or rods that are slightly bent.

In the case of main bearings, thermal distortion caused by over-torquing cylinder head and intake manifold bolts when the engine is hot often promotes an out-of-round bore. When the bearing housing bore deflects it forces the parting ends of the bearing closer to the crank reducing necessary oil clearance due to the pinching effect on the crank. With intermittent oiling, metal-to-metal contact occurs and, over time, the bearing fails.

Excessive bearing crush promotes a similar effect if the bearing housing bore is carelessly machined or the bearing cap is over-torqued. According to Clevite, excessive crush condition results in a wear pattern across more than three-quarters of the bearing surface with the worst damage near the parting line. In this

Close-up shows the fillet radius on the crankshaft journal and the bearing chamfer that prevents the bearing from riding against the radius.

case the ends of the bearing inserts at the parting line exhibit excessive wear caused by excessive crushing force that distorts the bearing shell insert.

The opposite of this is too little crush where radial pressure from the housing is insufficient to hold the bearing stationary. This allows the bearing to shift in its seat and may even lead to a spun bearing in some cases.

Insufficient crush is generally caused by improperly machined bearing seats, insufficient bolt torque, or poor fitment due to dirt or burrs contaminating the housing bore contact surfaces. Properly machined housing bores are also important for proper heat transfer from the bearing back to the housing bore material. This helps prevent overheating the bearing, which leads to flaking and early failure.

Another common failure mode is fillet ride, a condition seen with many racing crankshafts where the fillet radius is increased to improve strength. If the bearings do not incorporate enough clearance for the fillet in the form of a suitable chamfer, fillet ride occurs and damage ensues. Manufacturers of high-performance bearings now incorporate a generous chamfer on their racing bearings to eliminate this problem. Nonetheless, every bearing must still be checked and verified.

Indications of wiping are also a signal that oiling problems are lurking. This condition often displays a highly polished or worn bearing surface. It is typically caused by insufficient oil pressure and/or oil viscosity or excessive oil temperature. The polishing is generally even across the bearing, but uneven patterns or spots may indicate localized heating due to dirt contamination, bearing misalignment, or possibly an undetected bent rod.

Wiping may not always be severe, but it does indicate the onset of other problems that require attention. Advanced stages of wiping generally indicate oil starvation with the bearing often exhibiting discoloration and very excessive wear. Often this condition is cause by basic problems ranging from insufficient oil clearance to incorrect oil viscosity, blocked oil passages, plugged oil filter, poor sump design, or a partial pump failure.

Clevite advises obtaining oil pressure via cranking prior to ignition switch-on to help extend bearing life because it prevents engine startup until full oil pressure has reached the bearings. This is a good solution, and the use of a racing accumulator to store oil that pressurizes the engines oiling system prior to startup is also advised. The accumulator functions as a pre-oiler.

Many builders also advise preheating the oil supply with a surface heater either on the oil pan itself or on the dry sump storage tank. Heated oil flows to the bearings more quickly to provide immediate startup protection.

Coated rod bearings are particularly desirable because of their ability to withstand severe conditions such as detonation, which often pound out and destroy conventional uncoated bearings.

CHAPTER 8

CYLINDER HEADS

Race-prepared cylinder heads are the most important component in a racing engine. Most of the power an engine makes comes from the cylinder heads and their ability to fill the cylinders and evacuate them efficiently. Not surprisingly, a substantial portion of a racing engine budget goes to cylinder heads to ensure a competitive build. The difference between short blocks assembled by a range of competent engine builders is relatively small, but the builder with the superior cylinder heads always excels, often to a considerable degree.

There are hundreds of different sizes and configurations, each designed to meet very specific requirements dictated by their intended competition environment. The shape and specific dimensions of individual ports and combustion chambers exerts enormous influence on the shape and positioning of the torque curve and the overall powerband of the engine.

If maximum power spread across an application-specific powerband is the primary goal of competition engine building, cylinder heads have the greatest influence on the VE and cylinder filling ability that make this possible. Although the camshaft commands the precise timing of flow path events, the cylinder head flow passages (ports and valves) manage the rate and volume of flow into the engine based on engine speed and piston position as dictated by stroke length and rod length.

All of these components work in close concert and must be appropriately matched to ensure compatibility, optimum cylinder filling, and combustion efficiency. Incompatible components anywhere in the system not only fail to deliver the anticipated level of performance, they also restrict the optimum performance of other components operating within the flow path environment.

The cylinder head's intake and exhaust flow paths lead to and from the combustion space (chamber) where air and fuel are processed into power. In many ways the cylinder head is the heart of the matter. It

Highly refined canted-valve aluminum cylinder heads such as this Pro 1 head from Dart represent the gold standard in commercially available racing cylinder heads. Available in varying degrees of preparation they can be further finished to any degree of precision necessary to meet specific racing requirements.

COMPETITION ENGINE BUILDING: ADVANCED ENGINE DESIGN & ASSEMBLY TECHNIQUES 87

CHAPTER 8

Chevrolet RO7 cylinder heads start with these raw castings and undergo extensive precision machine work to bring them to the level of Cup competition. In addition to detailed porting measures, the valvetrain is set up with exhausting precision to ensure maximum durability in the extended high-RPM environment of Sprint Cup racing. (Courtesy General Motors)

provides the all-important combustion space where energy is harnessed from the reaction of the air/fuel mixture and it provides the valves and flow paths that escort the air/fuel mixture into the combustion chamber and usher it out via the exhaust system after the magic happens. How all of this is coordinated, managed, and properly tuned for high VE is largely a matter of sizing the ports and valves to suit the application.

To fully appreciate the dynamics of gas exchange it is logical to start by examining the combustion space for the critical keys to its function. For the purpose of discussion, think of the combustion space as having a roof (chamber with valves), a floor (piston top), and walls (the cylinder). Within this high-speed environment, the roof and floor approach each other rapidly as many as hundreds of times per minute. This motion exerts a profound influence on the fuel mixture as it enters the combustion space, combusts, expands, and exits at a very high rate. Since the spark ignition is initiated a selected distance before TDC, the piston (floor) is still approaching the roof with rising pressure creating negative work.

Turbulence driven by rising piston motion and quench against the roof drives the denser fuel charge toward the spark plug where it ignites with gusto. In the best cases the flame expands smoothly depending on mixture homogeneity, piston area, and the effects of any obstructions such as compression domes. The higher the mixture quality, the better the burn, resulting in smooth combustion. Most combustion chambers are designed to drive the advancing flame forward toward the exhaust valve, hastening the burn and improving the exhaust cycle, which often increases power.

In recent years combustion chambers have grown smaller and specific shapes have been refined to encourage swirl and tumble within the fuel mixture as it enters the cylinder through the intake valve. Swirl is a rotational motion of the incoming fuel mixture that tends to assume a circular path defined by the cylinder walls. Tumble is a similar but vertical motion where the mixture tumbles into the cylinder in a waterfall effect.

The mixture-enhancing qualities of swirl and tumble encourage power

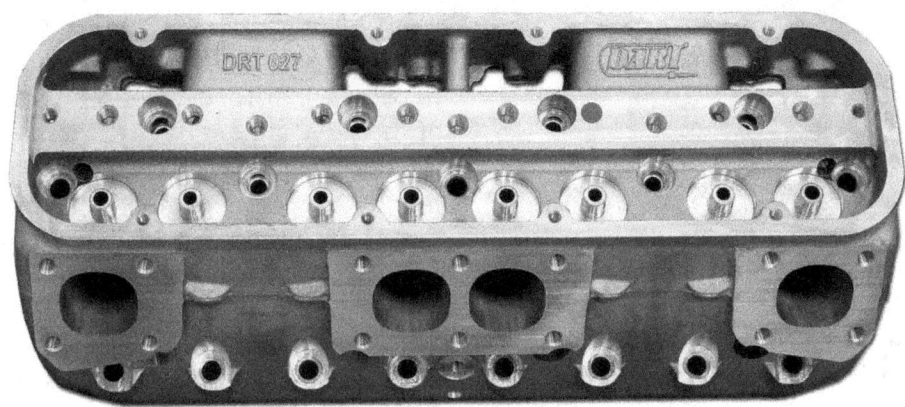

Dart's 9-degree aluminum small-block Chevy race head illustrates the ideal simplicity of an inline-valve configuration with optimum port placement and compact 38-cc combustion chambers to achieve superior power potential.

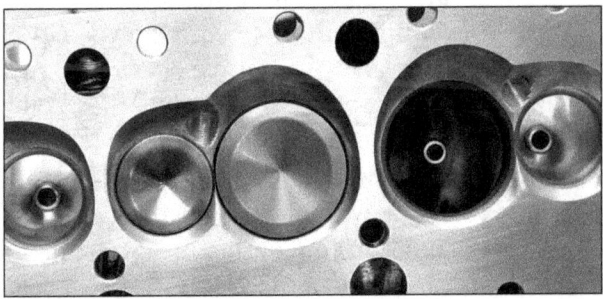

These high-end Dart race cylinder heads incorporate 50-degree valve-seat angles for enhanced high-RPM flow and exotic copper beryllium seats for optimum combustion chamber sealing.

improvements even though they tend to restrict net airflow to some degree. Along with advances in port design, spark plug placement, valve design and placement, and CNC machining processes, major cylinder head mods are no longer undertaken by many builders. The modern dilemma is to choose the ideal cylinder head from the vast selection offered by specialized cylinder head manufacturers.

With application specifics in mind builders tend to evaluate cylinder heads (when not specified or restricted by rules) based on mid-range and beyond flow numbers, port turbulence, chamber shape and efficiency, valve size and angle, spark plug placement, port shape, size and position, and other critical attributes that affect power production. Nearly all modern race heads now incorporate optimized valve placement, thicker deck surfaces, optimized cooling jackets, and better oil control.

It is commonly recommended to use the smallest ports and valves that support the power level you desire. Smaller ports with higher flow velocities offer superior flow and cylinder filling qualities accompanied by the more desirable mixture qualities that promote superior power. These qualities support strong low- and mid-range power even as they encounter a power ceiling based on the head's flow capacity. Larger ports and valves are superior at high RPM and when suitably cammed, they create big power upstairs. There is a critical balance that must be struck for every racing application and experienced engine builders routinely probe the limits while trying not to exceed the desirable flow velocities generated by smaller ports and the enhanced mixture qualities that promote good power.

Choosing a Cylinder Head

With the exception of Stock Eliminator drag racing and various lower level circle track applications, most racing engines use aluminum heads. Some applications are restricted to the stock-type iron heads and valve sizes with no porting allowed, but most applications allow aluminum heads with a variety of valve sizes and porting configurations. When selecting a cylinder head for a particular application it is important to closely match the desired RPM range based on port dimensions that include port length and cross section and the mid- and high-range flow rates.

The primary factors affecting cylinder head flow rate include valve size, port shape and dimensions, the bend radius before the valve, and the surface texture of the port surfaces. This is particularly true of the port floor and the port roof to prevent fuel separation. Inertia tends to push the bulk of the fuel mixture above the port centerline toward the roof where the runner makes the turn to the valve. The bend radius influences flow rates considerably and it is one reason high port heads with shallower valve angles have evolved.

Most manufacturers publish valve sizes and flow figures for their cylinder heads and some provide port volumes. The best ones also provide port dimensions including height, width, cross-sectional area, and port location. Port length along the centerline of the port is also useful, but few provide it.

The more of this information you have, the easier it is to pinpoint

CHAPTER 8

Dart Big Chief Pro 1 cylinder heads for big-block Chevys represent top-of-the-line racing cylinder heads. Enormous 2.400-/1.900-inch valves and large rectangular ports deliver outstanding flow for larger displacement engines with high-horsepower requirements.

the ideal head for your combination. Flow figures help determine the head's ability to fill and evacuate the cylinders efficiently. Port dimensions help calculate the torque peak and the spread of the powerband. This information is particularly useful if you are brainstorming combinations on one of the many engine simulation programs available for your PC.

Valves and Valve Sizes

Valves are a necessary evil in a racing engine. They represent a variable-flow restriction that must be dealt with to effectively feed the engine. Bigger valves are generally better for obvious reasons, but valve size is always limited by the bore size. Under naturally aspirated conditions, intake mixtures must find their own way into the cylinders at relatively low pressure, hence bigger valves are required on the intake side. Exhaust gases are discharged under higher pressures so smaller valves can be used.

In most racing circles, the intake valve is typically about 52 percent of the applicable bore size, while exhaust valves are generally about 72 to 76 percent of the intake valve diameter. These sizes are not set in stone, but they yield an effective combination in most high-speed, two-valve-per-cylinder applications.

Part of the complication with valves is shrouding caused by proximity to cylinder walls and some deeper combustion chambers. Shrouding presents a barrier that closes off part of the valve curtain or flow window. It reduces net flow, redirects the optimum flow path, and often influences the combustion process with negative results. This is the main reason that many successful racing heads use canted or splayed valves that move away from the cylinder walls as they open. Normally, the largest valve that fits works best, but in the case of severe shrouding, smaller valves may flow better because they are farther from the cylinder wall and present less restriction.

Valves are also somewhat delicate compared to most other components. It is very easy to burn or otherwise damage a valve to the point where the head breaks off and you lose an engine. Show them plenty of respect in order to avoid more serious consequences.

Valve seats must be perfectly concentric to seal properly and the valvetrain must be configured to minimize the severity with which it opens and closes the valves, avoiding

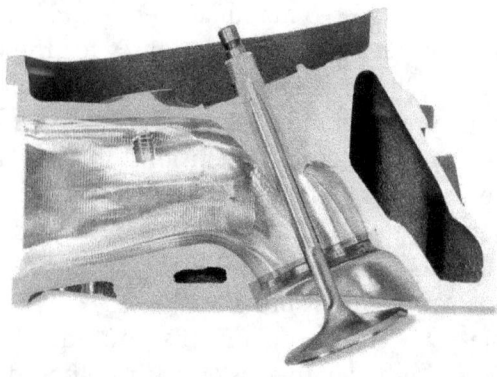

Note that the machining marks inside this ported Dart cylinder head are perpendicular to the direction of airflow. This creates small rolling vortices along the flow path boundary layer. These vortices act like miniature roller bearings to encourage smooth flow without boundary-layer drag. (Courtesy Dart Machinery)

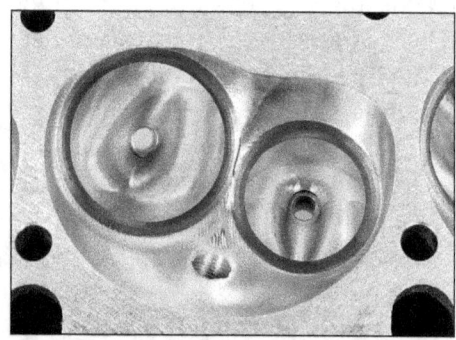

Big Chief CNC full-port versions illustrate the extreme degree of detailed preparation required in a racing cylinder head. Ports and chambers are fully CNC'd and the valveguide tapers are shaped and positioned to optimize flow into and out of the combustion chambers.

valve float at all cost. Valve angles are critical to maximizing performance. Many race heads use a radius seat or up to five different angles on each seat. While 45-degree seats are the norm, Pro/Stock–type applications now use 50- to 55-degree seat angles to take advantage of their superior airflow characteristics at higher engine speeds.

Valve weight is another important concern in high-speed engines. RPM potential and overall valvetrain dynamics are largely influenced by the mass of the valve and what it takes to open and close it with a perfect seal at very high engine speeds. Lightweight titanium valves are standard equipment in all serious racing engines except those applications where they are not permitted.

Cylinder heads are all about using ports, valves, and combustion chambers to manage and optimize airflow through the engine. To achieve the highest degree of success the cylinder heads must be carefully tailored to match the specific requirements of the desired powerband and its associated racing application. This is not difficult to achieve with the broad range of racing cylinder heads available today, but it is expensive. As a rule, top-performing cylinder heads are almost always the most expensive component of any superior racing engine.

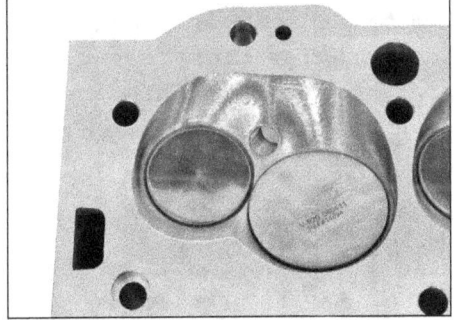

Titanium valves with optimized seat angles and a fully CNC'd combustion chamber are the recipe for high-combustion efficiency as long as the ports and flow paths are optimized to the target application.

This open intake valve shows the generous valve curtain, or flow window. Canted valve angles open the valves away from the cylinder walls to provide good flow with minimal valve shrouding.

Titanium valves are essential for all high-RPM environments. Their strength and light weight support impossibly high engine speeds without failure. Their minimal mass lessens valvespring requirements and reduces stress to related valvetrain components.

CNC-ported small-block head shows the perpendicular porting troughs that encourage efficient boundary-layer flow. Note the aerodynamically tapered valveguides shaped to minimize flow restriction.

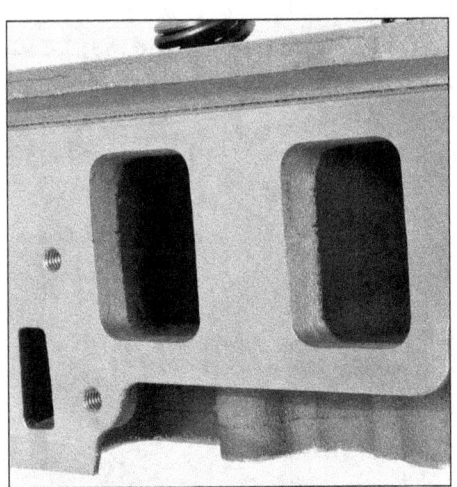

SuperMod ported, spread-port big-block Dart head illustrates basic port matching in the first 1/2 inch of the intake ports. Ports remain as cast, but chambers are fully CNC'd to encourage combustion efficiency.

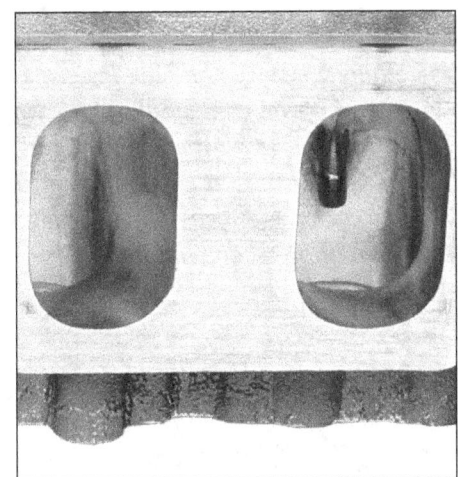

Dart's oval-port Big Chief heads with full port CNC treatment are designed to enhance mid-range torque without sacrificing top-end power. Note the carefully blended and tapered valveguide.

CHAPTER 8

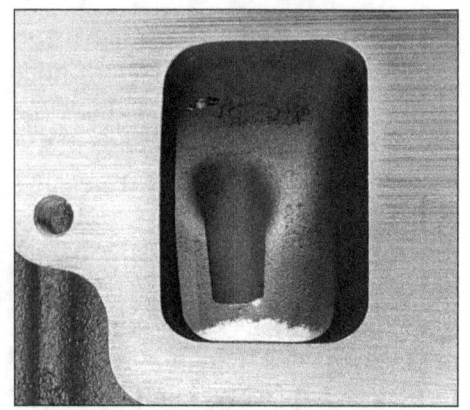

Here's an intake port on a Big Chief Pro 1 head. Even in unported condition it offers strong performance potential. Minor sportsman-style porting can be applied with good results even by amateur home porters.

Unported big-block Chevy exhaust port exhibits good efficiency as cast, but it really wakes up when treated to full-port CNC machining. The port size and shape are good, but the surface texture does little to support the effective evacuation of exhaust gases.

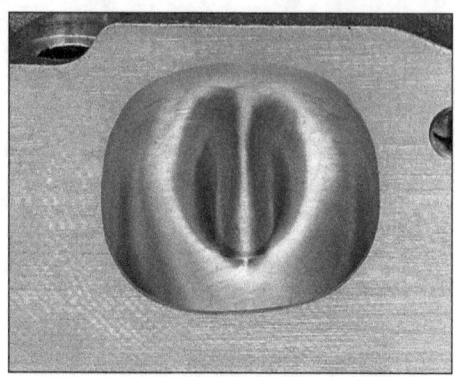

Here's a fully ported small-block exhaust port. Note the contoured and tapered valveguide boss and the polished surface texture. Higher-pressure exhaust gases don't necessarily need the assistance of CNC-generated vortices to exit the port effectively.

Valvetrain accuracy and stability are essential to take full advantage of well matched high-flowing cylinder heads. Valve gear like T&D Machine Products' shaft rockers stabilize the valvetrain and ensure the accuracy of valve timing in every cylinder. These rockers are the first line of defense against high-RPM engine damage.

T&D Machine's rockershaft system for Dart Big Chief heads has three different rocker arms; left offset, right offset, and straight. Each one uses its own unique rocker stand and shaft and they all use assorted shim sizes to set the proper height.

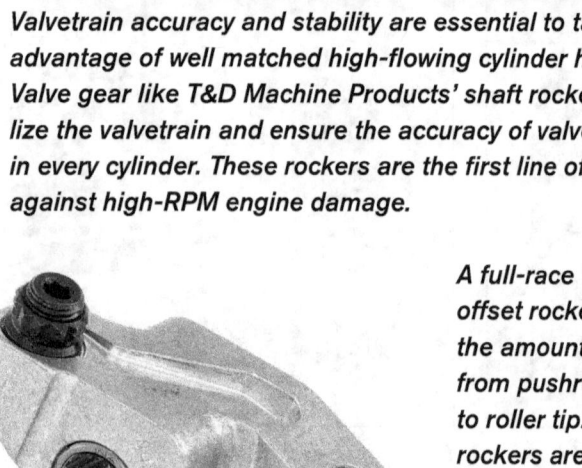

A full-race T&D offset rocker shows the amount of offset from pushrod cup to roller tip. These rockers are lightened on the top and they can be drilled for internal spring oilers for a small increase in price.

Here's another view of the diffferent rocker offsets necessary to obtain good valvetrain geometry and pushrod alignment on a big-block Chevy. Note that the left and right offsets are not the same.

COMPETITION ENGINE BUILDING: ADVANCED ENGINE DESIGN & ASSEMBLY TECHNIQUES

CYLINDER HEADS

CC'ing the combustion chambers is an important step in race engine preparation. Today's CNC-machined chambers are very consistent in shape and volume, but a good builder always checks everything.

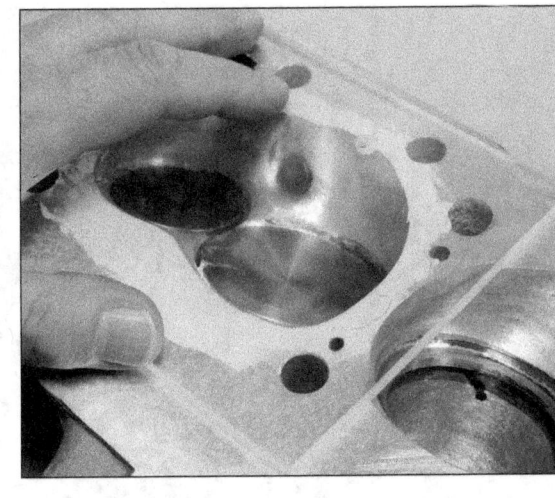

When cc'ing a chamber, it is important not to let any of the sealing grease press out into the chamber where it can alter the volume. This plate is perfectly sealed with the right amount of grease.

Most builders have a favorite gasket for the engines they build. This Fel Pro head gasket illustrates how the gasket bore is typically larger than the cylinder bore with an irregular shape around the valves.

Smoothed or polished ports on the exhaust side are beneficial to performance. There are no fuel-separation issues on the exhaust side. You simply want to provide the best possible exit path for the exhaust gases which are still under pressure.

Here's a typical CNC-prepped small-block combustion chamber with bowl blending. You can just see part of the contoured intake valveguide in this picture.

When using CNC-ported heads from top manufacturers you can be pretty sure the port volumes are close to advertised, but a good engine builder always checks every port.

COMPETITION ENGINE BUILDING: ADVANCED ENGINE DESIGN & ASSEMBLY TECHNIQUES

CHAPTER 8

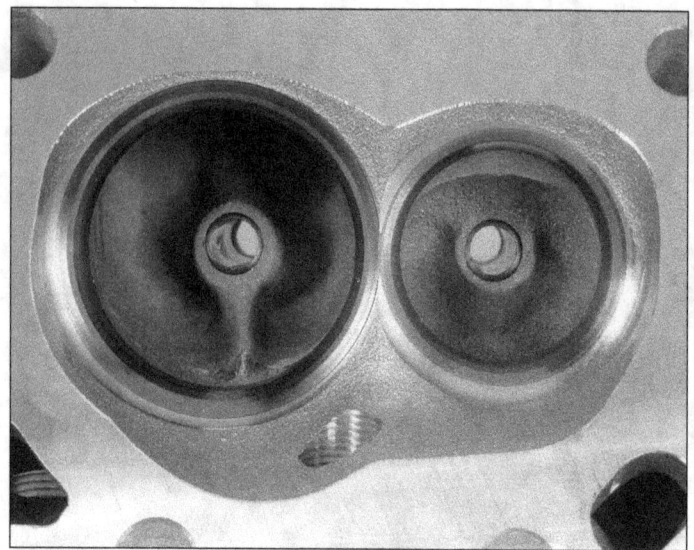

This is an as-cast Dart Pro 1 small-block combustion chamber with streamlined intake valveguide boss.

Here's the same Pro 1 chamber after full CNC porting. Note the precise valveguide blending and multi-angle valve job.

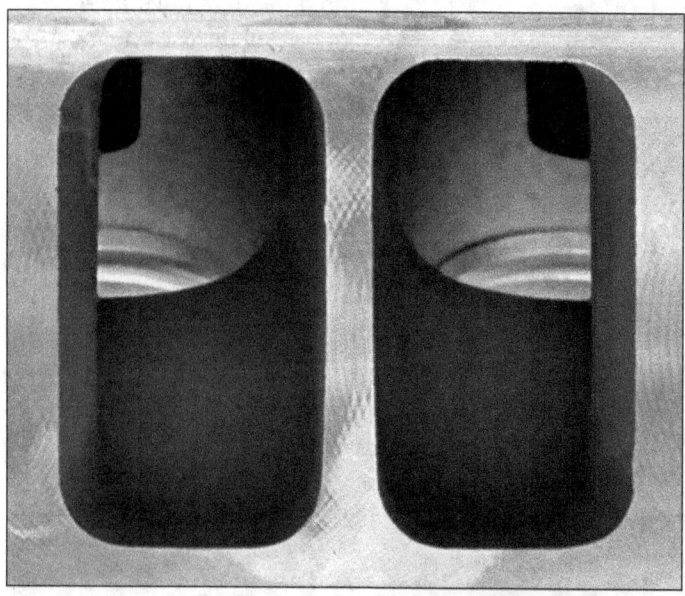

This is the as-cast Pro 1 intake ports with no modifications.

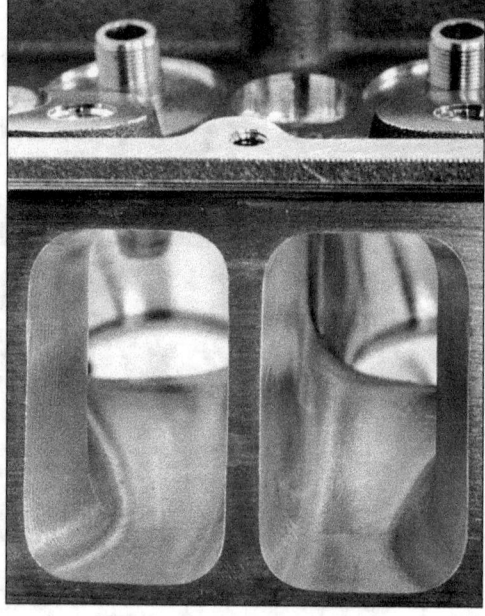

Here's the same Pro 1 intake ports with full CNC porting. Note how the porting cuts are all perpendicular to the direction of flow to provide a roller bearing effect that keeps the air flowing smoothly while resisting fuel separation.

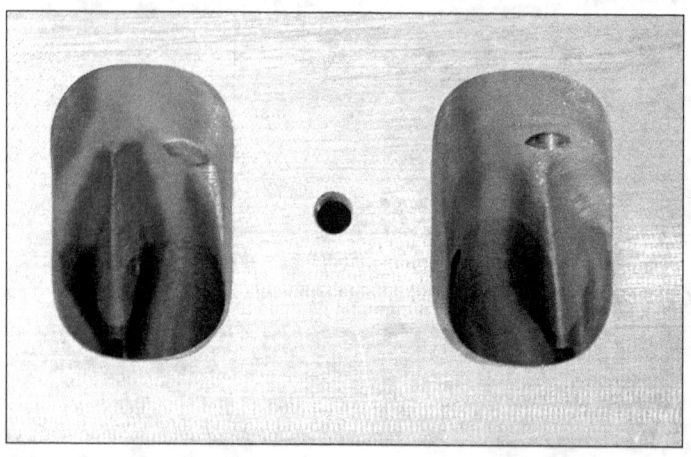

This Little Chief spread-port head shows similar porting and guide blending. The port to the right has a drilled and tapped hole in the roof for the rocker arm stud. Each port must be checked to ensure that threaded bolts or studs do not protrude into the port.

COMPETITION ENGINE BUILDING: ADVANCED ENGINE DESIGN & ASSEMBLY TECHNIQUES

CHAPTER 9

INDUCTION SYSTEMS

The intake manifold is one of the principal tuning components of any competition engine. Its configuration and dimensions actively influence the production of torque and horsepower and their placement within the engine's effective operating range. Consequently, a poor intake manifold selection is often a contributing cause of lost or misplaced power and/or poor throttle response.

Sonny's Racing Engines builds massive 932-ci fuel-injected Pro Stock drag racing engines delivering 2,050 hp at 8,100 rpm and that's no accident. They are equipped with highly refined induction systems that pinpoint the exact airflow requirements of the engine's operating range while providing nearly 1,450 ft-lbs of torque at 6,700 rpm.

Race applications deal with three basic manifold types: dual-plane intakes, single-plane intakes, and tunnel ram intakes (effectively a taller single-plane intake). Individual runner (IR) intakes are also employed in some applications, but not to the extent of more common plenum-style intakes. Each type has its strengths and weaknesses and tuning characteristics that make it suitable for particular high-performance or racing applications. Accordingly, manifold characteristics and dimensions exert considerable influence on engine performance with respect to powerband shape and positioning on the RPM scale.

Most applications employ commercially available intakes designed for broad application coverage while high-end applications lean more toward custom-fabricated manifolds that are built with specific dimensions applicable to their exact competition environment. This chapter examines each of them separately and identifies characteristics of each type that make it most suitable for a given racing application.

CHAPTER 9

Dual-Plane Intakes

Dual-plane intakes effectively divide a V-8 engine into two independent four-cylinder engines connected by a common crankshaft. The design divides intake runners into two separate groups, each exposed to alternating induction pulses, or airflow requests submitted by an opening intake valve and the accompanying pressure differential in a given cylinder.

When a manifold is divided into separate cylinder groupings with alternating and evenly spaced pulses it is said to have 2 degrees of freedom. This configuration produces stronger pressure waves, effectively emulating longer runners that tune to lower engine speeds. Dual-plane intakes are highly effective as high-performance street manifolds because they promote strong torque at street engine speeds. Similarly they are ideal for many sportsman racing classes that depend on low- and mid-range torque for optimum performance, particularly with heavier cars in various circle track applications.

Dual-plane intakes submit strong booster signals to the carburetor, promoting crisp throttle response and increased runner energy for effective cylinder filling at lower engine speeds. In effect, each cylinder only sees half of the carburetor or, in a sense, a 2-barrel carburetor with a single primary bore and a single secondary bore, each requiring individual tuning according to plenum size, configuration, and engine speed. Competition dual-planes are typically effective in the 2,500- to 6,500-rpm range. Their runners are dimensionally tuned to promote a torque peak between 4,000 and 5,500 rpm depending primarily on runner cross section and engine displacement.

If dual-plane intakes are required for various racing series, it is important to consider their unique characteristics and how they might best be manipulated to optimize power and performance in the most effective operating range.

Well-designed intake runners have a fixed cross-sectional area that you can use to calculate the RPM where the torque peak occurs. Once you identify the RPM where the intake builds maximum torque, you can manipulate supporting torque components to help boost torque above or below that point depending on how the car needs to perform. This broadens the overall torque curve and is the same procedure you can use to successfully pinpoint and position torque with single-plane and tunnel ram intakes. To accomplish this the cross-sectional area of the individual intake runners must be known.

To calculate the cross section of a given runner, measure the dimensions of the runner entry and the runner exit, then average the two. This yields the mean cross-sectional area of the runner, which can then be used to calculate the mathematically defined torque peak using the well-known McFarland formula.

$$\text{Torque Peak RPM} = (\text{runner mean cross section area} \times 88{,}200) \div \text{volume of a single cylinder}$$

Calculating the cross section by averaging runner entry and exit dimensions incorporates any degree of taper that may be present in the runners. Runner taper provides additional flow volume while preserving port energy by promoting a venturi effect with decreasing runner cross section along the length of the flow path.

Depending on the engine type, a dual-plane intake likely has unequal-length runners on the center

Dual-plane intake manifolds are a core component of many sportsman racing classes. They are widely recognized for their superior low- and mid-range torque.

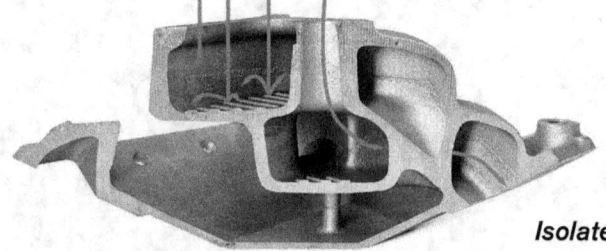

Isolated dual plenums differ in volume and booster signal strength. The larger volume of the deep-side plenum encourages an easier turn into the runners with less fuel dropout. The smaller high-side plenum can experience fuel separation due to high-charge velocity exiting the carburetor, close proximity to the plenum floor, and immediate turn into the runners.

INDUCTION SYSTEMS

cylinders as compared to the end cylinders. The longer runners tend to boost torque below the torque peak and the shorter runners promote torque above the peak. The peak location on the RPM scale is governed by the mean runner cross section.

This effect can be strengthened by providing complementary primary tube dimensions on the exhaust headers. Longer intake runners should be paired with longer primary tubes and shorter runners should be matched with shorter primary tubes to broaden the overall torque curve. Think of these efforts as torque shifting to bias torque one way or the other around the torque peak. You also have the option of employing larger or smaller primary tube cross sections on selected cylinders that are torque deficient due to a weak flow path, i.e., good port/bad port as found in big-block Chevys. This promotes a secondary torque peak that broadens the overall curve.

View from above the dual-plane's plenum shows the high-side floor (left) wetter and darker from fuel separation. Note gentle radius entering the runner. As the fuel charge decelerates coming out of the carburetor it makes the turn into the lower runners more easily and without fuel dropout.

Spacers with Dual-Plane Intakes

From a different tuning perspective, carburetor spacers and tuning adjustment may also improve the overall performance of the dual-plane intake manifold. As previously noted, dual-planes generate stronger pressure pulses and carburetor signals due to the separation of the plenum area into two smaller volumes. In many cases it can also be beneficial to investigate a different method of stagger jetting based on the high side as compared the low side of the divided plenum. The high side generates a stronger booster signal than the low side so it tends to dominate jetting selection for the engine. It's entirely possible that the deep side (generating a weaker signal because the booster is farther from the signal source and the plenum volume is greater) tends to deliver a leaner mixture because the weaker signal does not pull fuel through the jet as easily.

It may be beneficial to run slightly more jet on the deep side of the plenum. The amount of side-to-side jet stagger varies with plenum depth and volume, runner cross section, and engine speed. Dyno testing can establish the ideal difference between left-side (deep) and right-side (high) jetting based on power readings, EGT levels, and oxygen sensor readings if you have them.

Once you establish the optimum spread, you can adjust accordingly at the track. Automatically going richer on the deep side may not always be the best choice as that side may already be rich so it's best to take jet out of the high side until power falls off. Once you establish that point, you can tune the low side according to the best spread as indicated by the dyno or actual track performance.

As a rule, the low side often requires at least one jet size larger once you have optimized the high side. This varies depending on the height and type of carb spacer and whether or not the spacer permits cross-talk or pulse transfer between the divided plenums.

Depending on the type of spacer you elect to run, you may compound the problem and require more jet stagger to equalize fuel delivery. Remember, different-length runners resonate at different engine speeds, thus encouraging separate torque

TECH TIP: Intake Manifold Selection Criteria

- Carburetors or EFI?
- Cast or Fabricated?
- Required Torque Range
- Required Power Range
- Runner Length Requirement
- Runner Cross Section
- Plenum Volume
- Runner Volume
- Runner Taper
- Coolant Flow
- Carburetor(s) Position
- Throttle Body(s) Position
- Fuel Injector Bungs?
- Nitrous Injection Bosses?
- Carb Spacer?
- Throttle Linkage
- Dual Plane
- Single Plane
- Tunnel Ram
- Individual Runners
- Multi-carburetor?
- Throttle Body Type
- Weight
- Coatings

peaks and affecting the fueling requirement accordingly. A spacer's chief value is not in adding plenum volume per se, but rather in easing the ability of the high-speed air/fuel charge to make the sharp turn into the runners without depositing most of the suspended fuel against the plenum floor. With a dual-plane there is no practical way to equalize the distance from the signal source to the boosters on all four barrels of the carburetor.

Fuel droplets may hit the plenum floor and fall out of suspension on the high side because there is less room to make the turn into the runner. That means the low side of the manifold may generate better mixture quality than the high side. Juggling air bleeds might provide some relief, but they are generally too sensitive so stagger jetting is usually a more valid tuning strategy in the absence of a spacer design that would be open on the high side while incorporating throttle bore extensions to enhance booster signal on the deep side.

Clearly there are performance gains to be harvested for those willing to investigate booster signal and jetting requirements on separate sides of dual-plane intakes.

Intake Manifold General Characteristics

Different types of intake manifolds exhibit characteristics that make them particularly suitable for various racing applications.

Characteristic	Dual-Plane	Single-Plane	Tunnel Ram
Smaller Plenum Volume	x		
Larger Plenum Volume		x	x
Stronger Booster Signals	x		
Weaker Booster Signals		x	x
Small Unequal Runners	x		
Larger More-Equal Runners		x	
Larger Tapered Runners			x
Best Low-Speed Torque	x		
Best High-Speed Power		x	x
Maximum High-Speed Power			x

Single-Plane Intakes

The single-plane manifold's open plenum serves all eight cylinders at once and generally tends to promote even fuel mixture distribution at higher engine speeds. That said, the specifics of various runner entries and runner lengths may provide opportunity for selected runners to dominate others via pressure-wave exchange or cross-talk within the plenum, particularly on adjacent runners according to each cylinder's position in the firing order. A single-plane intake never achieves full resonance as found in dual-plane intakes. The lack of resonance limits low-speed torque, which can affect throttle response and drivability off slow corners, and also impacts fuel economy in the sense that it requires more engine speed and more throttle opening to produce effective torque.

A large, undivided plenum exposes all eight cylinders to the carburetor collectively, reducing booster signal and low-speed fuel metering consistency. Larger plenum volumes tend to dampen the effects of cylinder-to-cylinder pressure-pulse influence, but open-plenum manifolds in

An open spacer on a dual-plane intake increases plenum volume and exposes both sides of the plenum to inconsistent pressure changes. A four-hole spacer adds volume but maintains the separation between left and right plenums. Both can help ease the turn into the runner on the high-side plenum. Results vary depending on cam timing, carb size, and engine speed, hence careful testing is required.

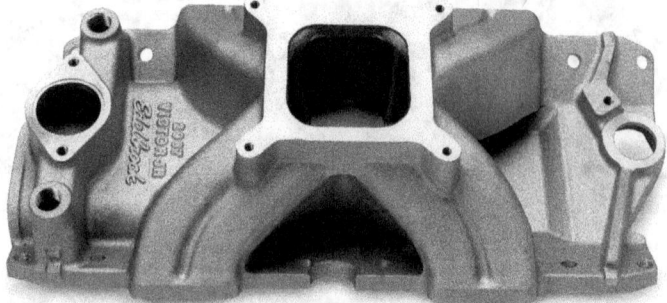

Single-plane 4-barrel intakes are a staple of contemporary sportsman drag racing. They are inexpensive and provide superior power and performance in a high-RPM drag racing environment.

INDUCTION SYSTEMS

general are sometimes subjected to fuel distribution issues caused by certain cam and/or cylinder head conflicts, or the undue influence of poor exhaust tuning.

It is generally conceded that properly configured combinations typically provide more even fuel distribution than most dual-planes particularly at elevated engine speeds. The point is that you can't assume this. There is power to be gained by investigating fuel distribution and mixture quality properties by whatever means possible. This is generally done on the dyno where precision instrumentation can lead the way, but you can gain some insight from plug readings, oxygen-sensor readings from side to side if you have them on the car, exhaust-gas temperature readings, and indications of reversion that may occur in individual intake runners or the plenum.

Despite potential problems, single-plane intakes offer superior high-speed power. They incorporate shorter runners that tune to higher engine speeds while promoting high-flow potential and greater charge density at high RPM. Single-planes can also be tuned with carburetor spacers.

Spacers with Single-Plane Intakes

Open spacers are commonly used to increase plenum volume, which soften the impact of cylinder-to-cylinder pressure influences that affect air/fuel ratio consistency. Open spacers also ease the transition of the fuel charge from vertical, exiting the carburetor throttle bores to near horizontal in the runners. Flow velocities through the carburetor can exceed 600 feet per second, which tends to slam fuel droplets against the plenum floor, as an attempt to change direction into the runner.

It has long been established that a mean flow velocity of 240 to 260 feet per second is optimal for best torque production. This depends on properly dimensioned ports and runners relative to engine displacement. An air/fuel mixture exiting the carburetor at 600 feet per second has to negotiate the relatively tight turn into the runners where velocity slows to the mean rather quickly. Air, being compressible, tends to make the turn and decelerate more easily than the incompressible fuel droplets that fall out of suspension due to greater high-speed inertia accompanied by rapid direction and volume changes. This becomes the first post-carburetor opportunity to practice mixture conditioning.

Highly atomized fuel produced by effective booster design changes direction more easily because smaller individual fuel droplets have less mass. Increased plenum depth and volume tend to support this cause. Engine dyno testing can help pinpoint spacer configurations that improve single plane performance by addressing mixture quality issues. Since the problem only increases with engine speed and associated higher mixture demand, efforts to improve these conditions are often surprisingly worthwhile.

Single-plane intakes like this Dart unit for a 4500 Dominator expose all eight intake ports to a common plenum chamber. They generally provide more even fuel distribution and superior power from about 5,000 to 5,500 rpm on up. Taller versions and those with open spacers often gain power because they soften the exchange of pressure pulses between cylinders due to increased volume and an easier flow path.

Most as-cast intake manifolds can be improved by specialized porting services like Wilson Manifolds. Most service providers excel at matching intake manifolds to your cylinder heads to achieve the proper turn-ins at the port interface and at the most desirable blending and port surface texturing.

Line of sight from the port to the carburetor throttle typically encourages superior flow. As shown here, that can't always happen with a single 4-barrel intake, but many aftermarket designs get very close.

Four-hole spacers and various hybrid or combination spacers are often used on single-plane intakes for similar reasons. In the long run, assisting mixture transition into the runner is usually more important than adding plenum volume to dampen plenum pressure excursions. Generally, a spacer assists both of these concerns, and to some degree they can also be fine tuned through other means such as individual cylinder adjustments to valve and ignition timing.

In the past plenum dividers were often added to single-plane intakes to boost carburetor signal strength. This was only partially successful as the uneven firing pulses acting on each side of the divided plenum did not permit second-degree freedom resonance. Instead, unpredictable resonant phases occur throughout the RPM range with inconsistent results that dramatically affect airflow and mixture quality.

Carburetor spacers typically accomplish two things. First, increasing the plenum volume tends to soften inter-cylinder pressure disturbances. Second, greater volume also reduces inlet airspeed and encourages the smooth transition of air and fuel into the individual runners with less fuel separation and puddling. Open spacers that provide a significant increase in volume sometimes allow a single-plane intake to modestly approach tunnel ram performance depending on the application.

In some cases where a manifold sees more action near the lower end of its powerband, a four-hole spacer improves booster signal and often sharpens low-speed throttle response. With fixed dimensions, all manifolds generate their own particular sweet spot (RPM) where they deliver maximum torque according to the displacement of the engine. Above and below this point they tend to fall in and out of tune according to dimensional influences on airflow and mixture quality that require evaluation and extensive tuning effort to optimize performance.

As a rule, try to accomplish tuning cylinder by cylinder if you have the instrumentation to accomplish it. The physical layout and dimensions of any intake manifold rarely promote perfectly equal conditions in each cylinder, so individual tuning consideration becomes compulsory to the extraction of maximum performance from each cylinder. More often than not, it is highly beneficial.

Tunnel Ram Intakes

Tunnel ram manifolds are highly desirable for all-out racing applications because they provide the very best configuration for equalizing runner lengths and volumes. They provide the most direct and unrestricted flow path from the carburetor to the intake valve and they offer the best possible design for optimizing flow velocity and mixture quality. They are particularly effective at engine speeds above 7,000 rpm.

If you don't consider packaging issues, a long-runner tunnel ram can be an effective high-performance intake and a good choice for heavier drag cars needing a torque boost at lower engine speeds. Short-runner tunnel rams with appropriate plenum volume provide superior high-speed performance, which is why you see them almost exclusively on professional drag racing cars (Pro/Stock) and their high-RPM Sportsman counterparts.

Tunnel rams present the best opportunity to optimize runner

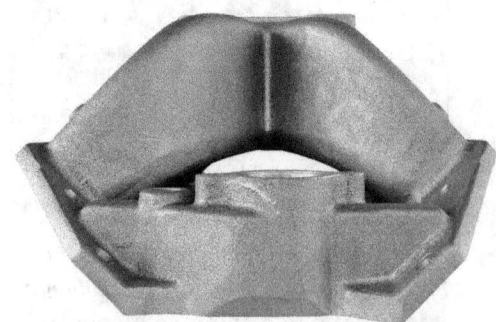

Taller, single-plane manifolds seek to emulate the superior flow paths of tunnel ram intakes. The raised carburetor location offers a straighter shot at the intake port on the cylinder head. This improves performance, but the fixed runner dimensions tune best to a specific engine speed and are not easily modified.

Tall, single-plane 4-barrel intake manifolds and carburetors are formidable racing attire. This Dart Big Chief spread-port intake and 1,150-cfm Holley Ultra HP aluminum Dominator pack a powerful punch when teamed with an appropriate-size, high-compression short block.

INDUCTION SYSTEMS

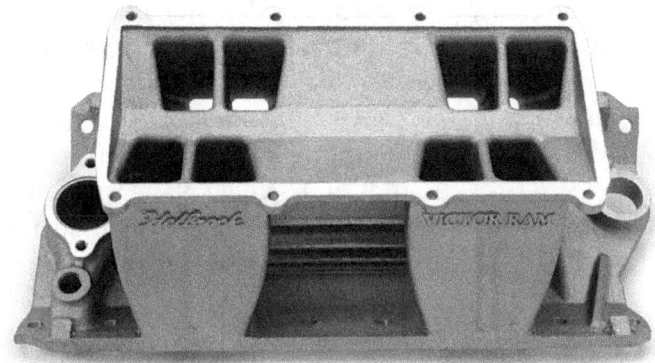

Basic tunnel-ram configuration like this Edelbrock Victor Ram incorporates specific tuned runner lengths, cross-sectional area, runner taper, and entry angles for superior performance with dual carburetors.

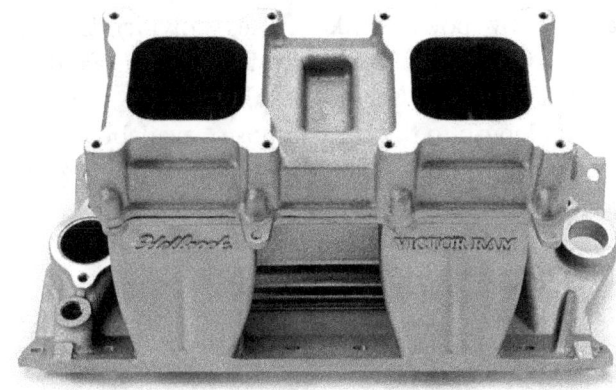

Position the carburetors directly above the intake ports to ensure a direct path to the valves. Plenum volume is often altered by fabricating a dedicated top to suit the specific application requirements.

length, volume, and taper. You're less likely to see variations in runner dimensions in these applications because they operate in a very narrow powerband that doesn't require the pursuit of multiple torque boosts via selective intake and exhaust dimensional matchmaking. A heavier drag car might respond to manifold modifications to complement alternating exhaust dimensions to help broaden the torque curve, particularly if it operates over a greater RPM spread than a Pro/Stock car.

The two basic types of tunnel ram intakes include fixed-dimension aluminum castings made by major intake manufacturers and hand-made sheet-metal intakes built by specialty manifold companies such as Wilson Manifolds or Hogan's Racing Manifolds. These intakes are custom built with very specific dimensions designed to closely match the engine's final application. Runner length, shape, taper, and cross-sectional area are specifically matched to the engine's requirements and the plenum shape, volume, and carburetor mounting surface are all sized to accommodate the exact requirements of the engine.

Unlike more universal cast tunnel ram manifolds, sheet-metal intakes are very much engine and application specific. The hand-made application permits the engine builder to pinpoint very specific intake characteristics depending on how the engine will be used. These intakes are very labor intensive to construct and are thus quite expensive. Used ones are often available through eBay and other outlets, but the chances of finding one that matches your exact requirements are pretty slim and you could easily do more harm than good if you don't thoroughly investigate the manifold's exact dimensions prior to purchasing it.

Most tunnel ram applications operate at extremely high engine speeds where it is important to accurately match plenum volume to displacement and the actual air demand in the engine's most effective operating range. The established rule of thumb dictates that optimum performance is derived from the smallest possible dimensions that adequately support the engine's airflow requirement. Runner cross section can position the torque peak relative to engine speed and vehicle requirements. Runner lengths returning multiple pulse reflections generally tune best to the second reflected pulse (wave) if the engine requires

Sheet-metal tunnel-ram intakes are the default power standard for naturally aspirated high-horsepower applications. These manifolds are labor intensive to construct, but they can meet the specific dimensions that produce big power within closely specified powerbands. (Courtesy Wilson Manifolds)

a peaky narrow powerband. Engines requiring a lower and slightly broader powerband are better served by tuning runner length to the third or possibly even fourth pulse.

To calculate the optimum runner length based on reflected pulses, use the following formulas, which are taken from Motion Software's Dynomation 5 engine simulation program.

Optimum runner length in inches
2nd pulse = 108,000/rpm
3rd pulse = 97,000/rpm
4th pulse = 74,000/rpm
5th pulse = 54,000/rpm

If you have correctly identified a powerband depicted by the desired RPM spread between peak torque and peak power, you can use the McFarland cross-sectional area formula (see page 96) to establish the optimum runner cross-section for your torque peak. Then use the reflected pulse formula (above) to pinpoint the supporting runner length.

These efforts are more effective than you might suspect, particularly when combined with other known strategies to effect individual cylinder optimization. When you tune each cylinder to its peak efficiency and take steps to boost torque across the required powerband it pays big dividends on the track. Accordingly, the intake manifold becomes one of the most influential components available for effectively tuning and positioning torque.

Plenum Characteristics

A cursory examination of manifold styles notes particular differences in plenum shapes and volume.

Dual-Plane Intakes

Dual-plane intakes typically have the smallest plenums because the manifold is divided into two separate manifolds functioning almost independently of each other. As previously noted, a major discrepancy of a dual-plane manifold is unequal plenum floor depth from one side to the other. This promotes uneven carburetor booster signals from side to side and leads to uneven fuel distribution if not compensated by jetting adjustments. The upper-side plenum is more susceptible to high-speed fuel separation due to minimal distance between the carburetor throttle bore exit and the plenum floor. The low-side plenum is more effective at directing the mixture into the runner with less fuel separation due to reduced velocity and an easier path approaching the floor and the runner. The downside is reduced booster sensitivity on that side of the manifold and the attending potential for uneven fuel distribution.

Also note that both plenum volumes are still smaller than that found in a single-plane manifold, and thus tend to provide superior throttle response at low to moderate engine speeds. Limited plenum volume supports this even though both sides may generate slightly different fuel curves.

If you accept that a fixed volume occupies the plenum at all times it's easy to see that this volume maintains a fixed amount of inertia or resistance to movement. One molecule has to get out of the way before the next molecule can replace it. This requires a certain amount of energy, which is easier to generate with reduced volume. Thus the higher

A glance inside the Wilson Manifolds sheet-metal intake shows meticulous workmanship with dimensionally correct runners, carefully radiused runner entries, and precision machine work to support the specific plenum and runner volumes required by the final application. (Courtesy Wilson Manifolds)

Those who regularly calculate the results of various runner lengths and cross sections will appreciate the value of PipeMax, a handy PC software program from Meaux Racing Heads. The program calculates induction system tuned lengths and provides predicted results based on sound mathematical models. You can download it from the website for less than $50.

energy state of smaller plenums makes it easier to move the mixture and provides higher sensitivity (even if unequal) to the venturi boosters.

Another important component of dual-plane intake operation is carburetor size. For many years builders sought to minimize carburetor size to maintain good flow velocity. But the newer generation of highly efficient dual-planes fly in the face of convention. Traditional thinking suggests that because each cylinder connected to a given plenum sees only half of the carburetor's total air capacity, the engine can effectively use a larger carburetor because the signal strength is greater.

While there is some truth to this, the greater benefit of using a larger carburetor is more often found in more effective mixture conditioning. The larger carburetor reduces venturi airspeed, allowing the air/fuel mixture to make the turn into the runners more easily and with less fuel separation. Therefore, like spacers, carburetor size can be an effective tuning aid for dual-plane applications when and if carburetor size is not restricted by the rules.

Single-Plane Intakes

Single-plane intakes are a different story. They may present more evenly matched signal requests to the carburetor boosters, but they are generally dampened due to increased plenum volume. This often requires more jet to compensate for weaker signal strength. When a spacer is added, volume increases, signal strength degrades further, and jetting must be readjusted to service fuel demand and establish adequate flow sensitivity at the jet. Spacers are a means of adding plenum volume to both single- and dual-plane intake manifolds. The primary purpose is to encourage mixture quality by easing the turn into the runners without detrimental fuel separation.

Tunnel Ram Intakes

There is a fine line between adjusting plenum volume for the promotion of mixture quality and the invisible dynamics of airflow inertia. Larger plenums as found in tunnel rams tend to soften intercylinder pressure excursions. Some engine builders feel that added volume is also necessary to ensure adequate mixture quantity at elevated engine speeds. In reality, every combination has a select "sweet spot" that strikes an ideal balance between mixture quality, pulse tuning, and airflow inertia management within the plenum. While it is sometimes difficult to pinpoint exactly, calculations to identify torque peak RPM and pulse-tuned runner lengths can put you not just in the ballpark, but well on the path to home plate.

Making the Choice

The best combination is not easy to determine, particularly on engines with a broad powerband. Still, it is possible to increase accuracy by conducting an airflow assessment of the manifold you intend to use, assuming of course that you are using a commercially available intake of fixed dimensions.

Builders with flow bench access can flow test the manifold and cylinder head together and it's a good idea to include the carburetor with throttle plates locked open. This often requires some jury-rigged props and adjustments to set up on the flow bench, but it's worth the effort. You then flow each runner and port combination separately with the other runners sealed off. This constitutes a basic airflow study that does not specifically contemplate wet flow conditions or potential pressure influences from adjacent runners.

It does establish a basic airflow map of the manifold and what each runner is capable of, independent of outside interference. It does not evaluate compensation for runner-to-runner pressure influence or the unsteady flow of dynamic valve operation, but it can illuminate airflow weaknesses and inequalities that should be corrected or compensated for if possible. With the carburetor in place it also considers plenum volume, at least to the extent that it affects total airflow and the identification of problematic flow paths.

For most race applications the valve opening action occurs so

Single-plane intake manifolds like this Dart Big Chief unit are particularly efficient single 4-barrel induction systems. Designed for spread-port cylinder heads, they encourage improved mixture quality by providing more efficient runner entry angles at the port interface.

quickly that it isn't generally necessary to evaluate low-lift flow except perhaps in the case of lower-performance circle track applications. It's also not necessary to flow at all valve opening increments, but you should evaluate intake flow at about 65 percent of net anticipated valve lift. If the manifold/port combination supports the calculated volume requirements and runner performance is relatively equal at this point, it is probably sufficient at peak lift as well. Recall that the valve is only at peak lift for a fraction of a second, but it typically resides at or above the stated percentages for most of the valve event. These percentages represent known values relative to piston position and port flow demand for optimum VE and efficient exhaust blow-down.

Cylinder-to-cylinder flow variations are often greatest with a dual-plane and least with a tunnel ram. In any case, careful flow mapping of the manifold in this manner helps to identify runners that may need individual tuning assistance in the form of rocker-ratio adjustments, individual cylinder cam lobe profiles, header dimension compensation, and even timing and jetting adjustment based on runners that exhibit weaker or uneven flow characteristics relative to the others. Once you have created this flow map, you'll be surprised at the follow-on thought process it provokes—all based on a keener awareness of your equipment's characteristics and recognized methods of compensation to increase and equalize torque.

Mixture Conditioning

Fuel atomization is central to the practice of mixture conditioning. This is particularly true for carbureted applications that are limited to wet-flow fuel delivery methods. First and foremost, you want the finest or smallest possible fuel droplets in the airflow mixture. You also want the highest degree of homogeneity (equality) of size among the smallest fuel droplets. For a given fuel volume, a higher percentage of smaller and evenly sized droplets presents more combustible surface area, which burns faster and more evenly. Droplets that vary in size slow the rate of combustion relative to smaller droplets because the larger ones are more difficult to burn. They also degrade mixture quality by falling out of suspension easier whenever they encounter abrupt changes in direction, cross-sectional area, runner volume, or mixture velocity.

Issues of mixture quality are particularly sensitive to booster design, plenum volume, runner configuration, surface texture, and flow path velocity. Any of these can lead to fuel separation and localized wetting of plenum and runner walls and floors. In severe cases fuel may actually puddle on the plenum floor, particularly on the upper plane of a dual-plane intake, making degraded mixture quality partially responsible for the diminishing efficiency of these manifolds at elevated engine speeds.

Successful mixture conditioning efforts incorporate all efforts to maintain the finest homogenous mixture while reducing dynamic influences that cause fuel separation. This includes fuel contact with runner walls, valves, cylinder walls, and piston tops, and the various surface textures they present.

Excessive velocity can separate fuel, transitioning the bowl area below the valve. It can also fling fuel against the opposing side of the combustion chamber causing fuel wash that is compounded by rapidly rising piston motion and potentially inhospitable piston dome configuration. In considering this environment, consider every portion of the flow path from carburetor to combustion chamber. This includes carburetors, plenums, runners and runner entries, port shapes, valvestems, valve seats, combustion chambers, cylinder walls, and piston top configuration—all potential sources of mixture degradation.

Smooth or polished surfaces are particularly troublesome and should be eliminated from the flow path wherever possible. Dimpling and/or port surface striations perpendicular to the flow path tend to support good mixture quality by reducing fuel separation. These depressions activate the boundary layer near

Some race intakes incorporate a separate cooling manifold to direct water to each cylinder head for additional cooling, particularly around the area of the exhaust valve. This example is a Chevrolet RO7 Sprint Cup manifold.

plenum and runner floors by providing a tumbling effect that tends to maintain flow velocity while keeping fuel droplets in suspension. In-cylinder mixture motion in the form of swirl and tumble as the mixture enters the cylinder also promotes mixture quality and cylinder filling.

In practice, most high-speed competition engines favor some degree of swirl to help direct the burn toward the exhaust valve, but tumble has generally been found to have little effect at very high engine speeds. Successful efforts to encourage quench and active mixture motion typically permit a reduction in spark timing, which lessens negative work against the piston as it approaches TDC. Accordingly, equalization of EGTs, lower BSFC numbers, and an increase in torque typically accompany successful mixture conditioning efforts.

Surface Texturing

Surface texturing is generally useful anywhere in the flow path, particularly in areas that are prone to fuel separation due to directional changes or changes in charge velocity due to area variations. Manifold runners should never be polished and any place in the plenum that has been ground to match a spacer or modify a runner entry should be retextured. (This primarily applies to carbureted wet-flow applications.) Fuel droplets tend to stick to smooth surfaces so avoid them wherever possible.

Depending on accessibility, plenum and runner floors can be dimpled with an appropriately blunt tool (1/8-inch rounded top) to promote rolling vortices or eddies that tend to return fuel into suspension and prevent further dropout. Dimpling is commonly used on piston tops and in combustion chambers that are easy to reach. Without prior engine operation there is no burn pattern to guide you relative to areas of fuel wash and incomplete combustion so you may want to reserve this tactic for after the engine has been run.

An interesting example of dimpling is found in the Tork-Link manifold offered by Hi-Tech Engine Components: a tall dual-plane intake specifically designed for some circle track applications. Hi-Tech also offers a Swirl-Quench piston design that incorporates dimples and a tapered ramp on the piston top to optimize homogeneity and direct mixture motion, and thus the burn toward the exhaust valve. Other applications attempt to do the same thing by reading combustion patterns on previously run pistons and dimpling clean areas that exhibit little or no combustion residue.

Some builders don't fully subscribe to these concepts, preferring instead to glass bead piston tops, apply piston top coatings, and texture manifold passages as best they can. Some racers have also tried extrude-honing manifolds to increase runner volume, but this is generally a bad idea for carbureted intakes since it tends to polish the runners and there is no practical way to retexture them. Extrude honing is generally reserved for "dry flow" manifolds on EFI systems where fuel separation is not an issue. At the very least, texturing manifold runners by glass beading improves mixture quality in manifolds with very smooth runners.

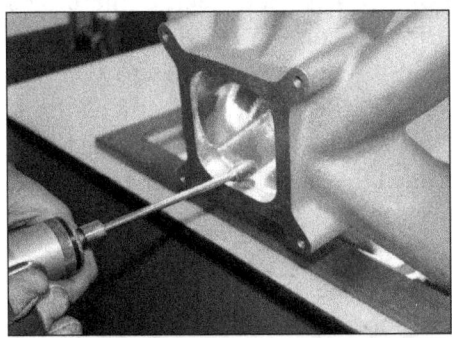

Part of the extensive work performed on intake manifolds at Wilson Manifolds includes proper surface texturing to optimize flow while minimizing the potential for fuel separation in the runners.

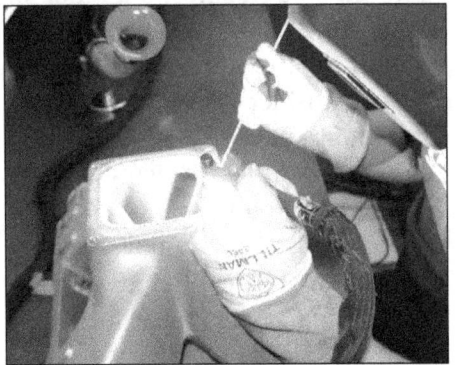

Wilson Manifold technicians modify and reshape the intake runners to accommodate the application in terms of runner entry angles, plenum-to-runner transitions, and other considerations to equalize each runner's airflow and mixture quality contribution.

Runner turn-ins are cut and reshaped to exactly match the cylinder head intake ports for optimum efficiency. The manifold-to-cylinder-head/runner interface must maintain the cross section and taper to prevent fuel separation due to rapid area and velocity changes.

CHAPTER 9

Reversion

Reversion is present in all engines to some degree. It varies with engine speed and the particular combination of parts and timing events that encourage it. Reversion occurs at intake valve opening when cylinder pressure is still greater than manifold pressure. This causes the remaining combustion residue to migrate into the intake manifold. This continues briefly until manifold pressure, cylinder pressure, and exhaust pressure equalize and a pressure drop is initiated in the cylinder. The incoming fuel charge then enters the cylinder contaminated with residual exhaust particles that previously entered the manifold.

Charge contamination reduces power by replacing useable fuel mixture with unburnable combustion residue—a version of EGR that works to limit power production in all competition engines. This typically forces the need to de-tune the system with more timing advance and more jet to get enough fuel into the engine and burn it as efficiently as possible.

More timing increases pre-TDC work against the piston (negative torque) and excessive fuel compounds the mixture quality issues that reduce power and increase fuel usage unnecessarily.

Manifolds are more or less resistant to reversion depending on the application. Dual-plane intakes with smaller plenums and high-energy runners tend to dampen the effects of reversion. Single-plane intakes with large plenums and larger runners are more sensitive to reversion pressure and frequently permit a greater level of charge contamination depending on the intake valve closing point and exhaust back pressure during the camshaft overlap period.

Efforts to reduce reversion include later closing intake valve timing to allow more time for cylinder pressure to fall. Properly timed exhaust-valve opening helps evacuate the cylinder and draw in the next fuel charge without the pressure difference that encourages reversion.

To some degree carburetor spacers tend to encourage reversion by weakening manifold pressure. This can usually be corrected with properly matched cam timing.

Consult your cam supplier with the specifics of your package to determine cam specs that resist the effects of reversion, particularly in the useable powerband of your engine.

Secondary Intake Considerations

If you're opting for a maximum-effort, custom-built intake make sure it incorporates all of the following considerations and any others that you may determine to be necessary. While the specific runner and plenum dimensions, shape, and style of manifold hold the most potential for power production and powerband positioning, there are additional factors to consider depending on the exact requirements.

Very few universal racing engines deliver top performance outside their intended environment. Once you have established the ideal manifold configuration and dimensions for your application, you may wish to apply additional techniques to help the manifold do its job at peak efficiency.

Some of these modifications include heat management in the form of thermal coatings and/or types of insulation to isolate the plenum and runners from radiant engine heat. These coatings may be applied to the entire manifold or specific areas such as the bottom, which is exposed to splash oiling from the lifter gallery.

For marine applications, companies such as Dart Machinery offer specialized anti-corrosive coatings and marine jacket coatings to prevent saltwater corrosion in the water jackets of cylinder heads and intake manifolds, or a shielding treatment that resists galvanic corrosion in blocks and cylinder heads.

You may also wish to incorporate modifications for "four-corner" or "center" cooling fittings to optimize coolant flow through the cylinder heads. Some manifold manufacturers specifically accommodate these needs. Others do not so you have to pick and choose from commercially available intakes or specify your exact requirements in a custom manifold.

Even if you are only running carburetors, it may be prudent to select or build a custom manifold that already incorporates bosses for nitrous oxide injectors or bungs for fuel injectors. This saves time and expense later if you decide to switch to port fuel injection or nitrous oxide injection. Most good racing manifolds now incorporate dual-distributor hold-down clamp bosses so you can choose the most convenient location for locking down the distributor. Many also incorporate threaded openings at the front and rear water jacket openings where bleeders can be installed to eliminate all air from the cooling system.

While you may incorporate some form of carburetor spacer, depending on your final application, you should never choose to incorporate a carburetor adapter if you are seeking top performance. Most manufacturers plenum and runner floors by providing a tumbling effect that tends to maintain flow velocity while keeping fuel droplets in suspension. In-cylinder mixture motion in the form of swirl and tumble as the mixture enters the cylinder also promotes mixture quality and cylinder filling.

In practice, most high-speed competition engines favor some degree of swirl to help direct the burn toward the exhaust valve, but tumble has generally been found to have little effect at very high engine speeds. Successful efforts to encourage quench and active mixture motion typically permit a reduction in spark timing, which lessens negative work against the piston as it approaches TDC. Accordingly, equalization of EGTs, lower BSFC numbers, and an increase in torque typically accompany successful mixture conditioning efforts.

Surface Texturing

Surface texturing is generally useful anywhere in the flow path, particularly in areas that are prone to fuel separation due to directional changes or changes in charge velocity due to area variations. Manifold runners should never be polished and any place in the plenum that has been ground to match a spacer or modify a runner entry should be retextured. (This primarily applies to carbureted wet-flow applications.) Fuel droplets tend to stick to smooth surfaces so avoid them wherever possible.

Depending on accessibility, plenum and runner floors can be dimpled with an appropriately blunt tool (1/8-inch rounded top) to promote rolling vortices or eddies that tend to return fuel into suspension and prevent further dropout. Dimpling is commonly used on piston tops and in combustion chambers that are easy to reach. Without prior engine operation there is no burn pattern to guide you relative to areas of fuel wash and incomplete combustion so you may want to reserve this tactic for after the engine has been run.

An interesting example of dimpling is found in the Tork-Link manifold offered by Hi-Tech Engine Components: a tall dual-plane intake specifically designed for some circle track applications. Hi-Tech also offers a Swirl-Quench piston design that incorporates dimples and a tapered ramp on the piston top to optimize homogeneity and direct mixture motion, and thus the burn toward the exhaust valve. Other applications attempt to do the same thing by reading combustion patterns on previously run pistons and dimpling clean areas that exhibit little or no combustion residue.

Some builders don't fully subscribe to these concepts, preferring instead to glass bead piston tops, apply piston top coatings, and texture manifold passages as best they can. Some racers have also tried extrude-honing manifolds to increase runner volume, but this is generally a bad idea for carbureted intakes since it tends to polish the runners and there is no practical way to retexture them. Extrude honing is generally reserved for "dry flow" manifolds on EFI systems where fuel separation is not an issue. At the very least, texturing manifold runners by glass beading improves mixture quality in manifolds with very smooth runners.

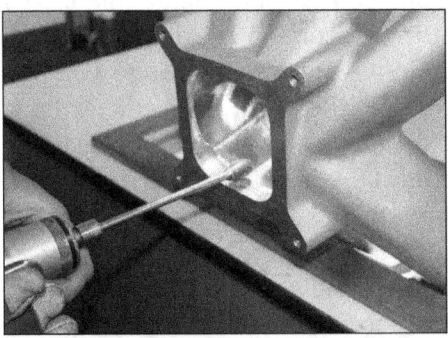

Part of the extensive work performed on intake manifolds at Wilson Manifolds includes proper surface texturing to optimize flow while minimizing the potential for fuel separation in the runners.

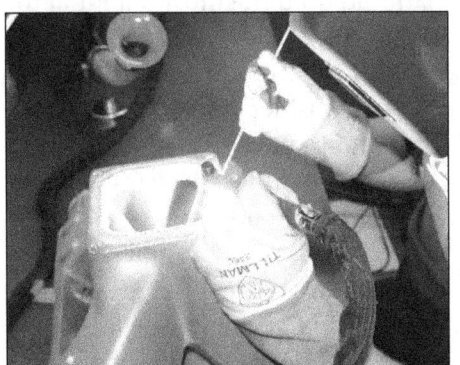

Wilson Manifold technicians modify and reshape the intake runners to accommodate the application in terms of runner entry angles, plenum-to-runner transitions, and other considerations to equalize each runner's airflow and mixture quality contribution.

Runner turn-ins are cut and reshaped to exactly match the cylinder head intake ports for optimum efficiency. The manifold-to-cylinder-head/runner interface must maintain the cross section and taper to prevent fuel separation due to rapid area and velocity changes.

Reversion

Reversion is present in all engines to some degree. It varies with engine speed and the particular combination of parts and timing events that encourage it. Reversion occurs at intake valve opening when cylinder pressure is still greater than manifold pressure. This causes the remaining combustion residue to migrate into the intake manifold. This continues briefly until manifold pressure, cylinder pressure, and exhaust pressure equalize and a pressure drop is initiated in the cylinder. The incoming fuel charge then enters the cylinder contaminated with residual exhaust particles that previously entered the manifold.

Charge contamination reduces power by replacing useable fuel mixture with unburnable combustion residue—a version of EGR that works to limit power production in all competition engines. This typically forces the need to de-tune the system with more timing advance and more jet to get enough fuel into the engine and burn it as efficiently as possible.

More timing increases pre-TDC work against the piston (negative torque) and excessive fuel compounds the mixture quality issues that reduce power and increase fuel usage unnecessarily.

Manifolds are more or less resistant to reversion depending on the application. Dual-plane intakes with smaller plenums and high-energy runners tend to dampen the effects of reversion. Single-plane intakes with large plenums and larger runners are more sensitive to reversion pressure and frequently permit a greater level of charge contamination depending on the intake valve closing point and exhaust back pressure during the camshaft overlap period.

Efforts to reduce reversion include later closing intake valve timing to allow more time for cylinder pressure to fall. Properly timed exhaust-valve opening helps evacuate the cylinder and draw in the next fuel charge without the pressure difference that encourages reversion.

To some degree carburetor spacers tend to encourage reversion by weakening manifold pressure. This can usually be corrected with properly matched cam timing.

Consult your cam supplier with the specifics of your package to determine cam specs that resist the effects of reversion, particularly in the useable powerband of your engine.

Secondary Intake Considerations

If you're opting for a maximum-effort, custom-built intake make sure it incorporates all of the following considerations and any others that you may determine to be necessary. While the specific runner and plenum dimensions, shape, and style of manifold hold the most potential for power production and powerband positioning, there are additional factors to consider depending on the exact requirements.

Very few universal racing engines deliver top performance outside their intended environment. Once you have established the ideal manifold configuration and dimensions for your application, you may wish to apply additional techniques to help the manifold do its job at peak efficiency.

Some of these modifications include heat management in the form of thermal coatings and/or types of insulation to isolate the plenum and runners from radiant engine heat. These coatings may be applied to the entire manifold or specific areas such as the bottom, which is exposed to splash oiling from the lifter gallery.

For marine applications, companies such as Dart Machinery offer specialized anti-corrosive coatings and marine jacket coatings to prevent saltwater corrosion in the water jackets of cylinder heads and intake manifolds, or a shielding treatment that resists galvanic corrosion in blocks and cylinder heads.

You may also wish to incorporate modifications for "four-corner" or "center" cooling fittings to optimize coolant flow through the cylinder heads. Some manifold manufacturers specifically accommodate these needs. Others do not so you have to pick and choose from commercially available intakes or specify your exact requirements in a custom manifold.

Even if you are only running carburetors, it may be prudent to select or build a custom manifold that already incorporates bosses for nitrous oxide injectors or bungs for fuel injectors. This saves time and expense later if you decide to switch to port fuel injection or nitrous oxide injection. Most good racing manifolds now incorporate dual-distributor hold-down clamp bosses so you can choose the most convenient location for locking down the distributor. Many also incorporate threaded openings at the front and rear water jacket openings where bleeders can be installed to eliminate all air from the cooling system.

While you may incorporate some form of carburetor spacer, depending on your final application, you should never choose to incorporate a carburetor adapter if you are seeking top performance. Most manufacturers

INDUCTION SYSTEMS

offer adapters for 2-barrel carbs or to adapt 4150-style intakes to 4500 carbs or vise versa. While these components offer tremendous convenience and utility they almost never complement the ideal flow path and volumetric requirements that promote optimum power, and more importantly, powerband positioning. If you are a top level engine builder you already know to avoid them.

Shear plates (such as those offered by Wilson Manifolds) are an exception. They are not really adapters but rather specifically designed airflow enhancement plates designed for tunnel ram intake manifolds. They integrate 1/2-inch-thick carburetor plates with 5-degree tapered throttle bore extensions with anti-reversion grooves that may be beneficial if you have made a poor camshaft selection.

Although, if you need them, you have no doubt really missed your cam selection. Their primary benefit comes from the throttle-bore extensions that help maintain velocity and mixture quality via fuel shearing at the lower openings. Some builders really swear by them. Decide for yourself by observing what other winning combinations are running, but make sure your cam designer is onboard with it and definitely do the math to see how it will affect plenum volume and flow velocity.

If light weight and top performance are your goals, a sheet-metal manifold is the best choice.

Flow Testing

Flow testing your intake manifold with the carburetor(s) and cylinder heads you intend to use can be very instructive even if not always scientifically precise. Most commercially available intake manifolds incorporate necessary compromises to accommodate manufacturing and production necessities. More often than not they meet broad marketing demands that require a more universal approach with regard to application and fit.

Custom sheet-metal intakes are a different story, but it is still a beneficial exercise to flow test the manifold and companion components together to investigate potential anomalies and gather an overall snapshot of the airflow characteristics of the entire intake flow path. While this approach lacks the essential dynamics of a running engine environment it identifies the overall capability of the components and exposes any major flow path deficiencies that may exist in one or more inlet paths.

Most intake manifold castings reduce cylinder head airflow by 10 to 15 percent, which may give you cause to rethink your overall airflow and cylinder head requirement for achieving optimum VE. Proper intake manifold selection does not include choosing the best flowing head and then handicapping it with the most convenient manifold selection. Complementary components and the attending mathematics are compulsory for top performance and you may find it worthwhile to return a poor performing manifold for a refund if it doesn't pass the flow test with your high-dollar heads and carburetor(s). In many cases flow problems can be addressed and corrected with various modifications, but this may not be cost effective and a different manifold may provide a better solution.

In order to perform these tests successfully, you have to isolate and flow each runner in an identical manner to determine the available airflow potential absent outside influences that may affect individual runners via dynamic pressure wave influences in the actual environment of engine operation. Recognize from the outset that this is an imperfect evaluation designed in a sense to help determine which way is up. Still, you can learn from it if you consider the data thoughtfully.

When mounting the manifold to the head, pay as much attention to port matching as you would when

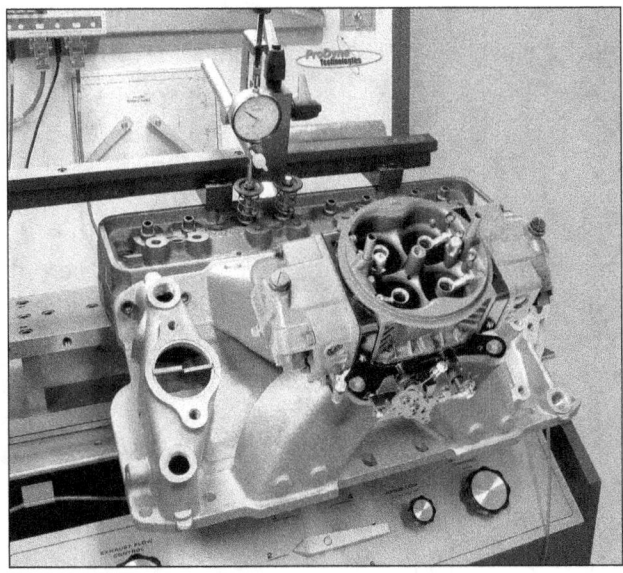

Flowing cylinder heads with the intake manifold attached can illuminate manifold issues that might otherwise go unnoticed. For optimum results add the carburetor and flow with the throttle plates locked open. This helps evaluate the entire flow path for each cylinder in terms of airflow, but does not specifically contemplate mixture quality issues.

CHAPTER 9

Nitrous oxide systems do not typically complicate a well-built induction system. When the manifold is already correct for the application, a properly plumbed and tuned nitrous system delivers consistent and equal cylinder-to-cylinder performance gains.

F.A.S.T. electronic fuel injection provided the fueling consistency to propel this 369-ci Mike LeFevers-built turbocharged small-block Pontiac Firebird to a 300-mph record at Bonneville with Joe Kugel at the wheel.

Big Stuff 3 EFI systems are found on some of the fastest Pro Mod cars because they provide exceptional control over all fuel and ignition events, particularly when using nitrous oxide.

EFI systems replace the carburetor with a billet throttle-body assembly of the appropriate size for the application. Since fuel is added via the electronic injectors the throttle body only flows air.

actually building the engine. Do the same for the carburetor(s) and make certain you are able to achieve WOT and lock it open. If your application is other than drag racing (oval track, road racing, or other), you may wish to also evaluate flow at several part-throttle openings such as 50 to 75 percent. All of this almost always requires some fancy rigging to support the whole thing while it is attached to the flow bench. Don't despair. What you will learn is almost always worth the effort.

Tape off every port that is not being flowed. You're not going to see any pressure influences but you can observe how much air each individual port and flow path is capable of flowing and identify any paths that are much better or much worse; then decide how they might be corrected. It is tedious work, and some builders are tempted to only spot-check a few ports, but you should check everything twice, three times, four times, or more—as many times as it takes to make it perfect. No doubt the port you may pass over will turn out to be flow deficient. The engine will be down on power in that hole and you may never figure out why because everything else seems correct.

Electronic Fuel Injection

The learning curve for EFI is still rather steep for many racers and engine builders, but it gets better and easier every day. Among the most consistent and easy-to-use systems are the F.A.S.T. systems and the Big Stuff 3 sequential units that permit very precise individual cylinder control for both fuel and spark curves.

Engine building per se does not require many changes to incorporate EFI, but you may want to study the available systems to decide what best suits the requirements of your application.

F.A.S.T. XFI fuel-injection kit provides all the necessary components to incorporate a race-ready EFI system. This system would be ideal for a fast drag-race bracket car seeking maximum consistency.

108 COMPETITION ENGINE BUILDING: ADVANCED ENGINE DESIGN & ASSEMBLY TECHNIQUES

Tuning Tips for Manifold Discrepancies

Various modifications and adjustments can be applied to intake manifolds to fine tune them for specific performance requirements.

1. Port matching the intake manifold to the cylinder head port is important to high-speed power unless it significantly degrades runner velocity. Changes in flow path cross section have the potential to separate fuel unless the change is minimal and does not occur abruptly.

2. A carburetor spacer usually assists fuel mixture transition into the runners. Re-jet accordingly and investigate timing reduction based on potential improvement to mixture quality.

3. Check runner and plenum surface texture and retexture any areas that have been ground or polished (if permitted).

4. If you identify runner discrepancies, consider using plenum floor dams or slots to redirect flow. Single-plane intakes can also utilize modified Brodix "turtles," which are plenum floor attachments that can be shaped according to flow requirements.

5. Some single-plane intakes can improve fuel distribution in problem runners (fuel separation) by laying back the base of the divider wall between the runners. If this fails to correct the problem you can reconstruct the divider with epoxy.

6. By whatever means possible check the port/runner interface for misalignment. If permitted, slot or elongate the manifold bolt holes to facilitate proper alignment.

7. During mock-up assembly install the manifold and distributor to check distributor depth in the block. Be certain that any oil passages around the distributor housing are properly aligned and that the oil-pump drive stub meshes properly with the oil-pump driveshaft.

8. Make certain the manifold does not bottom against the cylinder block end rails, which can affect runner seal at the port interface. You must have clearance for sealer on the end rails and to prevent misalignment of the ports and runners.

9. Check gasket fit to ensure that intake gaskets do not overhang port openings. Also check water passages to ensure the water ports do not leak. Add silicone sealer if required.

10. Use appropriate-length carb studs instead of bolts to prevent eventual stripping of the manifold bolt holes.

11. Use a silicone bead to seal the end rails. Allow it to set up prior to installation and then add a dab of sealer at each corner.

12. Use sealer on all plenum and runner accessory plugs to eliminate air leaks.

13. Apply a coating of light grease or cooking spray to both sides of the intake gasket so the manifold can be removed without damaging the gasket.

14. Block carburetor heat and/or EGR passages.

15. Investigate individual cylinder tuning via runner-length and cross-section mods and potential match-ups with individual header-pipe tuning and/or timing adjustments.

16. With boosted applications pay particular attention to intake manifold sealing issues.

17. Modifications that improve naturally aspirated performance also enhance boosted applications, sometimes to the extent of requiring less boost and less timing for a given power level.

18. If you have to use a plenum divider to improve throttle response, you probably need a different manifold, especially on a single-plane application.

19. On engines that have been run, examine the plenum and runners for signs of reversion or fuel separation. A colored stain (often reddish) indicates separation. Darker stains indicate reversion.

20. For any given manifold configuration, think critically about the movement of air and fuel through the plenum and runners. In particular consider the effects of abrupt turns in the flow path, runner length, and area variations, and the influence of individual runners on adjacent runners. Direct paths to the valve are always more desirable.

CHAPTER 10

CARBURETORS

Despite the widespread acceptance of electronic fuel injection and recent advances in tuning ease, carburetors remain the primary fueling device for most racing applications from Saturday night drag racers to top-level Sprint Cup racing. While electronic fuel injection offers desirable advantages in applications that have a wide operating range with frequent throttle changes, it is still pretty hard to beat a well-tuned carburetor for maximum WOT power.

You must consider the carburetor as a fundamental part of the total engine package by sizing it and configuring it to suit the final application. Carburetors have the potential to dramatically improve a racing engine's performance if they are properly sized and tuned to suit the application. Conversely they can also severely restrict an engine's performance if misapplied.

Most racing applications use either single 4-barrel (4150/4500-style Holley) or dual 4-barrel (4150/4500-style Holley) carburetors. Holley 4-barrels remain the industry standard. Surprisingly, many competent engine builders do not have a thorough understanding of basic carburetor function and how it affects the performance of the engines they so carefully assemble.

In a nutshell, a carburetor uses atmospheric pressure to provide inlet airflow through an orifice (barrel, throat, or venturi) to draw fuel from the fuel supply (within the fuel bowl). Various carburetor circuits control how much fuel is drawn and how it is mixed with air before it is passed into the engine's induction system.

An important principle of carburetor operation is the Bernoulli

Holley's Dominator line of carburetors were designed for competition use. They flow large amounts of air and fuel, as 1,050-, 1,150-, and 1,250-cfm models are available. The Dominators offer a wide range of adjustments to tailor the air and fuel flow curves to an engine's specific needs on a given day.

CARBURETORS

effect, which describes the degree of vacuum, or low-pressure increase, that accompanies an increase in velocity through an orifice such as a carburetor venturi. The greater the air velocity through the venturi, the lower the pressure, which in turn allows atmospheric pressure in the fuel bowl to push fuel into the airstream where it is atomized via the venturi booster.

The important controlling factor is atmospheric pressure, which remains relatively constant except for weather and altitude considerations. Whenever a descending piston provides an empty cylinder to fill, atmospheric pressure rushes in to fill it via the carburetor and intake system. Along the way it picks up atomized fuel in the appropriate amount at the booster. Carburetor size and manifold flow path dimensions control the rate of filling and the carburetor controls the fuel mixture based on air speed and the degree of throttling applied.

The carburetor feed or fuel nozzle is located in the path of highest air velocity and lowest pressure (the venturi booster in each individual barrel). The venturi is a narrowed region in the flow path that increases the velocity of the air flowing through it. In a carburetor, a booster venturi is placed within the main venturi to further increase the airflow velocity and lower the pressure. The pressure differential controls fuel delivery. The fuel nozzle distributes fuel to the airstream at this point based on a higher air pressure (atmospheric) in the fuel bowl. Below the venturi and the booster, a throttle valve or blade restricts the airflow entering the engine thus controlling the amount of air/fuel mixture entering the engine and providing the necessary throttling effect that ultimately makes the engine drivable.

The carburetor fuel supply is located on each end of the carburetor in the fuel or float bowl. Fuel is stored in the float bowl and a needle-and-seat arrangement is used to maintain a constant fuel level within the bowl at all times. When the engine draws fuel from the supply, the float drops with the fuel level and opens the needle valve to admit more fuel from the fuel tank. Various baffles and float shapes are utilized to accommodate and control application specific conditions, such as high g-force loading due to acceleration or side force in the corners. In some cases jet extensions are incorporated to ensure that the jet or supply orifice for the booster venturi always remains submerged in fuel.

Each barrel of the carburetor has its own connection to the fuel supply via a main jet or (sizeable) restrictor that controls the amount of fuel available to the engine at any given time. Atmospheric pressure in the fuel bowl (via the bowl vent) pushes fuel through the jet orifice to the booster venturi. Along the way the fuel is aerated or emulsified via air bleeds located at the top of the carburetor. The air bleeds also prevent fuel from being siphoned from the bowl during non operation by equalizing pressure on both sides of the jet.

Note the basic components on a Holley carburetor. The main body incorporates the throttle bores (or barrels) and the individual booster venturis in each venturi bore. The fuel bowls contain the floats and the needle-and-seat assemblies that maintain a constant fuel supply for the venturis to draw from. Most

Atmospheric pressure (P_1) is provided to both float bowls via the bowl vents (arrows). Bowl vents and air bleeds (small brass jets in line behind the boosters) must remain unrestricted and exposed to the same pressure as the throttle bores to ensure proper carburetor function.

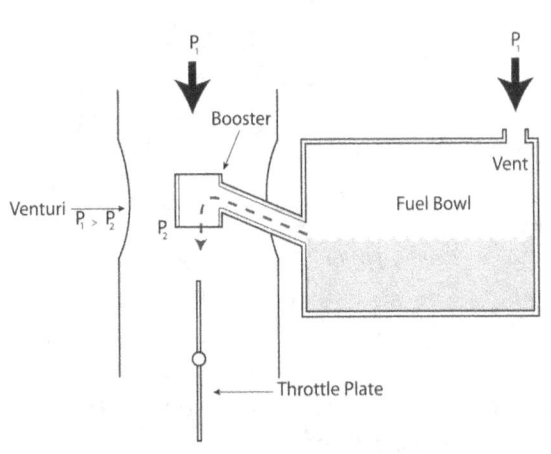

Atmospheric pressure (P_1) represents the reference pressure (atmospheric) above the throttle bore and the bowl vent. Pressure in the venturi (P_2) is reduced by high-velocity airflow, allowing atmospheric pressure in the bowl to push fuel into the booster through the jet, internal circuitry, and the booster.

CHAPTER 10

Carburetor Selection

Carburetors perform best when their airflow capacity closely matches the flow demand of the engine, particularly within the specific powerband or effective RPM range demanded by the application. This is largely controlled by engine displacement (size), engine speed, and VE provided by appropriate flow path dimensions and other contributing factors. Carburetor flow capacity is rated in cubic feet per minute (cfm), which defines the amount of air a particular carburetor can flow at WOT at a standard vacuum of 1.5 inches of mercury. It is important to remember that a carburetor must always have at least 1 inch of pressure differential between the intake manifold below the throttle bores and atmospheric pressure above the carburetor. This minimum differential is necessary to maintain adequate airflow velocity through the carburetor at WOT.

Carburetor size is commonly calculated by a basic formula that defines engine air capacity as a function of displacement (volumetric capacity) and engine speed (RPM). The displacement is divided by 1,728 (the number of cubic inches in a cubic foot) to convert it to cubic feet. The RPM is divided by 2 because the engine only intakes on every other revolution. The formula can be simplified as follows:

$$\text{Air Capacity (cfm)} = (\text{displacement} \times \text{RPM}) \div 3{,}456$$

In practice this formula should be used only as a preliminary indicator since it does not specifically accommodate an engine's actual VE or its ability to ingest more air than its volumetric capacity at operating speed based on flow path efficiency and appropriately matched valve events. Even if you are able to verify VE on a dyno, a carburetor can still be too small for some applications depending on the engine's dynamic range and transient response characteristics, which are affected by inlet and exhaust tuning, camshaft profile, and external influences such as gearing, tire size, and vehicle weight.

As a rule, engines with narrower powerbands such as Pro/Stock drag racing call for more capacity than the

Holley race carburetors incorporate an accelerator pump on both the primary and the secondary float bowls. Airflow capacity is determined by venturi and throttle bore size and the amount of restriction presented by the boosters.

applications also have a power valve to provide additional power enrichment during high demand. Others have a power valve plug and rely on larger jet orifices to provide the required fuel delivery. In either case an auxiliary accelerator pump is also provided to deliver the instantaneous fuel enrichment required when the throttle plates are opened rapidly.

Holley Ultra HP aluminum 950 carb in new Hardcore Gray is nearly 40-percent lighter with 20-percent greater fuel bowl capacity. Race-calibrated carb also offers billet throttle body and metering blocks, fuel bowl baffles, new idle bypass system, adjustable secondary link, and other race-only features.

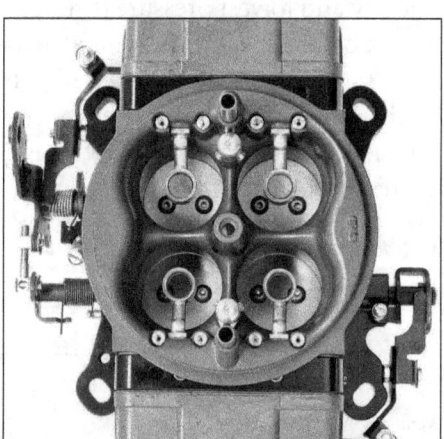

New Holley Ultra HP carbs also incorporate contoured button-head butterfly screws, revised air bleed locations, and aero contoured squirter screws—all features builders appreciate in a race-only carb.

CARBURETORS

effect, which describes the degree of vacuum, or low-pressure increase, that accompanies an increase in velocity through an orifice such as a carburetor venturi. The greater the air velocity through the venturi, the lower the pressure, which in turn allows atmospheric pressure in the fuel bowl to push fuel into the airstream where it is atomized via the venturi booster.

The important controlling factor is atmospheric pressure, which remains relatively constant except for weather and altitude considerations. Whenever a descending piston provides an empty cylinder to fill, atmospheric pressure rushes in to fill it via the carburetor and intake system. Along the way it picks up atomized fuel in the appropriate amount at the booster. Carburetor size and manifold flow path dimensions control the rate of filling and the carburetor controls the fuel mixture based on air speed and the degree of throttling applied.

The carburetor feed or fuel nozzle is located in the path of highest air velocity and lowest pressure (the venturi booster in each individual barrel). The venturi is a narrowed region in the flow path that increases the velocity of the air flowing through it. In a carburetor, a booster venturi is placed within the main venturi to further increase the airflow velocity and lower the pressure. The pressure differential controls fuel delivery. The fuel nozzle distributes fuel to the airstream at this point based on a higher air pressure (atmospheric) in the fuel bowl. Below the venturi and the booster, a throttle valve or blade restricts the airflow entering the engine thus controlling the amount of air/fuel mixture entering the engine and providing the necessary throttling effect that ultimately makes the engine drivable.

The carburetor fuel supply is located on each end of the carburetor in the fuel or float bowl. Fuel is stored in the float bowl and a needle-and-seat arrangement is used to maintain a constant fuel level within the bowl at all times. When the engine draws fuel from the supply, the float drops with the fuel level and opens the needle valve to admit more fuel from the fuel tank. Various baffles and float shapes are utilized to accommodate and control application specific conditions, such as high g-force loading due to acceleration or side force in the corners. In some cases jet extensions are incorporated to ensure that the jet or supply orifice for the booster venturi always remains submerged in fuel.

Each barrel of the carburetor has its own connection to the fuel supply via a main jet or (sizeable) restrictor that controls the amount of fuel available to the engine at any given time. Atmospheric pressure in the fuel bowl (via the bowl vent) pushes fuel through the jet orifice to the booster venturi. Along the way the fuel is aerated or emulsified via air bleeds located at the top of the carburetor. The air bleeds also prevent fuel from being siphoned from the bowl during non operation by equalizing pressure on both sides of the jet.

Note the basic components on a Holley carburetor. The main body incorporates the throttle bores (or barrels) and the individual booster venturis in each venturi bore. The fuel bowls contain the floats and the needle-and-seat assemblies that maintain a constant fuel supply for the venturis to draw from. Most

Atmospheric pressure (P_1) is provided to both float bowls via the bowl vents (arrows). Bowl vents and air bleeds (small brass jets in line behind the boosters) must remain unrestricted and exposed to the same pressure as the throttle bores to ensure proper carburetor function.

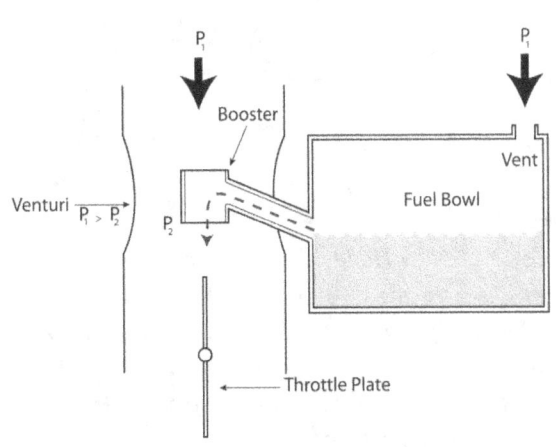

Atmospheric pressure (P_1) represents the reference pressure (atmospheric) above the throttle bore and the bowl vent. Pressure in the venturi (P_2) is reduced by high-velocity airflow, allowing atmospheric pressure in the bowl to push fuel into the booster through the jet, internal circuitry, and the booster.

CHAPTER 10

Holley race carburetors incorporate an accelerator pump on both the primary and the secondary float bowls. Airflow capacity is determined by venturi and throttle bore size and the amount of restriction presented by the boosters.

Carburetor Selection

Carburetors perform best when their airflow capacity closely matches the flow demand of the engine, particularly within the specific powerband or effective RPM range demanded by the application. This is largely controlled by engine displacement (size), engine speed, and VE provided by appropriate flow path dimensions and other contributing factors. Carburetor flow capacity is rated in cubic feet per minute (cfm), which defines the amount of air a particular carburetor can flow at WOT at a standard vacuum of 1.5 inches of mercury. It is important to remember that a carburetor must always have at least 1 inch of pressure differential between the intake manifold below the throttle bores and atmospheric pressure above the carburetor. This minimum differential is necessary to maintain adequate airflow velocity through the carburetor at WOT.

Carburetor size is commonly calculated by a basic formula that defines engine air capacity as a function of displacement (volumetric capacity) and engine speed (RPM). The displacement is divided by 1,728 (the number of cubic inches in a cubic foot) to convert it to cubic feet. The RPM is divided by 2 because the engine only intakes on every other revolution. The formula can be simplified as follows:

$$\text{Air Capacity (cfm)} = (\text{displacement} \times \text{RPM}) \div 3{,}456$$

In practice this formula should be used only as a preliminary indicator since it does not specifically accommodate an engine's actual VE or its ability to ingest more air than its volumetric capacity at operating speed based on flow path efficiency and appropriately matched valve events. Even if you are able to verify VE on a dyno, a carburetor can still be too small for some applications depending on the engine's dynamic range and transient response characteristics, which are affected by inlet and exhaust tuning, camshaft profile, and external influences such as gearing, tire size, and vehicle weight.

As a rule, engines with narrower powerbands such as Pro/Stock drag racing call for more capacity than the

applications also have a power valve to provide additional power enrichment during high demand. Others have a power valve plug and rely on larger jet orifices to provide the required fuel delivery. In either case an auxiliary accelerator pump is also provided to deliver the instantaneous fuel enrichment required when the throttle plates are opened rapidly.

Holley Ultra HP aluminum 950 carb in new Hardcore Gray is nearly 40-percent lighter with 20-percent greater fuel bowl capacity. Race-calibrated carb also offers billet throttle body and metering blocks, fuel bowl baffles, new idle bypass system, adjustable secondary link, and other race-only features.

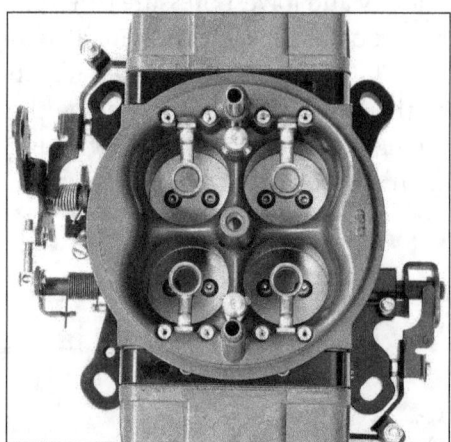

New Holley Ultra HP carbs also incorporate contoured button-head butterfly screws, revised air bleed locations, and aero contoured squirter screws—all features builders appreciate in a race-only carb.

CARBURETORS

formula indicates because they have a minimal range of operation between gear changes and spend all of their time at WOT. For lower-class circle track and road racing applications with more frequent throttling and a broader dynamic range, the formula can more closely predict a proper carburetor size. A notable example of appropriate carburetor sizing is found in Reher-Morrison's recommendations for basic sportsman and professional class drag racing.

Of course there are always exceptions, hence you need to carefully evaluate the specific requirements of the application including such things as the racing environment. For example a car racing at Bonneville might require carburetors slightly smaller than indicated simply because of the altitude (4,200 feet elevation with DA (density altitude) ranging from 4,200 to as much as 8,500 feet depending on conditions) and the reduced atmospheric pressure available to act on the carburetor. While this is a specific application, there are many instances of unintended over- or under-carburetion for the application. A cardinal rule of thumb states that race engine performance is maximized with the smallest possible induction components that do not cause a reduction in horsepower.

When an engine is over-carburated, air velocity through the venturis is reduced and the venturi/booster combination cannot pull enough fuel to support the engine. A lean condition ensues and the engine falters due to lack of fuel. This condition cannot be corrected by installing larger jets because the engine will run too rich at higher engine speeds when air velocity finally catches up. You can never balance mixture delivery across the full operating range of the engine and performance suffers across the board.

While a slightly smaller carburetor sometimes helps sharpen throttle response in a circle track or a road racing car, under-carburetion is often just as bad as over-carburetion in terms of overall engine performance. When the airflow capacity is too low, the air velocity is too high causing a potentially richer mixture, a flow restriction and a subsequent loss of power at higher engine speeds even though the engine may exhibit crisp throttle response and strong low-end power. The great majority of racing applications use square-bore, single, 4-barrel carburetors with progressive mechanical secondaries.

Most racing applications incorporate progressive throttle linkage for optimum control of mixture delivery and engine response. Progressive linkage opens the primary (front) throttle blades first for low-speed efficiency and the secondaries at a later point for high-speed power. Hence it is critical that the final carburetor size be properly matched according to the engine size and specific racing application.

Exit Air Speed

Other things to consider concerning carburetor selection and sizing may include the exit airspeed from the carburetor throttle bores. In some cases (specific applications and components) conditions may exist where a larger carburetor makes more power on a smaller-than-indicated engine. This result is largely tied to the mixture quality produced by the carburetor and influences acting upon it immediately after exiting the carburetor. A unique correlation exists between carburetor exit velocity and mixture quality as affected by engine speed and the proximity of the plenum floor.

Reher-Morrison Recommended Carburetor Sizes

Engine Size	Carburetor CFM	Total CFM
327 to 366 Sportsman	(1) 650 to 800	650 to 800
400 to 460 Sportsman	(1) 780 to 850	780 to 850
500+ Sportsman	(1) 1,050 to 1,150	1,050 to 1,150
350 to 366 Pro	(2) 850 to 1,050	1,700 to 2,100
500+ Pro	(2) 1,150 to 1,300	2,300 to 2,600

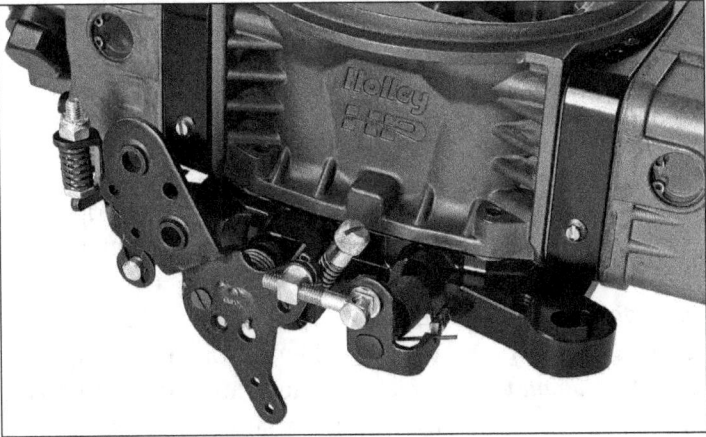

Adjustable secondary throttle linkage allows tuners to alter secondary operation for greater response according to application and prevailing track conditions.

CHAPTER 10

It is entirely possible for a larger carburetor to produce more power because the lower exit speed from the larger throttle bores reduces the mechanical separation of fuel being flung against the plenum floor. Slower air speed enables the fuel mixture to make the turn into the runners more easily with less fuel dropout. This may require different jetting (or even staggered jetting in the case of dual-plane intakes) to accomplish optimum results, but the relatively easy tuning adjustments are often worth the effort. This also suggests that an area of opportunity exists where other gains may be acquired by carefully examining all the influences affecting fuel mixture quality from the time it exits the carburetor until it enters the combustion chamber.

Holley Ultra HP race Dominators feature all aluminum construction with three circuit-billet metering blocks, 12-hole billet booster inserts to boost the fuel signal, and improve atomization, adjustable progressive linkage, glass sight plugs, four-corner idle circuits, and dual -8 AN fuel inlets for maximum utility on single 4V or dual-carb tunnel ram applications.

Bottom view of Holley Ultra HP 1150 Dominator shows dual 50-cc accelerator pumps, billet metering blocks, dual side-inlet fuel bowls, adjustable progressive secondary linkage, and button-head throttle plate screws.

Tuning Elements

As you may have surmised, carburetor size is actually an effective tuning element in terms of optimizing airflow and throttle response for a particular engine and operating conditions. Beyond that there are basic tuning components available to tune the carburetor for ambient track conditions. These include the idle mixture screws, main jets, air bleeds, power valves, boosters, accelerator pumps, float adjustments, and exit air speed. Each of these makes an important contribution to the engine's overall performance and in some cases they can assist an engine and/or vehicle combination that may have been saddled with other ineffective choices such as a poorly matched intake manifold, a bad cam choice, or improper gearing in the rear end or transmission.

Idle Mixture Screws

While not critical to a racing engine's performance, the idle mixture screws still provide a necessary adjustment that helps keep the engine idling at the desired speed at the starting line or during pit stops. They still require the basic adjustment to the highest vacuum reading or the highest RPM when the throttle is set to the desired idle speed. Failure to do this may result in stalling or stumbling on a poor transition to the main circuit.

Main Jets

The main jets represent the primary fuel-feed circuit and largely control the air/fuel ratio. When the carburetor is properly matched to the application, jetting rarely requires much departure (up or down) from the factory selection, but adjustments are necessary under some conditions and jetting largely accomplishes this. The accepted target air/fuel ratio for maximum power ranges from about 12.5:1 to 13.2:1 with 13.1 being the most common ratio on engines that have good mixture quality and combustion characteristics. Main jets richen or lean the fuel mixture throughout the RPM range and they can effect a big change in power even with small incremental changes.

Air Bleeds

Air bleeds control the rate of circuit startup. They work the opposite of a jet. While a bigger jet richens the mixture, a bigger air bleed leans the mixture by introducing more air to the fuel emulsion. This can be an effective fine-tuning correction for a condition that is clearly supported by hard data, but air bleeds are highly sensitive and are generally not a good means of making tuning adjustments that are likely to require changing over the course of the same day or event. It is very easy to go too far and lose track of the combination to the point that it is difficult to find your way back to the starting point. Experienced tuners may use air bleeds to correct an unusual condition or alter the high-speed fuel curve, but most effective carburetor tuning is accomplished with jetting, accelerator pump adjustments, or even float level changes.

Power Valves

Power enrichment from cruise or a part-throttle condition, particularly on a plenum-style intake, is most effectively accomplished with a power valve. Power valves are generally not found in drag racing applications where throttle transitions are relatively unimportant. But they are effective in other forms of competition such as road racing, oval racing, off-road racing, and some marine applications. When manifold vacuum drops below a certain point during a throttle transition a diaphragm in the power valve opens an auxiliary jet that routes additional fuel to the booster venturi to help support the additional load and consequent fuel demand. When this occurs, fuel is drawn through the main jet and the auxiliary jet at the same time, based on the vacuum rating of the power valve and the load applied.

Boosters

Booster mods are best left to experienced carburetor tuners, but it is important to understand their contribution to fuel delivery and the atomization process. Boosters allow carburetors to have main venturis properly sized for maximum output according to the engine's air demand while still providing the sensitivity required for effective fuel metering. Boosters are designed to increase the pressure drop created by airflow through the main venturis, thus providing greater sensitivity at the jet. When properly configured they significantly improve mixture atomization while providing greater calibration accuracy via finer control.

The booster is located in the minor diameter of the main venturi and is thus exposed to the greatest pressure-drop effect. This creates an even greater pressure drop in the minor diameter of the booster, which increases sensitivity and improves mixture atomization. Finer fuel droplets are the result. In a race engine, high velocity is maintained and the enhanced mixture remains relatively consistent all the way to the valve unless acted upon by bad influences such as a flow path area change, restrictive turns, and so on.

Accelerator Pumps

Another tuning aid frequently adjusted to suit the application is the accelerator pump. Race carbs typically have an accelerator pump for both the primaries and the secondaries as found in Holley 4-barrels. Their function is to provide fuel enrichment to support the temporary lean condition that occurs during rapid transient throttle movement. When the throttle opens rapidly from idle or a part-throttle condition, manifold pressure rises as air rushes in, and fuel condenses on the walls of the plenum and runners. This leans the mixture at a time when the airflow

Wilson Manifolds four-hole combination spacer provides transition from four-hole to open-spacer with central flow cone to optimize flow. Combo spacers like this often provide the best power increase, particularly on single-plane intake manifolds.

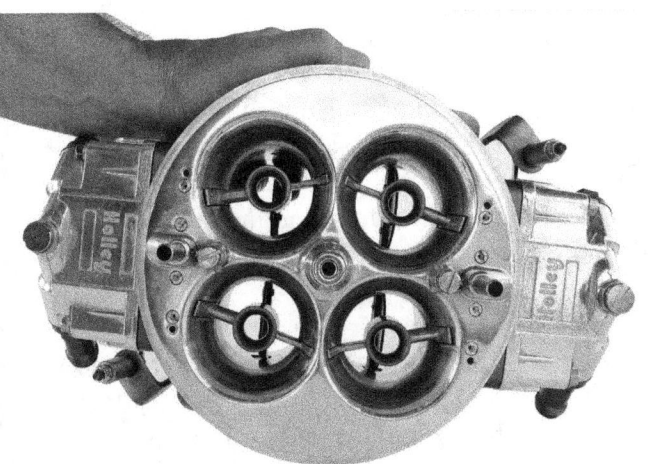

Seen from above with throttle plates held open this HP Dominator shows its massive airflow capability, which is controlled by the venturi bore size, booster restriction, and throttle plate diameter.

increase requires a fuel mixture increase. The accelerator pump provides temporary enrichment until engine speed rises sufficiently for the main circuit to re-establish control of the fueling process.

Accelerator pumps are tunable to adjust the rate and length of the supplemental fuel shot and further adjustment is available via the orifice size of the pump shot squirter above the venturis. Different-shaped accelerator pump cams attached to the throttle arm are used to adjust the pump's delivery characteristics according to the requirements of the application.

Float Adjustments

Many tuners like to make fine adjustments quickly by raising or lowering the fuel level in the bowls via float-level adjustments. Raising the float level slightly increases the head pressure against the jets and tends to provide a subtle enrichment. Lowering the float accomplishes the opposite. Pro/Stock racers often use this method to adjust the fuel mixture when racing at higher altitude tracks such as Denver International Raceway.

Basic Tuning and Maintenance

Numerous factors may combine to influence or otherwise deteriorate the performance of an engine once you have achieved the optimum tune via previously discussed methods. The following are some characteristics and functions that require regular inspection and attention to avoid a subtle deterioration in performance that may go unnoticed until the loss of performance reaches a critical state.

Float Level

Regular verification of the float level and float integrity is prudent insurance. A damaged, leaky, or saturated float can alter the fuel level and upset the calibration efforts. Inspection efforts should include checks for sticking or other interference, improper needle-and-seat operation, and leaky fuel-bowl gaskets. A hung float can quickly initiate a condition that can destroy an engine or the entire car if a fire occurs.

Needle and Seat

The needle-and-seat assembly is the gatekeeper for a precision fueling device or carburetor. The needle-and-seat assembly is also a tuning element in that it must be properly sized to support the fuel demand of the engine. This is particularly important on alcohol-fueled engines that require twice the fuel delivery of a gasoline application. While rare, conditions do exist where dirt or trash can enter the assembly, hanging it open with potentially disastrous results. This often occurs when frequent jet changes are made or when fuel lines are disconnected and reconnected for various reasons.

Fuel Pressure

Some tuners also try to use fuel pressure as a tuning element, but in most applications you should restrict fuel pressure to 7 psi at idle and 6 psi at maximum RPM. A good way to ensure consistent fuel pressure is to incorporate a bypass regulator with a fixed restriction. In most cases fuel pressure remains steadier and falls off less with higher RPM. Alcohol applications can generally use 9 to 11 psi at maximum RPM depending on the effective jet size.

Fuel Bowl Vents

Bowl vents must see atmospheric pressure at all times or calibration is incorrect. This is the same pressure that the carburetor entry sees because jet flow characteristics are relevant to equivalent pressure exposure. Many factors affect this including the proximity of air scoops, hoods, vehicle speeds, and so on. This is one reason dyno jetting rarely translates to correct track jetting.

High-Speed Air Bleeds

The best advice is to leave them alone. Carbs with removable high-speed air bleeds invite calibration problems initiated by the unwitting tuner. Holley air bleeds control the rate of circuit startup; they can influence when and how quickly the circuits change. Air bleeds are very carefully calibrated and they are extraordinarily sensitive and should not be track tuned or even dyno tuned without the aid of a fuel flow meter and a reliable oxygen sensor and plenty of time to correct any mistakes.

Power Valves

Power valve failure due to backfires has been dramatically reduced with the newer carburetors, but it is prudent to check them often. Most 4-barrel race applications work best with a 6.5 power valve. When vacuum drops below the preset point, the power valve opens and additional fuel is provided to the main well to help accommodate the temporary increase in load.

Air Cleaner

The air cleaner and/or scoop design can radically affect carburetor operation. Make certain any filter you use is absolutely clean and that the top cover is at least 1 to 2 inches above the carburetor air horn to prevent flow restrictions and undue influence on calibration. Air bleeds are also easily plugged on dirt track cars, which is a surefire way to upset calibration enough that performance suffers or engine damage occurs. The base design of the air cleaner should feature a large, gentle radius to direct air smoothly into the carburetor.

Carburetor Spacers

Carb spacers are generally a beneficial addition that improves performance. Open spacers are usually more effective on a race engine, particularly on intakes that suffer excessive inter-cylinder pressure influences. Smaller carbs generally like taller spacers and all spacers should be carefully blended to the plenum entry.

Fuel Filters

A good 20-micron filter should be installed close to the carburetor. If a larger-capacity filter can be installed without greater fire potential during an accident, it provides a larger reservoir of fuel for the carburetor to draw from in the immediate vicinity. Use a second filter near the fuel tank outlet and install a fuel shutoff valve that can be turned off before shutting down the engine.

Jets and Fuel Flow

Carburetor jets flow more fuel in proportion to the pressure drop until the jet reaches its saturation point beyond which fuel flow stalls. The amount of fuel passing through a given jet changes according to the pressure drop applied to it. If the pressure drop is less than the jet's maximum rated capacity, the jet flows proportionately less. Once the maximum is exceeded a larger jet is required. When carburetor signals are weaker (for whatever reason) it may be necessary to increase jet size to initiate adequate flow and achieve the desired air/fuel ratio.

Final Thoughts

Beyond these basic tuning adjustments, many experienced engine builders are adept at additional fine-tuning methods that further support their specific application or the types of engines they regularly build. Sometimes these modifications are not legal in certain series, but when they are (and sometimes when they're not) tuners specifically tailor a carburetor's internal circuits to suit their needs. Fuel emulsion characteristics are often modified and some passages are either enlarged or restricted to achieve the desired effect.

A properly selected Holley racing carburetor delivers better than 95 percent of the performance available from the engine. The small amounts that tuners often seek are generally pursued in an effort to correct a condition or characteristic of the overall engine configuration or changes in operational requirements that require adjustment outside the normal range of carburetor calibration.

Most builders achieve surprisingly good results with effective application of the previously mentioned tuning aids. If you require much more than that, your engine combination is likely misapplied or you are a highly experienced tuner seeking a very subtle change to gain a small advantage in fuel economy or perhaps a combustion characteristic of a particular cylinder head that you favor for other reasons.

Dual carburetors on a cast or sheet-metal tunnel ram intake are the optimum setup for most very high horsepower drag engines. Smaller displacement engines use 4150-style 4-barrels while large-displacement engines typically require a pair of Holley Dominators.

Supercharged engines typically employ dual carburetors to meet the increased air and fuel demand created by the blower.

CHAPTER 11

CAMSHAFTS

Camshafts are the command center of the engine. As a primary contributor to VE they govern the precise valve action that controls the intake and exhaust system and thus exert enormous influence on an engine's power potential. Choosing a camshaft for any given racing application can be a daunting experience for even the most experienced engine builder. While the primary mechanical processes are well understood, the actual physics of engine airflow and camshaft timing are considerably more challenging, particularly as they relate to the requirements dictated by each individual racing application.

Some engines today are built strictly for dyno work—just to see how much peak power they can make. That seems like a lot of fun, but most of us are racers seeking an optimum combination to reinforce our racing requirements. The question of defining the power curve requirement becomes paramount. What is the required optimum operating range for the intended application? Is the powerband requirement broad or narrow and how does this relate to the overall engine speed, gearing, tire diameter, and shift frequency for the application?

The builder/cam designer must determine how much duration, lift, lobe separation angle (LSA), and other factors are required to optimize the engine's performance in the required operating range. Consideration must also be given to valvetrain stability and durability and their long-term contribution to the precision operation of all the relative components.

Like many other functions within a competition engine, mathematical specifics govern the operating principles and dictate the physical and mechanical limits of operation as they relate to the application in terms of engine displacement, stroke and rod length, compression ratio, flow path dimensions, vehicle weight, gearing, rear axle ratio, tire diameter, and a host of other factors each of which contributes to or affects the overall VE equation. Arriving at a suitable compromise among all these factors is often a formidable task for race engine builders and cam designers alike.

Many races have been won by cars with less power than their competitors. Usable power that

The camshaft is the command center of the engine. It controls the intake and the exhaust events and plays a major role in the power-making process. Flat-tappet cams are used in some racing series, but roller cams are the prevailing camshaft type in most professional series.

CAMSHAFTS

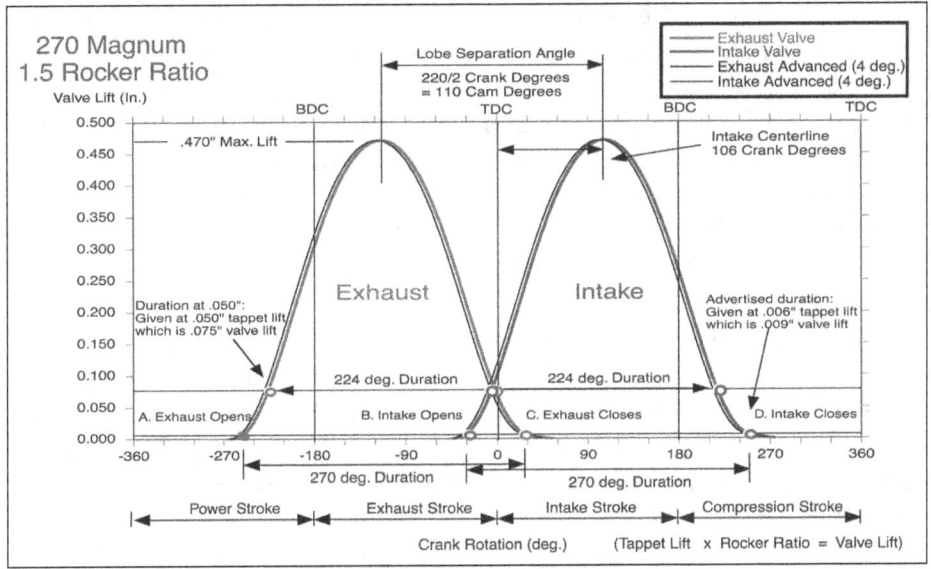

This illustration explains everything about camshaft operation. In addition to lift duration and overlap, it also indicates the intake and exhaust centerlines, lobe separation angle, and the location of timing events relative to the four cycles. Note that .050-inch tappet lift equals .050 times the rocker ratio to indicate valve lift at the checking point. (Courtesy Comp Cams)

complements the specific requirements of a racing application is what's being sought. Peak numbers are irrelevant if the powerband is not properly shaped and positioned to support the final application.

Understanding Cam Specs

In terms of opening and closing valve events, the intake opening (IO) and exhaust opening (EO) represent the intake and exhaust opening points in crankshaft degrees. Intake closing (IC) and exhaust closing (EC) are the intake and exhaust closing events. Cam cards show these points based on the manufacturer's chosen reference points: typically .006 inch for advertised duration and .050 inch for a universal checking reference based on an agreed amount of lobe lift where reasonable flow is initiated.

The following formula is used to calculate intake and exhaust duration. It applies to any lift as long as your cam card specifies opening and closing figures for a particular lift value. (Note that all camshaft specifications are designated in crankshaft degrees except the LSA, which is measured in camshaft degrees.)

Duration at Specified Lift = opening point + 180 degrees + closing point

For example, a Comp Cams XE274H-10 hydraulic cam lists the following opening and closing points for a checking lift of .006 inch:

IO = 31° BTDC   EO = 77° BBDC
IC = 63° ABDC   EC = 29° ATDC

Intake Duration = 31 + 180 + 63
= 274° at .006-inch lift
Exhaust Duration = 77 + 180 + 29
= 286° at .006-inch lift

From these numbers you can calculate the intake centerline of our example using the following formula:

Intake Centerline = (duration ÷ 2) − IO
Intake Centerline =
(274 ÷ 2) − 31 = 106°

Sometimes with a very mild or stock cam the IO occurs after TDC (ATDC). In this case just add the IO figure to half of the duration.

On the exhaust side the formula is similar, but instead of subtracting the IO point, you subtract the EC point.

Exhaust Centerline =
(calculated duration ÷ 2) − EC
Exhaust Centerline =
(286 ÷ 2) − 29 = 114°

Once you know these numbers, it's easy to find LSA, which is the difference between the two centerlines. You add the centerlines together and divide by 2. Continuing our example, the LSA is calcualted using this formula:

LSA = (intake centerline + exhaust centerline) ÷ 2
LSA = (110° + 114°) ÷ 2 = 110°

If a cam is ground "straight up" both centerlines are the same.

More commonly, cam companies grind their street cams 4 degrees advanced to help boost low-speed torque on longer duration cams. Our Comp XE274 is an example of this: the IC is 106 degrees, and the LSA is 110 degrees (4 degrees advanced). Note that 110 degrees is exactly halfway between 106 degrees and 114 degrees (the EC).

This practice moves the IC event 4 degrees ahead, which diminishes top end power in favor of more low-speed grunt for street engines. Another point to note is the use of parentheses around some timing

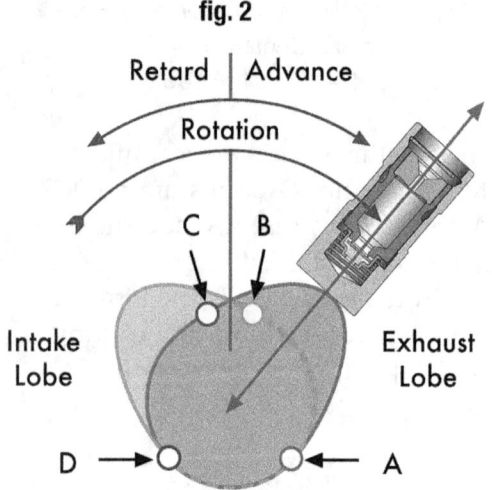

fig. 2

A. Exhaust Valve Opens - Power Stroke
B. Intake Valve Opens - Exhaust Stroke
C. Exhaust Valve Closes - Intake Stroke
D. Intake Valve Closes - Compression Stroke

The basic cam lobe shape is an eccentric with the lifter riding on the base circle. As the cam rotates, the lifter moves up the flank of the lobe and over the top to open the valve. (Courtesy Comp Cams)

points (on a cam card). This notation indicates that the cam actually closes the valve ATDC instead of before, even though the card indicates BTDC. This is only found on short-duration cams, but it is important to note if you're making calculations with a small cam.

Calculating Valve Lift

Net valve lift is a function of camshaft lobe lift and rocker arm ratio. Lobe lift (sometimes called cam rise) is the height of the eccentric portion of the cam lobe above the base circle. The rocker arm transfers the motion of the valve lifter riding on the cam lobe to the valve and increases the lobe lift by the amount of the rocker ratio, which is typically 1.5 to 1.7:1. It provides a convenient means of increasing valve lift. This is very evident in a pushrod engine where the valvetrain is compact and easily packaged compared to the complication and excessive size required for single- and double-overhead cam arrangements.

Net valve lift varies according to the type of lifter. To accommodate thermal expansion, clearance is built into the system in the form of clearance ramps and valve lash for mechanical (solid) lifter cams. The valve lash clearance must be subtracted from the total valve lift to obtain the net valve lift for this type of camshaft.

Mechanical Lifter Cam Net Lift = (lobe lift x rocker ratio) − valve lash

For example, an engine with a lobe lift of .300 inch and a 1.5:1 rocker ratio with a .022-inch valve lash:

Net Lift = (.300 x 1.5) − .022 = .428 inch

Hydraulic camshafts that are often used in lower-tier circle track applications automatically adjust for thermal expansion via lifter preload against an internal hydraulic plunger. No clearance is necessary and these lifters are typically adjusted with a specified amount of preload or a preferred degree of turn down from zero lash—usually one-quarter to one-half turn down. In this case the net valve lift is based on the lobe lift and the rocker ratio alone.

Hydraulic Lifter Cam Net Lift = lobe lift x rocker ratio
Net Lift = .300 x 1.5 = .450 inch

Mechanical cams are typically smaller than their hydraulic counterparts due to loss of lift attributable to valve lash. But mechanical cams, unlike hydraulic cams, can be tuned slightly by altering valve lash. Tightening the lash adds lift and starts the valve event sooner, effectively mimicking a larger cam.

To accommodate various tuning changes, lash changes are often limited to either the intake valves or the exhaust valves and sometimes only on the end cylinders to accommodate variations in runner length. A racer might tighten the lash on the exhaust side to increase the exhaust event if he feels that the engine is exhaust limited. Or he might tighten the lash on the outer four corner cylinders to compensate for the longer intake runners on those cylinders. That's equivalent to running slightly more camshaft on those cylinders.

In many cases, dual torque peaks and a broader torque curve can be generated by running different-size (c/s area) primary pipes on alternating cylinders in the firing order. This is a worthy fine-tuning measure, and in some cases you can combine this step with valve-lash adjustments on selected cylinders to further tune the torque output at different speeds. In theory this is predictable, but in practice it almost always requires dyno verification to quantify gains.

Valve lash changes should be limited to a maximum of .004 inch, and consideration should be given to the known valve-to-piston clearance before going too far on the exhaust side. These tuning measures can net small gains, but the correct combination can effectively broaden a torque curve with surprisingly good results. This may be just enough to give you some added leverage on the competition without making major engine modifications.

Finding TDC

Locating TDC accurately is absolutely essential to proper camshaft installation. Exact TDC is the timing basis for all camshaft timing events. The method for locating it varies according to the engine's state of assembly. Whatever that is, a temporary piston stop is used to stop the piston at some arbitrary distance before and after TDC. For fully assembled engines that are not already equipped with an accurately set TDC indicator, a threaded piston stop can be installed in the spark plug hole of the number-1 cylinder.

On most V-8s, the number-1 cylinder is almost always the farthest one forward in the V configuration. Paired rod-and-piston assemblies on each crank throw dictate that one is always offset farther forward than its counterpart. Study the front of the block to see which of the front cylinders is farther forward. That is the number-1. If the degree process is being performed during engine assembly, it is best to do it with only the number-1 piston-and-rod assembly installed on the crankshaft. Rotating the engine to degree the cam is much easier this way. In this case a flat-bar piston stop is bolted to the block deck surface above the number-1 piston. This type of piston stop has a center bolt that can be adjusted to stop the piston at any desired point below TDC.

Begin by installing the degree wheel on the crank snout or on the balancer if it is already installed.

Before installing the piston stop, rotate the engine until the piston top appears to be at TDC. You should be able to see this through the spark plug hole on an assembled engine. It does not have to be exact—just close.

Install a temporary wire pointer and adjust it so that the tip is close to the graduated marks on the degree wheel.

Adjust the degree wheel so the pointer indicates TDC (0 degrees) and snug it lightly.

Rotate the engine counterclockwise approximately one half turn and install the piston stop.

Tighten it securely so it won't move when the piston contacts it.

Slowly rotate the engine clockwise until the piston contacts the piston stop.

Note the pointer reading on the degree wheel. It will be in degrees BTDC. Record that number and then rotate the engine in the opposite direction (counterclockwise) until it completes a revolution and contacts the piston again.

Record the reading on the degree wheel and note that it indicates degrees ATDC.

If your calibrated eyeball is very accurate, the recorded numbers indicate the same number of degrees on either side of TDC and the pointer reads zero with the piston stop removed and the piston brought to the top. In practice, most of us aren't that accurate, so locate TDC based on a common reference point on either side of TDC. That's the piston stop. The reason you can't accurately locate TDC visually is because the piston experiences a brief period of dwell (stationary) at the top of its stroke as the rod angle transitions from one side to the other. The piston is stopped at this point and you have to split the dwell point exactly to find true TDC.

Since the piston stop does not move, it represents a fixed reference point before and after TDC. True TDC is found by splitting the difference between the degree-wheel readings.

For example, let's say your recorded numbers are 34 degrees BTDC and 30 degrees ATDC. The exact number depends on the depth of the piston stop in the cylinder bore, but it is all relative. TDC is halfway between the recorded readings. Loosen the degree wheel and rotate it only until the pointer reads 32 degrees. Lock down the degree wheel and make sure not to touch or move the pointer from now onward. Check your work by rotating the engine back and forth to the piston stop in both directions. The pointer reading should be the same in both directions (32 degrees in our example). If it is not the same, repeat the steps until the pointer indicates the exact same number of degrees before and after TDC. Once it does, remove the piston stop and degree the cam with confidence that you are locating the timing events based on exact TDC.

Degreeing the Cam

There are two methods for degreeing a camshaft. One compares the opening and closing points of the intake valve to see if they match the manufacturer's specs on the cam card. The other method locates the intake lobe centerline relative to TDC. Both methods are successful, but the intake centerline method does not verify the intake opening and closing points according to the cam card. Both methods are described below, but the intake opening and closing method is recommended for initial setup. Then you can check your work with the intake centerline method. In either case you need an accurate means of reading lifter travel.

I prefer the cam checking tool available from Jegs, Summit, and

CHAPTER 11

Comp Cams Magnum and High Tech double-roller timing chains are suitable for most basic performance applications and many lower tier racing series. This is the most affordable cam drive for racers seeking solid performance per dollar. Standard cam bushings are used to adjust cam timing.

Comp's fully adjustable billet timing sets feature multiple adjustment keyway crank sprockets and 2-degree incremental adjustment of the cam sprocket for up to plus-or-minus 6 degrees from TDC. These cam drives represent top-of-the-line chain drive systems for race engine applications.

many other suppliers, but successful results can be obtained using a solid lifter or a modified hydraulic lifter with the internal plunger reversed to give the dial indicator plunger a flat surface to bear against. You can also locate the plunger against the edge of the lifter. Make sure that the contact is stable and that the direction of the indicator travel is parallel to lifter travel. Then adjust the dial indicator to ensure that it has enough available range to read total intake lifter travel for the number-1 cylinder.

Intake Opening Method

Install the cam with the timing marks correctly aligned for the engine. Set up your dial indicator and checking lifter, or the cam checking tool in the number-1 intake lifter hole as described above. Zero the dial indicator and rotate the engine in the normal direction of rotation for several revolutions to verify that the dial indicator reads full lifter travel and returns to zero each time. You can take this opportunity to verify that lifter travel matches the indicated lobe lift on the cam card. If the lifter does not return to zero on the base circle, determine the cause and correct before continuing.

Once you're satisfied, begin with the lifter on the base circle and slowly rotate the engine clockwise until the indicator shows .050-inch lifter travel. Note the reading on the degree wheel. It should match the intake opening (IO) point indicated on the cam card for .050-inch lift.

Continue rotating the engine through full lifter travel and down the other side of the lobe until you reach .050-inch lift before the intake closing point. Since you know the lobe lift and the recommended closing point from the cam card, you should be able to anticipate the closing point as you rotate the engine. If you miss it, simply back up about 60 degrees to compensate for timing chain slack and approach the .050-inch closing point again. Compare it to the cam card and then continue rotating to verify that the lifter returns to zero again.

Your readings should show the intake opening and closing points and the total lifter travel or lobe lift. If the IO event doesn't match the cam card, you advance or retard the cam to bring it into spec.

For example, if your cam is supposed to open the intake valve at 36 degrees BTDC and close at 70 degrees ATDC (at .050-inch lift), but your measurements show that it is opening at 34 degrees BTDC and closing at 72 degrees ATDC, the cam is retarded. The valve event is occurring later than the recommended spec. If it were to open at 38 degrees BTDC and close at 68 degrees ATDC, it would be 2 degrees advanced because the valve event is occurring 2 degrees earlier than specified.

CAMSHAFTS

Belt drive systems like this Comp Cams big-block Chevy unit are the most desirable cam drive devices for all-out max-performance race engines. They deliver rock-solid timing with broad adjustability and durability. The belt also isolates crankshaft harmonics better than most mechanical drives.

Gear drive systems have been popular cam drives for racing applications for many decades. They provide very steady cam timing and they generate the distinctive whine that some racers love. However, gear drives are a mechanical connection that transfers crankshaft harmonics that can affect accurate cam timing.

In either case it is easy to correct using offset cam bushings or a crank gear with multiple keyways. Both allow you to adjust the position of the cam and then recheck it for compliance with the cam card specs. They can also be used to reposition the cam if you deliberately choose to advance the cam to promote low-end torque or retard the cam for a little more top end power.

If degree results are plus-or-minus 1 degree of the published specs, consider leaving the engine as assembled because it is entirely possible that the degree wheel you are using is not that accurate. Larger-diameter degree wheels space the degree marks farther apart and therefore have a greater chance of improved accuracy.

You can check the accuracy or your wheel by placing it on a large sheet of paper and marking the four 90-degree positions of the wheel. Then move the wheel to various positions and check to see that each 90-degree mark is an equal number of degrees from 90. Your wheel might not be completely accurate. This is why fussing over less than 2 degrees (unless for example, the cam is retarded 2 degrees and you want 2 degrees advanced) may not be worth the effort.

Intake Centerline Method

The intake centerline method finds the location of the intake lobe centerline relative to TDC. The recommended intake centerline is indicated on the cam card, and when correct it should yield the specified intake opening and closing points when you degree the cam.

Finding the centerline is easy. Rotate the engine clockwise until you find the maximum lobe lift, and then zero the indicator. Now rotate backward about .100 to .150 inch to compensate for timing chain slack. Then rotate clockwise until you reach .050 inch. This is .050 inch before maximum lift.

Note the reading on the degree wheel. Then continue over the nose of the cam until you reach .050 inch again. This is the .050 inch after maximum lift.

Note the degree wheel reading again. Now add the two readings together and divide by two to find the centerline. It should match the cam card. Let's use an example of 80 and 132.

$$(80 + 132) \div 2 = 106° \text{ centerline}$$

The cam card indicates the correct installed intake centerline. If it calls for 106 degrees and you come up with 108 degrees, the cam is early and you have to retard it 2 degrees to bring it into spec. If you get 104 degrees the cam is retarded and you have to advance it 2 degrees to correct it.

If you have degreed the cam with the intake centerline method, check

Digicam Digital Degree System

Altronics' Digicam digital degree system is an easy-to-use crankshaft and camshaft position tool that enables engine builders to determine TDC, find the camshaft centerline measurement, and find the cam duration. With the use of a separate dial indicator reading off a lifter or the valve it can help pinpoint valve events relative to crank position within .1-deggree accuracy. Builders can use either the piston stop method or dial indicator method to determine exact TDC and camshaft position.

This also allows you to display the installed camshaft centerline using the same .050 inch before-and-after method. Once you find maximum lift with the dial indicator, rotate the engine counterclockwise to approximately .100 inch before maximum lift and press the menu button. The prompt tells you to rotate clockwise to .050 before maximum lift. The Digicam notes that position.

When you press the BTDC button you are instructed to continue clockwise to .050 inch after maximum lift. When you press the ATDC button the display indicates the crank centerline.

Pressing any button after this returns to display the crank position.

To determine camshaft duration rotate the engine to zero lift with the lobe on the base circle of the cam. Adjust the dial indicator to zero. Press the menu button until "Cdur" is displayed.

When you press select the prompt instructs you to rotate clockwise to .050-inch lift at which point you press the BTDC button.

Continue rotating over the nose and back down to .050 inch before valve closing at zero lift.

Pressing the ATDC button displays the cam lobe duration.

Note you can use any checking point such as .006 inch, .020 inch, or whatever your cam card indicates for seat-to-seat timing. And you can verify opening and closing points at the same time.

Again, pressing any button returns to showing crank position.

The Digicam adapters fit Chevy small- and big-blocks, LS1s, Mopars, Oldsmobiles, and Pontiacs. It runs on a pair of AAA batteries. The supplied bolt and spacer may or may not fit your particular engine depending on the particular combination of crankshaft and timing cover. You can also use it with the heads off by making a spacer to fit directly to the timing cover mounting surface. Then you can use a cam-checking dial indicator directly off the lifter to accomplish the same measurements.

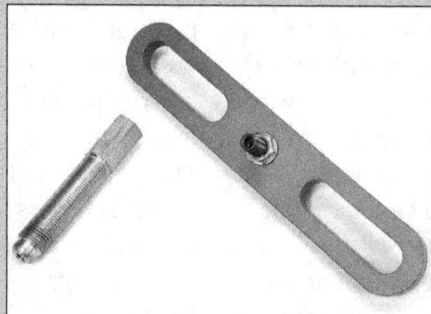

You can use Summit Racing's plug hole piston stop (left) or deck surface piston stop (right) to provide a solid stop for the piston while determining TDC.

The Digicam kit includes the rotary encoder assembly and an assortment of interchangeable sleeves to fit all popular crankshafts.

The appropriate sleeve adapts the encoder hub to the front snout of your crankshaft. Set screws are tightened into a groove to lock the sleeve solidly in place.

CAMSHAFTS

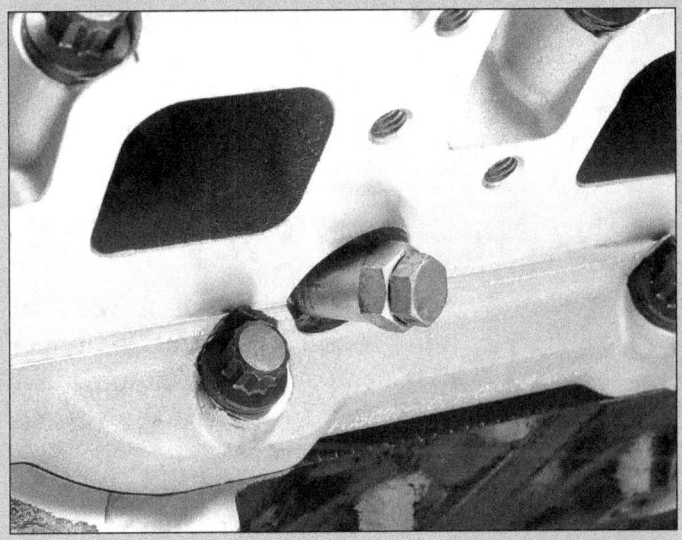

A piston stop installed in the number-1 cylinder helps you find TDC.

ProForm's dial indicator cam-checking tool is used to read lifter travel with the heads off the engine.

The encoder runs against a rubber tread surface with the proper amount of friction to provide precise measurement of the crank's rotational progress.

The Digicam kit installs onto the crank snout and is secured in place with a long bolt and spacer installed in one of the timing cover bolt holes. This holds the unit steady so the rotary encoder can be turned with a ratchet.

Here the digital readout is indicating an installed centerline of 110.7 degrees.

CHAPTER 11

To ensure accuracy when degreeing the cam use a precision cam checking device like this ProForm adjustable cam checker that fits snugly into the lifter bore and reads directly off the camshaft lobes.

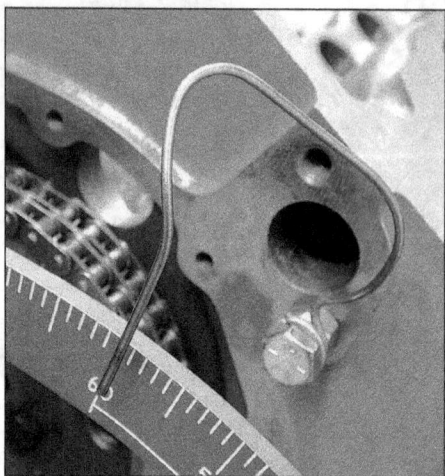

All camshafts must be degreed to establish their precise position in the engine relative to the crankshaft. A large-diameter degree wheel is recommended to ensure absolute accuracy.

to see if the intake opening and closing points match those indicated on the cam card. If incorrect, determine the direction of error and reposition the cam accordingly.

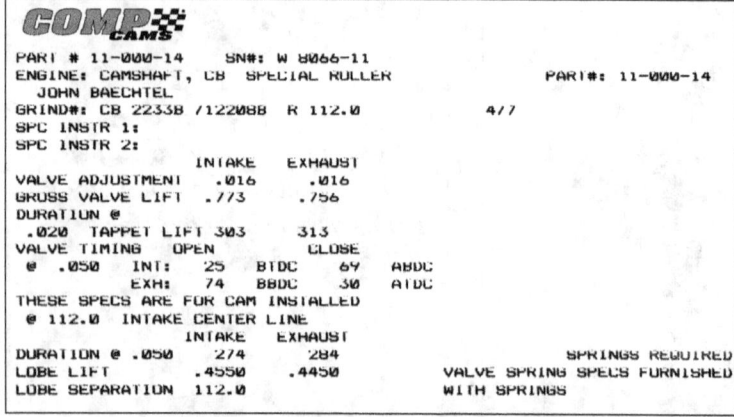

Cam card nomenclature includes the part number and serial number on line one. Line two indicates the engine family and a special custom roller cam. Line three is the customer name and line four is the grind number. In this case the grind number indicates a 2233 intake lobe and a 2208 exhaust lobe on 112-degree centers per Comp's Master Lobe Catalog. The valve adjustment and gross lift are shown next and then the advertised duration for the .020-inch lift-checking spec. Below that you see the actual timing figures for .050-inch lift. At the bottom is the duration at .050-inch lift, the actual cam rise or lobe lift, and the lobe separation angle. The 4/7 at the upper right indicates that the cam is ground for a 4/7 swap in the standard Chevy firing order. The 11 in the part number specifies a big-block Chevy, the 000 indicates a custom grind, and the -14 denotes core type and price code.

Calculating Valve Overlap

Overlap is the number of degrees where both valves are off their seats at the same time. It is a combination of the intake opening event and the exhaust closing event. Adding these two points together yields valve overlap.

Valve Overlap = IO + EC

For example, a cam with an intake opening point of 29 degrees BTDC and an exhaust closing point of 23 degrees ATDC has a valve overlap of 52 degrees.

29° + 23° = 52° overlap

Camshaft Terminology

Numerous terms and acronyms are used to describe camshaft operation. The following definitions are provided to explain camshaft lingo and make it easier for you to work the associated math.

ABDC (after bottom dead center): Position where the piston is accelerating away from BDC. Intake valve closing occurs in this area.

ATDC (after top dead center): Piston position where the piston has passed TDC and is accelerating away from it. The exhaust closing event usually occurs in this area.

BBDC (before bottom dead center): Piston position before reaching BDC. Normal area for exhaust opening event.

BDC (bottom dead center): Position of the piston at the exact bottom of its travel; exactly 180 degrees opposite of TDC.

BTDC (before top dead center): Piston position (typically number-1) before or approaching TDC. The piston is decelerating and the intake valve opening normally occurs in this area.

EC: Exhaust closing point in degrees ATDC.

EO: Exhaust opening point in degrees BBDC.

IC: Intake closing point in degrees ABDC.

IO: The intake valve opening point, usually in degrees BTDC.

LDA (lobe displacement angle): The number of camshaft degrees separating the centerlines of the intake and exhaust lobes. Also referred to as lobe separation angle (LSA) or simply "lobe center."

LSA (lobe separation angle): Same as lobe displacement angle. Most commonly used reference.

TDC (top dead center): Position where the piston is at the exact top of its travel in the cylinder. It splits the dwell point where the rod changes its angle and represents the zero degree reference point for crankshaft degrees and cam timing events.

Pro/Stock cam compared to standard roller cam illustrates larger-diameter journals and cam lobes that permit more aggressive profiles with less spring pressure. The larger, stiffer cam maintains more accurate camshaft timing while raised camshaft position permits shorter pushrods that deflect less. (Photo Courtesy Comp Cams)

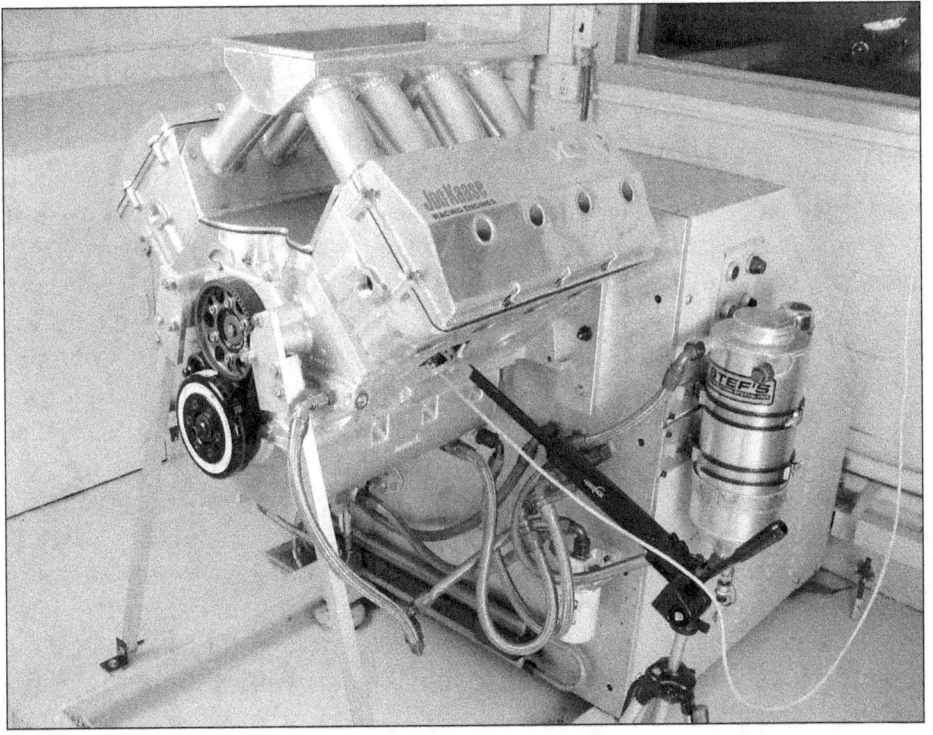

Spintron unit at Comp Cams permits development of more radical camshaft designs. The Spintron is a dyno-like motoring device that independently drives racing engines at elevated RPM to evaluate valvetrain dynamics. (Photo Courtesy Comp Cams)

Rocker Ratio Tuning

You can fine tune a mechanical or solid lifter cam to some degree with small valve lash adjustments, but you can further tune any pushrod-style cam with a rocker arm change. For example, a Chevy 1.5:1 rocker arm can be replaced with a 1.6:1 ratio rocker to achieve a 10-percent gain in rocker ratio. That doesn't mean a 10-percent increase in lift, but the effective increase is substantial and often quite useful. This increases valve lift on a Chevy, for example, by about .030 inch. As a general rule, the higher the lobe lift, the greater the increase. To be certain of the gain, multiply your known lobe lift by the new rocker arm ratio.

Net Lift = lobe lift x new rocker ratio

For example, a lobe lift of .350 inch provides a net lift of .525 inch except with a mechanical cam. A 1.65:1—rocker arm bumps that value by more than .050 to .577 inch—a substantial increase. Equally important are the other effects a ratio change brings to the table.

A higher ratio rocker arm accelerates valve opening and closing events at a faster rate, effectively increasing duration with the same opening and closing points. The rule of thumb is 1 degree of duration for every 1/2 point of rocker ratio increase. Hence, a switch from 1.5 to 1.6:1 can net a 2 degree increase in duration. Power gains acquired through ratio changes are split between the increase in lift and the increase in duration.

Rocker ratio increase may affect valve to piston clearance, valve-spring coil bind, and retainer-to-seal clearance; the faster valve action may induce valve float in some cases. Generally these problems don't occur, but you have to check for them and take appropriate action if necessary.

Ratio changes are often made on either the intake or the exhaust only to help mask a deficiency elsewhere, and tuners sometimes run more rocker ratio on the end cylinders to compensate for differences in runner length. Whatever the case, rocker ratio is an effective tuning tool for racers who understand the advantages it can provide.

COMP CAMS SOLID ROLLER

HXL SERIES ROLLERS

The HXL Series rollers are intended for high lift applications that require maximum torque and extended rpm. These fall somewhere in between the RX and TK Series in terms of aggressiveness but provide more lobe lift. They are closest to the High Torque .440" lobes but have incorporated our latest profile advancements that should allow higher engine speeds and improved dynamics.

CAMSHAFT TYPE	LOBE NUMBER	RATED DURATION	DURATION IN DEGREES		LOBE LIFT	TAPPET LIFT @ TDC		THEORETICAL VALVE LIFT @ "0" LASH ROCKER ARM RATIO		
			@ .050"	@ .200"		106°	110°	1.6	1.7	1.8
HXL Series Rated Duration @ .020" Tappet Lift	2222	281	252	175	.434	.118	.102	.694	.738	.781
	2223	283	254	177	.436	.122	.106	.698	.741	.785
	2224	285	256	179	.438	.126	.110	.701	.745	.788
	2225	287	258	181	.440	.130	.114	.704	.748	.792
	2226	289	260	183	.442	.135	.118	.707	.751	.796
	2227	291	262	185	.444	.139	.122	.710	.755	.799
	2228	293	264	187	.446	.144	.126	.714	.758	.803
	2229	295	266	189	.448	.148	.130	.717	.762	.806
	2230	297	268	191	.450	.152	.135	.720	.765	.810
	2231	299	270	193	.452	.157	.139	.723	.768	.814
	2232	301	272	195	.454	.161	.143	.726	.772	.817
	2233	303	274	197	.454	.166	.148	.726	.772	.817
	2234	305	276	199	.454	.170	.152	.726	.772	.817
	2235	307	278	201	.454	.174	.156	.726	.772	.817
	2236	309	280	202	.454	.178	.161	.726	.772	.817
	2237	311	282	204	.454	.183	.165	.726	.772	.817
	2208	313	284	206	.454	.187	.169	.726	.772	.817
	2209	315	286	208	.454	.191	.173	.726	.772	.817
	2210	317	288	210	.454	.195	.177	.726	.772	.817

Take a look at the lobe family Comp specified for our 565-ci Dart big-block Chevy. Recall from the cam card on page 126 that the selected lobes are 2233 and 2208 which, according to the lobe family chart, spec out at 274 and 284 degrees at .050-inch lift for the intake and exhaust respectively.

Wherever not prohibited by the rules, roller lifters are the choice of top-level engine builders. Various types and sizes are available with different methods of retaining lifter pairs. Tie bars (shown) are the most common, but some engines use guided lifters and/or other means of maintaining roller alignment with the cam lobes.

Duration

The difference between advertised duration and duration at .050-inch lift doesn't have to be confusing. Cam manufacturers select an opening and closing lift point to specify the duration of their cams. This is typically a point of discernable lifter motion such as .006 inch for Comp Cams or .004 inch for Crane Cams. These lift points are the basis for the advertised duration that all cam manufacturers use because bigger numbers sound better from a marketing standpoint. Advertised duration is problematic because manufacturers all seem to use different lift points to specify duration, thus making cam comparisons difficult.

Years ago, at the urging of Harvey Crane, all manufacturers finally settled on a universal checking point of .050-inch to compare cam specs from different companies. This standard was adopted by the SAE and is currently the standardized checking point for all camshafts. Later, Harvey Crane introduced the concept of hydraulic intensity, which is the time in crankshaft degrees that it takes for the lifter to move from its advertised duration checking point to the universal .050-inch lift point. It's determined by subtracting the duration at .050 inch from the advertised duration. The smaller the number, the greater the hydraulic intensity, which indicates a more aggressive cam. Naturally comparisons can only be made between cams with the same advertised checking point relative to the .050-inch standard. Cams with a more aggressive hydraulic intensity typically exhibit more valvetrain noise due to the steep lift curve, but they generally deliver more performance without sacrificing idle quality.

CAMSHAFTS

Camshaft Selection Criteria

In a nutshell, camshaft selection must be painstakingly matched to the application's required engine speed range, the flow rates of the inlet and exhaust systems within the given RPM range and how well they complement piston motion, and cylinder pressure differential according to rod length.

Engine builders are often required to contemplate a specific engine speed or operating range, engine breathing characteristics within that speed range, and the mechanical requirements suitable to sustain durable high-speed operation based on the type of camshaft and valvetrain being used. This typically includes accommodations for potential mechanical conflicts such as inadequate piston-to-valve clearance, valvespring coil bind issues, and other critical interference issues typically associated with high-lift, long-duration cams.

The primary goal of the camshaft designer is to achieve and maintain optimum intake and exhaust flow velocity across the specified operating range. The intent is to maintain a minimum flow velocity of 240 to 260 feet per second in the ports, but high-speed engines frequently exceed those values by a factor of two or three. As lift and duration increase, the engine must run faster to make sufficient power.

Many factors contribute to the engine airflow equation. Superior breathing is a highly variable function of engine size and operating speed, inlet and exhaust flow path characteristics, and how closely they are matched along with intake manifold design and carburetor or throttle body size. Typically, short-stroke, small-displacement engines do not accept as much camshaft lift and duration as larger-displacement, longer-stroke engines that produce higher flow velocities with longer-duration, high-lift cams.

While the intake closing event has traditionally been viewed as the most important point in effective camshaft selection, more and more designers are now basing their design criteria on the valve overlap period and its relationship to engine speed and final application. The overlap period is critical to taking maximum advantage of exhaust pressure wave scavenging and its potentially optimizing effect on intake tuning. The second most important criteria is the LSA or lobe centerline angle (LCA, the angle between the centerlines of the intake and exhaust lobes). As compression ratio increases it calls for a wider LCA. The same goes for valve acceleration rate. Higher ratio rockers and quick action cam lobes also tend to require a wider LCA.

Firing Order Swaps

For some time now, many Chevy engine builders have routinely rearranged the firing order of their racing engines. The debate as to whether this accomplishes anything is ongoing, but it's become common practice and the naysayers appear to be fading. The most common reordering is the 4/7 swap, where the firing positions of cylinders 4 and 7 are swapped in the standard V-8 firing order (18436572). This yields a firing order of 18736542 and was a well-kept secret in Pro/Stock drag racing for years; many builders now favor it. Interestingly the power claims are generally not substantial (something on the order of 4 to 7 hp), although numbers as high as a 40-hp gain routinely circulate on Internet forums, particularly with regard to dual-plane-equipped circle track applications.

More common are claims of a broader, smoother torque curve with improved drivability and component durability. With the original firing order, cylinders 5 and 7 firing in sequence tend to saturate heat around those chambers, which could encourage detonation and dimensional issues with valves and seats.

Cooling issues are said to be resolved by separating cylinders 5 and 7 in the firing order, but the problem is really only transferred to cylinders 4 and 2, which are admittedly closer to the water pump in a domestic V-8.

Offset lifters are often required to compensate for poor pushrod alignment or the need to shift a pushrod's position to clear an obstacle on the cylinder head. In many cases builders mix and match lifters according to their specific needs. The Comp roller (left) shifts the pushrod .180-inch off center and is available in left or right versions.

CHAPTER 11

Modern high-speed engines require precise valve control to deliver the extraordinary power levels currently achieved. Titanium retainers and 10-degree locks with lash caps are required for lightweight titanium valves. In some cases valvespring pressures approach 1,000 pounds or more, hence the need for very stiff top-quality components that include spring seat cups and centering guides.

More recent advancements in valvespring technology have rendered the beehive or ovate wire spring with reduced mass that requires less pressure to control the valve. These springs also use smaller, lighter retainers.

Durability claims may hold some merit since the standard firing order has numbers 6, 5, and 7 cylinders all hammering the number-4 main bearing in sequence. The 4/7 swap relieves this, but transfers similar loading to the center main with cylinders 6, 5, and 4 all hitting in sequence. These issues are more prevalent on big-inch stroker applications where you're slinging a good bit more mass in the crankcase.

In the case of GM's Gen III firing order (18726543), loading is transferred from front to back and then cycled through the center cylinders (where the thrust bearing is now located) before hitting the end cylinders again. This firing order replicates the Ford Windsor and the later 5.0 HO firing order if you re-number the cylinders to match the Chevy. More importantly, this firing order cycles between cylinders with longer runners and cylinders with shorter runners, which must be tuned to different torque peaks, potentially broadening the overall curve.

Cam profile selection varies according to application and covers a broad spectrum. Many professional engine builders are well acquainted with the basic requirements of camshaft selection, but they still defer to the cam designer's judgment in most applications and often the selection is a collaborative effort depending on the engine builder's level of experience and recognition of the power curve requirements. The cam designer or profile builder can draw from a deep well of experience and engine builder feedback, which often translates to better camshaft selection for builders down the line.

A high-speed drag race profile, for example, requires very specific timing for successful operation, particularly on large-displacement engines running very high engine speeds, high compression ratios, and large-tube open headers. This type of engine generates a lot of exhaust volume at high RPM so the designer may emphasize early exhaust valve opening to minimize pumping losses during the exhaust stroke. Depending on the cylinder head, these engines may experience difficulty discharging the high volume of exhaust gas they produce, hence the emphasis on exhaust timing.

Shaft rockers like these from Comp Cams are preferred for serious high-speed valvetrains. Shaft setups anchor the rocker arms more securely and provide added stability that translates to more accurate valve timing.

---

130 COMPETITION ENGINE BUILDING: ADVANCED ENGINE DESIGN & ASSEMBLY TECHNIQUES

CHAPTER 12

SUMPS AND OILING

Lubrication is the critical lifeblood of every racing engine. Without it, the engine's lifespan is measured in seconds. The oiling system is designed to deliver a constant supply of clean, filtered oil to properly lubricate all of the engine's moving parts. This includes the engine bearings, pistons and piston pins, camshaft and valve gear, and all the associated parts that make the engine run. In concert with its lubricating function the oiling system may also be utilized to cool certain parts such as the valvesprings and piston crowns.

When the oiling system is functioning correctly the camshaft and crankshaft journals ride on a hydrodynamic wedge of oil that prevents the journals from ever touching the bearing inserts. This wedge is provided by the oil pump and companion components and its effectiveness depends largely on the oil's viscosity, pump speed, proper bearing clearances, oil temperature, crankcase pressure, and bottom end components optimized for minimum drag. There are two basic lubrication systems currently utilized in racing engines: wet sumps and dry sumps. With either setup the primary components of the oiling system include:

- Oil Pump and drive mechanism
- Pump pickup
- Pan and associated baffles
- Oil filter
- Oil cooler if required
- Internal and external oil passages
- Windage control components

Engine designers and builders treat oil control as a major factor of engine design and construction. Considerable effort is devoted to ensuring that adequate pressurized oil is available to the engine's moving parts at all times. Designers are

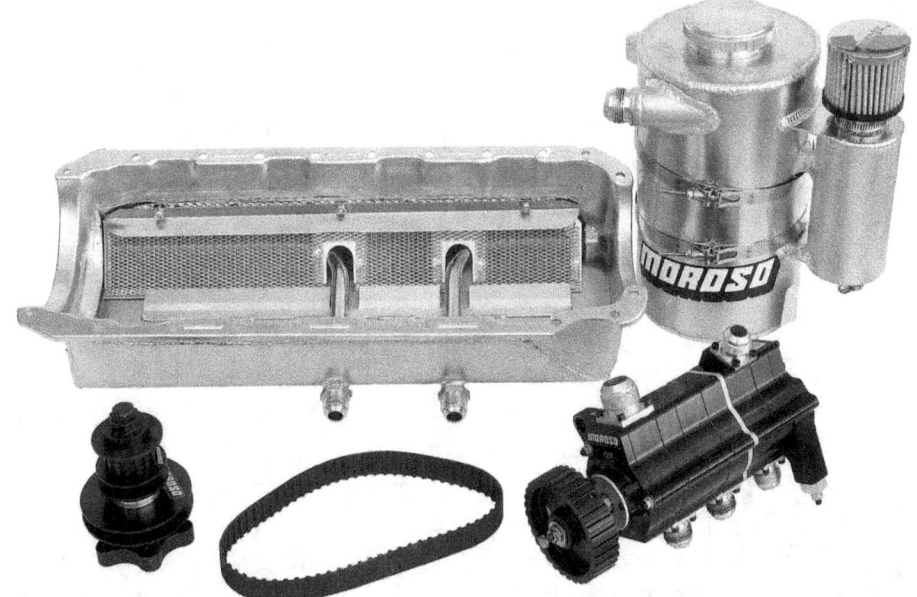

Moroso dry sump oiling systems incorporate a shallow oil pan with multiple pickup points, remote dry sump storage tank with integral breather, multi-stage pump, and drive mandrel with cog belt.

COMPETITION ENGINE BUILDING: ADVANCED ENGINE DESIGN & ASSEMBLY TECHNIQUES 131

also concerned with where the oil is stored, how it is retrieved from the engine, and how the engine's oil supply is affected by moving internal components, oil temperature, pumping effort, and the dynamic influences of vehicle motion—all of which have a profound impact on the quality and consistency of a critical lubrication process that must not falter even for a second.

Of particular concern is the strict control or elimination of aeration and the formation of air bubbles in the oil supply (commonly known as cavitation). Lubrication efficiency virtually ceases to exist in the presence of air bubbles and designers make every effort to control oil movement and exposure to conditions that promote oil foaming. Extreme turbulence caused by the rapidly spinning crankshaft assembly can grab oil returning to the sump and spin it into a nasty taffy-like mixture that exerts considerable parasitic drag on the engine's internal parts. This crankcase condition, called windage, creates drag and has the potential to encourage the formation of air bubbles in the oil supply. This not only degrades oil pump and filter efficiency, it reduces the efficiency of the hydrodynamic oil wedge that supports moving components.

Aerated oil also tends to be less efficient at removing heat from components and its lubrication efficiency may become diminished to the point where important companion components undergo conditions of intermittent or insufficient lubrication. These include rocker arms, lifters, pushrod tips, valveguides, valvesprings, distributor gear, timing gears, and even the oil pump itself. In some cases these conditions may be partially helped by the improved lubricating qualities of synthetic oils, but only minimally. Moving parts need a filtered, cooled, and bubble-free supply of fresh engine oil at all times to ensure optimum performance and durability.

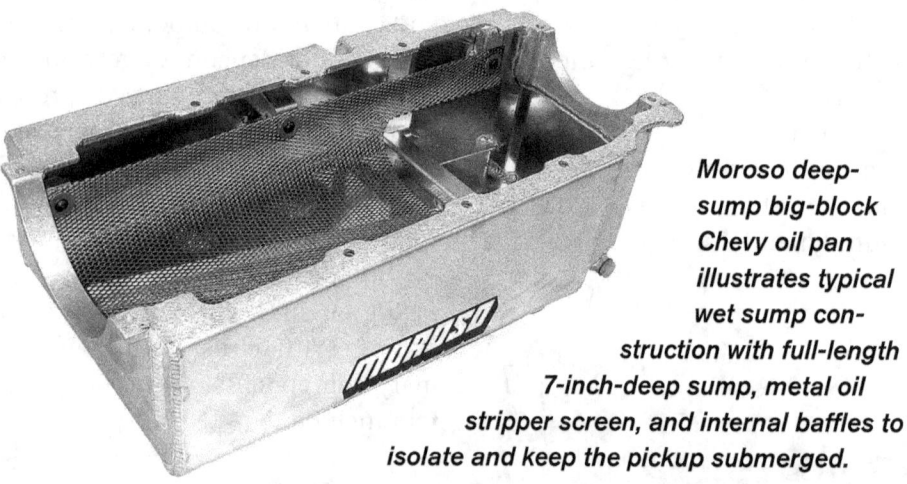

Typical wet sump oiling system incorporates an internally mounted gear-driven oil pump with windage tray and an extended submerged pickup in a deep-sump pan. Oil is picked up, pumped through the engine, and returned to the sump. (Courtesy Moroso Performance Products)

Moroso deep-sump big-block Chevy oil pan illustrates typical wet sump construction with full-length 7-inch-deep sump, metal oil stripper screen, and internal baffles to isolate and keep the pickup submerged.

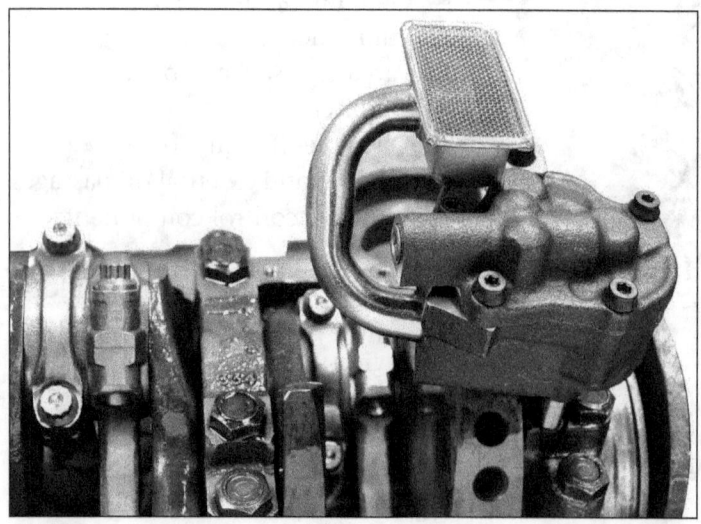

Wet sump pans often require pump extensions and/or pickup extensions to properly position the pickup near the bottom of the sump.

Basic performance wet sump oiling systems usually incorporate a deeper, expanded-capacity oil sump to store the oil farther below the crankshaft assembly. A blueprinted stock pump or a specially designed race pump uses an extended pickup to scavenge oil from the bottom of the pan. (Courtesy Don Cooper, Reher-Morrison)

Racing wet sump pans often incorporate an extended kickout section on the passenger side of the engine. It provides an escape route for oil being flung off the crank assembly so it can't rebound off the side of the pan, creating additional drag. (Courtesy Don Cooper, Reher-Morrison)

Wet Sump Systems

Wet sump oiling systems are the most commonly used oiling strategy in sportsman class racing and a few select professional classes because they are effective and relatively inexpensive. A wet sump system stores a reservoir of oil in the bottom of the oil pan and pumps it through the engine with an internally-mounted pump that is typically driven off the bottom of the distributor via a short driveshaft. An oil pump pickup attached to the pump extends to the bottom of the oil pan to pick up the oil. For best results the pickup is usually positioned within 1/4 inch off the pan floor to make certain it remains submerged.

This is the same basic oiling method used in most production cars, but it can be significantly enhanced with specialty components that improve oil control and increase power via drag reduction. Racing applications typically use higher capacity oil pans, racing oil pumps, extended pickups, windage trays, oil control kits, racing oil filters, and other components designed specifically to boost oiling efficiency under competition conditions. In some wet sump applications an external oil pump is used, allowing the windage tray or screen to extend the full length of the oil pan for more effective oil control.

Oil control is a key concern in a wet sump oiling system. The movement of sump oil initiated by constantly varying vehicle motion is a major contributor to intermittent conditions of oil starvation and the adverse effects of crankcase windage. The importance of steps to keep the oil pickup submerged in the sump oil supply at all times cannot be overstated. Under hard acceleration, oil climbs up the back of the oil pan and lateral acceleration tends to slosh the oil supply to one side or the other depending on the direction of turning. Even hard braking can initiate conditions where the pickup is briefly uncovered by oil movement and air is sucked into the pump to encourage aeration.

Various baffles, compartments, and trap doors within the oil pan sump section are employed to limit oil movement so the sump remains submerged under all dynamic conditions. Competition oil pans are constructed with sump extension compartments on one or both sides to increase capacity. Depending on the racing application pan baffles, compartments, and trap doors are configured to direct oil to the pickup at all times. On most oval track cars the oil tends to move to the outside (or right side) of the engine. With road racing cars, it moves to both sides depending on the direction of loading. Drag racing engines are typically concerned with preventing oil from stacking to the back of the sump and uncovering the pickup.

Windage Trays and Scrapers

Among the various oil control strategies, windage trays and crankshaft scrapers are a primary consideration. Sometimes they are an integral part of the overall pan design and often they are installed separately depending on the application and the specific control strategy employed. Some windage trays are mounted on extensions of the main cap bolts or studs and some are built right into the pan as permanent fixtures. The purpose of a windage tray is to mitigate the hurricane whipping effect of the spinning crankshaft and rods. In a high-RPM engine, windage can be strong enough to whip the oil supply in the sump into a stormy sea of aerated oil much like the ocean in a violent windstorm.

The windage tray serves to separate the primary oil supply from the eye of the storm and helps to preserve its liquid state while still permitting oil drainage via slots and channels in the tray itself. Some windage trays only cover part of the sump depending on the pan design and application. Other types employ louvers or expanded metal screens that help shield the oil supply while shearing oil from the spinning mass with minimal aeration.

Crank scrapers attempt a similar but more direct shearing by fixing their scraper edges very close to the crankshaft throws. Scrapers are typically hand fitted to provide the minimum required clearance between the scraper and the spinning crankshaft assembly. Generic-style scrapers that are fitted inside some pans do not follow the exact contours of the crankshaft and rods. These scrapers provide some benefit by shearing a given quantity of oil from the oil mass, but they are typically not as effective as a closely fit crankshaft scraper.

Scrapers also perform another important function by directing separated oil toward a special kickout section built into the pan on the upward side of crankshaft rotation (usually the passenger side). When the side of the pan is very close to the spinning crankshaft it encourages parasitic drag due to the proximity of the spinning oil mass. The kickout provides an escape route for oil being flung off the crankshaft. At higher engine speeds, increased mass inertia tends to toss the oil off the crankshaft toward the side of the pan in the direction of crankshaft rotation. Instead of hitting the side of the pan and rebounding into the oil mass to create more drag, oil is thrown into the kickout cavity where it drains back to the sump. Most scrapers support and encourage this effect and work in concert to separate crankshaft oil and minimize windage.

In many cases a well-configured scraper and kickout combination can be worth up to 20 hp, depending on the engine speed, the size of the concentrated oil mass, and the overall layout of the scraper/kickout combination. One problem with the effectiveness of this arrangement is that most GM engines and others have the starter located on the same side of the engine as the kickout, effectively limiting the length of the kickout to accommodate the starter. Shortened kickout cavities are the result and they lose some of the overall effect. Still, some kickout is better than none provided there is enough room in the chassis.

Deeper sumps attempt to isolate the oil reservoir by placing it farther from the crankshaft. This is common practice on wet sump oil pans that are typically 2 to 4 inches deeper than stock.

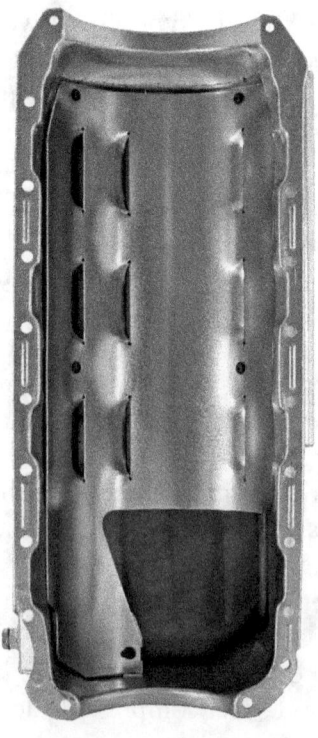

Side kickouts are an effective component of wet sump oil pans, but their efficiency is often compromised by the starter location, which prevents a full-length kickout to control oil coming off the rear crank throws. Internal windage control (right) features rear cutout for the pump and pickup, and a full-length curved windage tray incorporating louvers to direct oil back to the sump. (Courtesy Moroso Performance Products)

SUMPS AND OILING

Wet Sump Oil Pumps

Wet sump oiling systems have been highly developed in part by tremendous demand for effective wet sump components that help curtail excessive expenses in sportsman applications. At a minimum this includes blueprinted and reworked factory pumps, high-efficiency internal and external pumps, custom extended oil pickup designs, and various support components designed to ensure the effectiveness of any wet sump system. Factory-style pumps and all external pumps are positive displacement designs, meaning the pump transfers the exact volume of oil that it takes in.

The different styles of pumps are distinguished by the type of gears used inside them—gerotors or spur gears. Spur gears are common to General Motors pumps while gerotors are found in most Ford and Chrysler applications. Spur gear pumps use one driven gear to drive a second freewheeling gear on a fixed shaft. Gerotor pumps typically use a four-tooth gear to drive a multi-cavity rotor that traps oil and transfers it in a similar fashion to a spur gear pump, but for the most part with greater efficiency at slower pump speeds.

If a wet sump pump is not completely submerged, the connection where the pump pickup enters the pump must be fully sealed to prevent the pump from sucking air above the sump level. Aftermarket racing pumps have special pickups designed for virtually every oil pan they offer. This is to ensure optimum pickup placement and performance under all operating conditions. If a factory-style pump is used, most builders disassemble it to deburr the gears and check the end clearance, which is typically limited to about .002 inch. Many blueprint the pump housing by grinding and straightening internal passages to ensure smooth uninterrupted oil flow with no cavitation.

Spinning a pump faster generally increases flow volume as long as steps are taken to prevent oil cavitation. As a rule this can only be done with an external pump where it is possible to change the pump's drive ratio. Internal pumps gain flow volume with taller gears—up to a point. The use of a big-block Chevy pump on a small-block is an example. The big-block pump has taller gears that transfer a greater volume of oil, but they also have more drag, which may be detrimental unless you absolutely need higher oil volume.

Savvy race engine builders consider the drag penalty and the loads incurred with higher oil pressure when contemplating higher flow volume or higher pressures. In most applications, 60 to 80 psi adequately meets lubrication needs. Wet sump pumps maintain pressure at any given flow rate by bypassing excessive oil. In the best case scenario, bypass oil should be limited so that the minimum volume needed to support the desired pressure is applied. Of course pressure should be limited to the amount required to fully support the hydrodynamic wedge in the bearing journals at maximum engine

The severe dynamics of race vehicle motion vary according to the application. In almost every case, wet sump systems are challenged to maintain control of the sump oil supply and keep it separated from the crank assembly at all times. Inertia typically prevails, thus all manner of internal baffles and trap doors are required to restrict unwanted oil movement. (Courtesy Moroso Performance Products)

CHAPTER 12

speed. To accomplish this, purchase the correct pump and pickup according to the manufacturer's recommended specs.

Determining Oil Pump Clearance

Maintaining the proper clearance between the oil pump pickup and the bottom of the oil pan is critical to proper pump operation. The pump pickup must never suck air, hence the pump and/or pump pickup must be accurately located in reference to the floor of the pan. With the oil pan removed, this measurement is easily taken using a combination square with a sliding rule. Position the square against the block's pan rail and slide the rule to measure the distance to the bottom of the pickup. Then lock the rule in place. Without changing the setting, check the depth of the oil pan from its rail down to the bottom. The difference indicated should be a 1/4- to 3/8-inch gap between the end of the rule and the pan's bottom. A clearance greater than 3/8 inch may result in aerated or inadequate oil flow, while clearances less than 1/4 inch could disturb or restrict oil flow patterns and cause cavitation.

Some builders claim the pump can draw hard enough to close up the gap if the pan material is too thin. A common trick is to weld a small 3/8-inch metal tab to the bottom of the pickup to position it accurately. This works very well, but it requires careful prepositioning of the pickup in the pump before final assembly. Once this is done many builders like to tack weld the pickup to the pump or even braze it in place. If you choose to do so be sure to remove the bypass spring to prevent heat damage and recheck the pump mating surfaces for distortion that might affect proper gear alignment and rotation.

Dry Sump Systems

Dry sump oiling systems store their oil supply in a separate tank leaving the oil pan virtually dry because multiple scavenge pumps suck it out as fast as possible. An external pump assembly incorporating multiple scavenge stages (typically three, four, or more) sucks oil out of the shallow pan and delivers it to the storage tank. The pressure section of the pump sucks oil from the tank to pressurize the engine's oiling system. A single pressure stage is normally used to return oil from the tank to the engine while the scavenge section may incorporate anywhere from two to six pickups, some

Drive systems vary considerably depending on the application. Most manufacturers have auxiliary hardware such as this water pump mounting plate for a Moroso alternator and vacuum pump. Appropriate-drive mandrel components are also required to properly position the drive belts.

Dry sump plumbing is sometimes difficult. This system uses a single large -16 AN return line to the tank instead of more typical multiple lines. Where the chassis configuration permits, it also mounts directly to the oil pan, eliminating the clutter of external lines from the pan to the pump.

136   COMPETITION ENGINE BUILDING: ADVANCED ENGINE DESIGN & ASSEMBLY TECHNIQUES

of which are often used to scavenge oil from the valve covers or the lifter valley beneath the intake manifold.

A dy sump's primary advantage in a racing engine is its ability to make more power. With minimal oil in the pan, the rotating system is not burdened with the weight and parasitic drag of the excess oil whipped up by the spinning crank. With no internal pump, the windage tray or screen, which normally isolates sump oil from the rotating assembly, can run the full length of the oil pan, keeping the rotating assembly free of windage so it spins more easily and delivers more power. Crankcase vacuum created by the dry sump scavenge stages also improves ring seal and encourages more power.

Dry sump systems provide increased oil capacity in a separate reservoir, more consistent oil pressure, and the ability to easily adjust oil pressure. Since the pan doesn't store any oil, it can be made relatively shallow to permit lower engine placement in the chassis to improve handling and weight distribution. Separate plumbing provides the opportunity to run a small in-line filter on each scavenge stage for maximum filtering effect. In some cases manufacturers also offer scavenge manifolds that accept scavenged oil from two or more pickups and route it through a single filter prior to delivery to the storage tank. In either case, the opportunity to send the oil through a cooler along the way presents itself.

Sometimes a manifold arrangement is also incorporated on the pressure stage to send pressurized oil to the engine at different points such as front and rear pressure entry ports.

It's pretty normal to use two or more scavenge ports on the oil pan. They are typically located as near the floor of the pan as possible and their location is often further dictated by the specific racing application and where the designers feel is the best point to scavenge the oil most effectively under actual racing conditions and the associated g-loading.

Drag racing pans tend to concentrate sump pickups toward the rear of the pan while oval track setups typically scavenge from the right side of the pan. In either case the actual pickup fitting may be on the opposite side of the pan with an internal extension pickup that helps ease plumbing problems in restrictive chassis arrangements.

Road racing, off-road racing, and many marine applications usually have the scavenge points located near the center of the pan for maximum effectiveness under constantly changing conditions. Some manufacturers actually mount the pump assembly directly to the oil pan to eliminate plumbing restrictions. This may be advantageous in certain chassis configurations.

There is a broad choice of steel or aluminum pans, either of which may present advantages depending on the application. Some builders also modify commercially available pans to suit their own particular requirements.

High-end systems like this Pro Mod setup incorporate up to five scavenge stages, some of which are dedicated specifically to pulling a vacuum on the crankcase. (Courtesy Don Cooper, Reher-Morrison)

Choosing a Dry Sump Pump

A leading manufacturer of race oiling systems, Moroso offers a full range of dry sump oiling system components all engineered to be fully compatible with one another. This helps you select the best combination of equipment to avoid potential problems that may occur when "mixing and matching" components from various manufacturers. According to Moroso, you need to consider the following before choosing a standard or custom oil pump:

- Weight of the oil
- Operating temperature range
- Oil consumption at idle
- Oil consumption at operating range
- Desired vacuum level

Pump selection requires a builder to determine the number of scavenge and pressure stages required for the application, the type of gears or rotors for a desired pump drive ratio, drive belt type, and mounting configurations according to operational chassis requirements. Further consideration must be given to pump materials, with coated aluminum being the most popular. Some applications also incorporate a cable-drive adapter to operate a remote mechanical fuel pump. Moroso, Barnes, and Weaver Brothers all offer high-end race pumps incorporating internal manifolds to minimize plumbing and space requirements.

Determining the required number of scavenge stages requires careful contemplation. In addition to scavenging oil from the sump, oil may also be taken from the valve cover or from the lifter gallery. Some dedicated racing engines route upper engine oil directly to an internal scavenge gallery so it never enters the sump at all. Multiple stages increase pumping volume and vacuum in the crankcase. More stages means that the pumps are sucking a lot of air in addition to oil. Air and other vapors must be separated from the oil before it can be routed back to the engine in pure liquid form.

Some applications incorporate a pump-driven air/oil separator to precondition scavenged sump oil on its way to the storage tank. The tank itself is configured to separate air and oil vapors, bleeding it off to a separately vented tank. Oil entering a circular dry sump tank from the scavenge stages is introduced tangentially with a swirling motion that encourages air and vapor to rise to the vent opening while oil drains to the storage section via additional baffles and separators. This design is very effective at eliminating aeration and collecting only liquid oil in the bottom of the tank.

As a rule, a taller tank is more effective and requires the least amount of internal baffling and oil

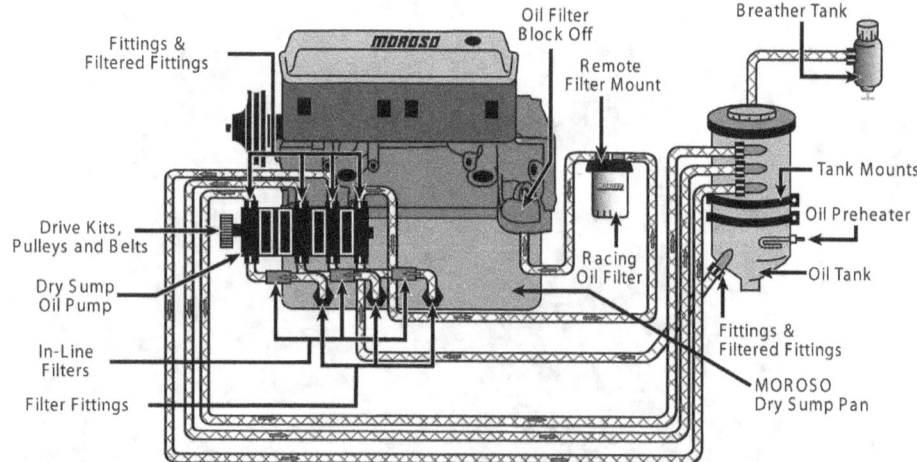

This illustration shows the major components of a dry sump system and how they are plumbed for maximum effectiveness. Most systems are plumbed this way or similarly depending on the application. The primary components include a multi-stage dry sump pump, drive mandrel with pulley and drive belt, racing oil filter, storage tank, breather tank, oil pre-heater and the accompanying plumbing that typically incorporates braided steel hoses, in-line filters, and the appropriate AN fittings to connect it all together. (Illustration Courtesy Moroso Performance Products)

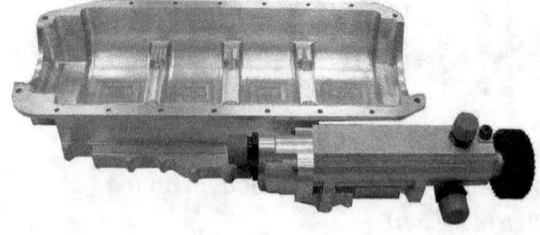

The dry sump pump incorporates a Gilmer belt-drive pulley on the front with multiple scavenge and pressure stages stacked behind it. The rear stage is the pressure stage that pumps oil from the tank to the engine. The front two lower fittings are scavenging stages attached to the dry sump pan. Both of them return scavenged oil to the tank via the single -16 outlet on top at the front. The unit hanging down at the rear is for oil-pressure adjustment.

With appropriate filter attachment, the CV Products remote oil filter mount offers a convenient way to plumb a filter between the dry sump pressure stage and the engine. It features dual- or single-inlet usage and it incorporates a fitting for reading oil temperature.

Dry sump pumps typically mount on the lower left or right at the front of the block with a pivot bolt for easy belt-tension adjustment.

control. Shorter tanks that may have space limitations often require more baffling and more complicated air separation. Some of this also speaks to the builder's preferred oil volume. Generally small-block engines require less volume than big-blocks, but the requirement is also tempered by the final application in terms of available oil capacity and the ability to cool the oil effectively. Where a drag car with a short event duration may work well with a small 1½-gallon tank, endurance applications generally require as much as 4 to 5 gallons. This is true for speedway operation, off-road racing, road racing, and some marine endurance applications like offshore power boat racing.

Pump Speed Drive Ratios

A dry sump system can regulate oil pressure according to pump speed via the combination of belt circumference and pulley sizes to achieve the required drive ratio. Manufacturers offer a broad choice of pulley sizes to accommodate a wide range of ratio options and crankshaft-to-pump-shaft centerline dimensions. With a given belt circumference, you can position the pump farther away from the crankshaft centerline using smaller-tooth pulleys with a specified drive ratio. By using larger-tooth pulleys for the same ratio, the area from centerline to the crankshaft can be reduced, but in either case they have the same drive ratio.

Builders with a good working knowledge of the requirements and chassis arrangement can consult the manufacturer to achieve the drive ratio and pump position that accommodates their pressure/volume and chassis fitment requirements.

Oil Pan Installation

A common-sense approach to pan installation suggests starting with a thorough cleaning and inspection for damage or potential leaks from cracks or other damage. While unlikely with a new pan, recall the prime directive of race engine construction: Check everything and then check it again. Use OEM-quality gaskets or the equivalent and a quality sealer. Apply a small dab of silicone sealer at each corner where the rubber seal meets the rail gaskets. Moroso technicians recommend installing the pan with the engine in the upright position if the pan incorporates internal trap doors. This prevents the doors from sticking open accidentally.

Minor rocking (approximately 1/4-inch is acceptable) may be encountered when installing the pan. This is normal even on high-quality pans; it stabilizes once the pan is tightened.

Start all the bolts before you tighten any of them, or if you are using studs, install all of the nuts loosely.

Moroso drive mandrel kit incorporates V-belt and Gilmer-belt drive pulleys and assorted spacers to adjust pulley positioning.

CHAPTER 12

Secure the mounting bolts or nuts in each corner, tightening them to less than 50 percent of final torque. Then move to the center bolts tightening them in an alternating "X" fashion working toward the ends of the pan in a circular motion similar to that used for head gasket torquing.

Repeat this procedure at 75-percent torque and then at the final torque setting to seat the pan correctly. Thread sealer, such as Loctite, is recommended on all fasteners and most true race applications may also require safety wiring.

Crankcase Vacuum Pumps

It is common practice to use an auxiliary vacuum pump to create vacuum in the crankcase. This helps control windage but its primary purpose is to reduce pressure below the piston rings so you can run lower tension rings that significantly reduce friction in the cylinders. Racers used to accomplish this with a "pan-evac" system consisting of one-way check valves and a vent whistle assembly installed in each header collector at a 45-degree angle to the direction of exhaust flow. A hose running from an air/oil separator on each valve cover to the check valve allowed the collector to pull a slight vacuum on the crankcase. Once the beneficial effects of this were confirmed it was found that more vacuum worked even better. Vacuum pumps were the next logical step.

Considerable research has determined desirable vacuum levels for various applications and the appropriate components to achieve it. Multi-stage dry sump pumps are often used to accomplish a certain level of vacuum and these may or may not be supplemented by a dedicated external vacuum pump. Many wet sump systems also incorporate an external vacuum pump with good results. Baffling is required at the suction side to separate oil and vapor and a breather is installed at the outlet side to accumulate any oil that migrates through the pump.

Optimum vacuum levels are a matter of considerable discussion. Leading engine builders and race teams all confirm that 10 to 14 inches of vacuum on a wet sump system creates additional horsepower while minimizing oiling-related problems. Dry sump engines function optimally in the range of 18 to 22 inches. While a good system with multiple pumps is normally capable of achieving greater vacuum levels, it is best to consult the pump manufacturer and your ring supplier if higher levels of vacuum are desired.

Manufacturers such as Moroso carry a variety of vacuum relief valves to adjust the maximum amount of vacuum an engine makes. The best time to check vacuum and oil pressure together on a drag race application is during the trans-brake check. At staging RPM, monitor vacuum and oil pressure to determine the state of the system. For other applications

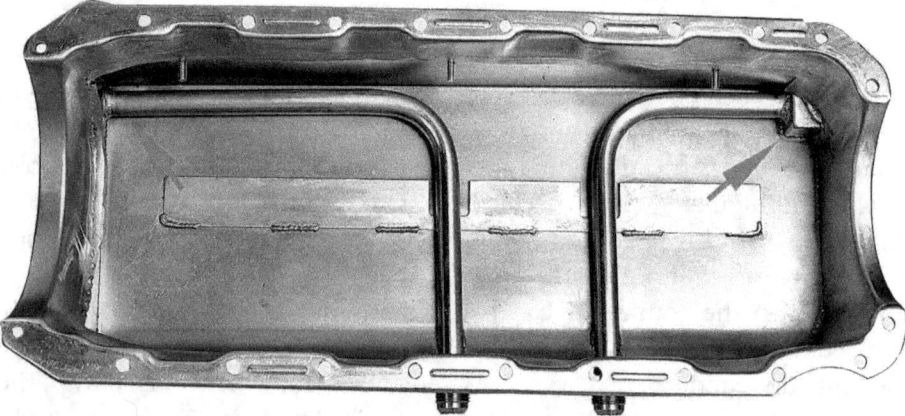

This dry sump oil pan has two pickup points on the side of the pan and one each at the front and rear in case the side pickup encounters chassis fitment issues. The tubes inside the pan are connected to the pan outlets. They have slots in the bottom to pick up sump oil from the bottom of the pan.

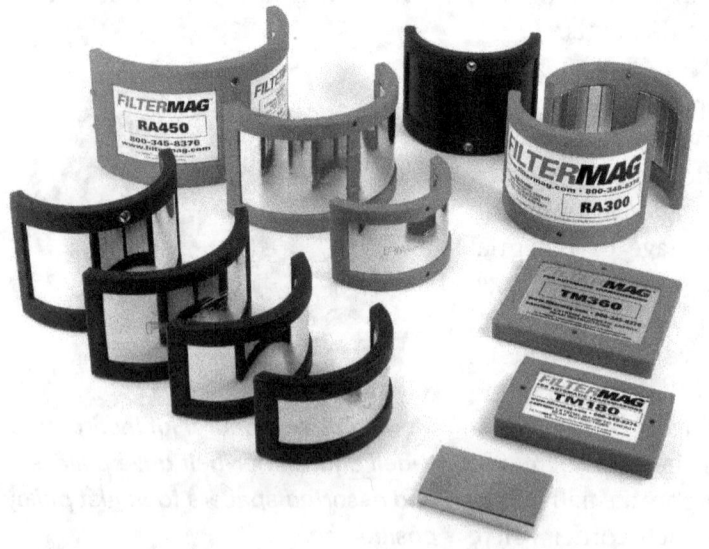

All race engines should incorporate a Filtermag as part of their overall oiling strategy. The Filtermag prevents contamination of the oil supply by trapping all metal particles inside the filter canister.

it is advisable to incorporate a data logging port to constantly monitor crankcase vacuum for comparison to other engine conditions that are also being recorded.

Vacuum levels depend on pump speed. As a major supplier of race engine vacuum pumps, Moroso recommends starting at 50 percent of engine speed. If more vacuum is required at lower engine speeds (at idle or staging RPM) or across the overall power range of the engine it is necessary to increase the pump drive ratio according to your specific requirements and the recommendations of the pump manufacturer. Some pumps are limited to 6,500-rpm shaft speed while others can turn up to 8,000 rpm so make certain you are using the correct pump and drive ratio.

Pump inlets are best attached to the front or top of a valve cover using a fitting with a built-in baffle that allows a small amount of oil to flow to the pump to lubricate the pump vanes.

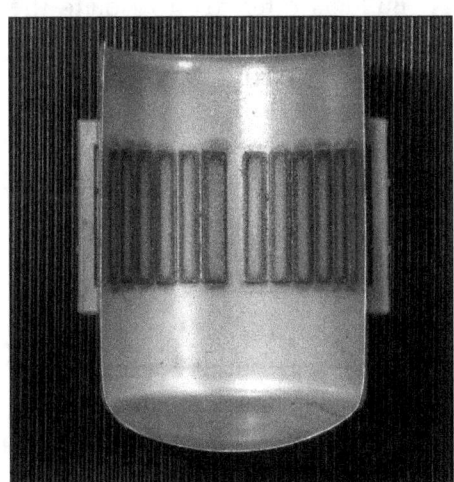

A Filtermag attracts all metal particles that pass through the filter housing. As shown here the captured material aligns itself according to the magnetic field created by attaching the Filtermag to the outside of the filter canister.

Oil Accumulators for Racing Engines

Oil accumulators are independent auxiliary oil storage tanks connected to an engine's oiling system that have pressurized air on one side of a moveable internal piston, and engine oil on the other side. If engine oil pressure drops or fluctuates due to oil surging away from the pickup during hard acceleration, severe cornering, or hard braking, the accumulator instantly provides a temporary supply of oil to the engine. When the fluctuation is over and full pressure is restored, the engine's oil pressure forces this reserve of oil back into the accumulator. Under normal engine oil pressure the accumulator is pressurized and refills automatically to reload the temporary oil supply. Some drag racing applications have successfully used accumulators to free up horsepower by lowering the oil level in the sump and relying on the accumulator to maintain adequate pressure if required.

On Moroso accumulators, the end cap on the air side has an air gauge and Schrader valve; the oil side has a 1/2-inch NPT fitting for plumbing into the oiling system. Accumulators require a valve assembly to function properly so they are equipped with a manual ball valve. The valve has to be manually opened before starting the car to pre-oil the engine (offering surge protection) while the vehicle is in use, and closed when the engine is turned off.

Moroso offers two styles of optional electric valves with its accumulators: A solenoid valve (electric) allows remote control of the accumulator. Solenoid pressure valve kits are the best performing for competition vehicles and are offered in different oil pressure ranges of 15 to 24 psi, 35 to 40 psi, and 55 to 60 psi discharge and refill. They have all the benefits of the solenoid valve but with quicker reaction times because the solenoid pressure valve allows only the necessary volume of oil to be released for faster filling and discharging. An internal sensor electronically activates when engine oil pressure drops below normal.

Independent tests have shown over 85 percent of engine wear is caused by starting an engine, and that these "dry starts" cause premature engine wear. Accumulators prevent cold-start scuffing by pre-oiling the engine before startup. Most race applications require a 3-quart-capacity accumulator for optimum protection. A single line is required to plumb it into the oiling system (either tee'd into the return line of an oil cooler or remote filter). An adapter mounts between the engine's spin-on oil filter and the engine or, in many cases, runs directly into a pressurized oil gallery port in the engine block.

Common Modifications

Engine builders have developed many tweaks and modifications over the years, some of them specific to the oiling system. Most involve increasing or decreasing oil flow to selected components as operating conditions warrant.

Restricting Flow

Among the more common modifications are efforts to restrict oil flow to components that don't necessarily require full-time oiling. The intent is to limit oil flow and lubrication in areas where it may increase parasitic drag or to minimize the amount of oil dripping on the crankshaft and rotating assembly. These may include

CHAPTER 12

An accumulator is a pressurized remote oil supply that provides temporary full-pressure oiling prior to engine startup or whenever a pump issue causes an interruption or complete failure of the oil supply.

roller rocker arms and other upper engine components that require only minimal lubrication. The reverse of this might include piston pin oilers designed to spray additional oil beneath the piston crown to lubricate the wrist pin and cool the piston crown.

Another example is a block equipped with roller cam bearings that obstruct the camshaft oiling holes and receive lubrication strictly by splash. In many cases the oiling supply to roller lifters and roller rockers is significantly reduced to minimize friction. When oil to the top end is reduced, there is less overall drainage through the crankcase, which helps to mitigate the effects of windage. Needle bearings and rollerized components help support these efforts when top-end oiling is restricted through the use of commercial restrictors in the oil galleries or special metered orifices installed to restrict oil flow. Priority main oiling, as found in modern race-bred blocks, supports this by directing oil to the mains first and then supplying other components as needed.

Non-race Chevy blocks typically use commercially available oil restrictors inserted in the back of each lifter gallery to limit upper engine oiling. The same effect can be accomplished by installing new metered jets in the gallery. These help support the reduction of parasitic drag including pumping effort required of the oil pump and subsequent loading against the distributor gear, which may have negative consequences for precision engine timing.

However, there are trade-offs. Too little oil upstairs may negatively affect valveguide and valvespring life and this must be weighed against the lifespan of these components versus the overall event duration of the specific racing application. It may not be of serious consequence in a drag race, but it may initiate unwanted problems in a durability application such as a 6- to 24-hour endurance race. In this case commercially available valve covers with integral spring oiler tubes usually solve the problem.

Directing Drain-Back

Efforts to isolate and limit lifter valley oil from draining onto the camshaft include installing tall standoff vent tubes in the valley drain holes and/or isolating the area completely by installing a sheet-metal block-off plate with epoxy. The idea is to force excess oil to drain at the front or rear of the block so its exposure to the crank throws is limited.

Some builders don't mind oil draining via the timing cover; others epoxy sheet-metal dams in the front drain holes to force all oil to the rear of the valley where it must drain on the rear main throw and distributor, or in the case of a dry sump, be evacuated at that point. The intent here is to isolate lubricant, not to prevent equalized pressure within the crankcase itself. While oil must be closely controlled, lifter valley pressure must remain equalized to prevent end gasket failure due to excessive crankcase pressure or vacuum (as the case may be).

Many specialized race blocks isolate the camshaft tunnel completely and provide separate internal drain paths leading directly to the sump area so none of this oil can affect the spinning crank.

Baffling the Crankcase

Builders often try to isolate the individual crankcase bays of paired cylinders to further reduce oil contamination. This is done in the form of baffles or dams that restrict oil motion without compromising bay-to-bay breathing where higher crankcase pressure might be created under select cylinders. The efforts most often accompany dry sump oiling systems where an individual scavenge port is assigned to each individual bay of the oil pan.

These efforts are often application specific and you must weigh the alternatives—both positive and negative—before finalizing specialized modifications that have the potential to dramatically aid crankcase breathing and oil control or just the opposite if proper care is not exercised.

CHAPTER 13

IGNITION SYSTEMS

As a rule, racing ignition systems aren't particularly complicated. All you need is a power source and a means of distributing a high voltage (spark) to each cylinder at the proper time. In reality, it is far more complex. Racing ignition requirements are complicated by numerous factors that require special consideration and specific hardware to ensure efficient and reliable performance. The wide range of possible operating conditions makes optimum ignition timing and delivery of adequate power to light the mixture vital parameters of overall engine efficiency, particularly when the system is challenged by high compression ratios, extreme engine speeds, and ever rising boost levels on supercharged systems.

Selecting an ignition system for a racing engine requires consideration of several important factors. Since timing is the basis of all engine functions it is critical that, above all else, the ignition system maintain rock-solid timing integrity.

The ignition system consists of the following components:

- Battery (power source)
- Ignition coil
- Ignition module
- Distributor
- Pickup
- Plug wires
- Spark plugs

Robust ignition systems are essential for engines to deliver maximum horsepower. Components include a precision calibrated distributor, top-quality wires, and spark plug boots all driven by a powerful coil and amplifier.

Each of these components require individual attention to ensure compatibility and successful operation. A full 12 volts of power is typically required for proper ignition operation. This makes the battery and its charging system vital contributors to successful ignition operation.

Modern racing ignition systems have largely moved to digital control to improve their accuracy and reliability. The triggering device may be located within the distributor itself or externally as in crank trigger ignition systems that rely on exact crankshaft position signal to trigger the spark in each cylinder.

Depending on the type of system, the triggering device may be a magnetic pickup, an optical trigger, or a Hall-effect transistor, which functions similarly to a magnetic pickup. Optical devices use an LED (light emitting diode) and a interrupter wheel to provide the trigger effect. The pickup sensor may be located within the distributor itself or externally as with a crank trigger system. Crank trigger systems are the most accurate because they eliminate timing inconsistencies caused by variables such as camshaft twist.

Digital controllers like MSD's Power Grid system provide full access to all ignition functions via dedicated computer software that runs on a laptop computer. The Power Grid controller uses camshaft synchronization to provide individual cylinder timing alterations to compensate for varying cylinder conditions caused by fuel ratio or runner length inconsistencies and other conditions that may affect individual cylinder timing requirements. It also provides tunable launch and shift retard functions, rev limiter control, individual timing curves for each gear, and ignition data acquisition for post run evaluation.

Ignition control has never been easier and you have seemingly endless choices, but basic engine building practices still apply. You must take great care to ensure that the distributor gear and the camshaft gear are materially compatible, properly meshed, and well lubricated. Race distributors are equipped with an adjustable collar that allows you to control the depth of the distributor in the engine. This prevents bottoming the distributor gear against the internal oil pump shaft or meshing the gears too tightly. The collar also permits compensation for variations in manifold mounting-flange height.

Ignition Choices

The development of both multi-firing and extended-spark ignitions added unique capabilities to high-performance ignition systems, particularly those that operate at engine speeds below 6,000 rpm. Instead of producing a single short spark for ignition these systems either produce multiple high-voltage sparks or one long-duration spark.

In multi-spark systems the number of sparks per ignition cycle at idle can be as many as six, when time between power strokes is the greatest. As engine speed increases, the number of sparks decreases to about two at high RPM. In extended-spark ignitions, a single, long-duration spark jumps the plug gap during the time a multiple-spark system would generate several sparks at the plug.

Potential horsepower increases from multiple-spark or long-duration systems depend on the flame propagation characteristics of the combustion chambers. Cylinder heads with

Digital ignition components like MSD's Digital 6AL and Power Grid system controller provide digital tuning convenience and full control of an engine's ignition requirements via computer software and a laptop interface.

This MSD race distributor accommodates individual cylinder timing adjustment by mechanical means. Note that each individual trigger can be adjusted by loosening the appropriate screw.

larger chamber volumes can benefit most from these ignitions, and although it's impossible to predict the benefits on any single engine, gains may vary from negligible to as much as 5 percent. Engines with small-volume chambers usually show little or no improvement from multi-firing ignitions. However, multiple-spark or long-duration ignitions almost universally help smooth out a rough idle and minimize plug fouling that can hurt engine performance during the first critical seconds after leaving the starting line.

The current trend to smaller, shallower combustion chambers has generally reduced timing requirements for many engines and perhaps lessened the need for multiple- or extended-spark systems except perhaps in lower-tier applications that operate in the 4,000- to 6,500-rpm range.

Magnets embedded 90 degrees apart in this MSD crank trigger wheel create an electrical current every time they pass by the pickup coil. This triggers the ignition module to discharge the coil at the appropriate time. Crank trigger systems provide exceptional timing accuracy because they read directly off the crankshaft.

The need for higher-energy systems with greater individual cylinder control has fostered a new age of precision ignition timing controllers that have revolutionized the precise control of racing ignition systems.

Other system designs found on racing engines include magnetos, crank-trigger systems, and more complex forms of MSD systems, including high-power multiple-coil ignitions with electronic advance curves, high-speed retards, and other exotica.

Magnetos have always been popular and reliable racing components. The faster they spin, the hotter the spark they produce. They are really a simple generator that operates without outside power. The instant a magneto begins to turn, it starts generating electrical power. If you have ever been the victim of the popular racer's prank of spinning a magneto while holding the lead you know how much kick they can produce. At low RPM they barely have the energy to fire the plugs, so they are usually reserved for high-RPM, race-only applications.

Many circle track venues limit ignition systems to stock-type systems that incorporate minimal changes like a cap and rotor and a high-energy coil as found in this HEI unit from Performance Distributors.

CHAPTER 13

The pickup coil is adjusted to within about .060 inch of the trigger wheel to provide a strong signal when the magnet passes by it. Ignition timing is set by loosening the pickup coil-mounting bolts and sliding the assembly up or down to achieve the desired timing.

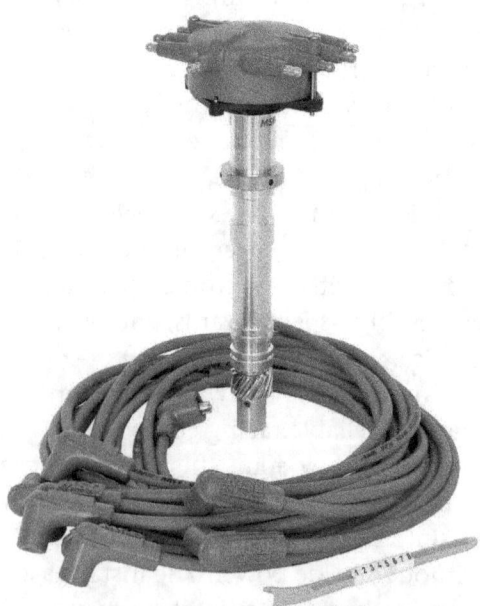

Space limitations caused by the use of tunnel ram intake manifolds often require the use of low-profile crab cap–style MSD distributors that fit within the tight space behind the rear intake runners. The crab caps have the added convenience of placing the correct terminals on each side of the engine for easy plug wire installation.

Spark Plugs

Spark plugs for an engine should have the proper heat range, and they must be gapped to match the ignition system's requirements. Greater secondary voltage often permits the use of a slightly colder plug. Dyno tests often indicate that plugs of one or two heat ranges colder than stock can produce an increase in power, although this may not occur in every case. In addition, a higher secondary voltage has more energy to jump across an air gap, so increasing spark plug gap by .010 to .020 inch may provide a fatter spark that more reliably ignites the air/fuel charge. This can be of particular help with lean mixtures or high compression ratios (but don't exceed .050-inch gap since secondary voltages may go high enough to damage ignition components, and electrical emissions also dramatically increase). More reliable ignition can, in turn, increase the speed of flame-front propagation, and this may require slightly less total ignition advance to re-establish optimum power. This can be beneficial in reducing negative work against the piston before TDC. If the ignition timing is not optimized when the flame propagation times are altered, the result can be a reduction in power. A small change is usually all that's needed, assuming the ignition advance was right-on prior to modifications.

Spark Plug Wires

Secondary wires used with modern electronic ignition systems must withstand higher voltage levels and prevent spillover into vehicle electronics, including engine-control computers. High-temperature silicone-jacketed wires are available for racing applications. MSD, Mallory, Moroso, and others make excellent 8-mm, heat-resistant cables that are substantially superior to the carbon-impregnated, string-core versions that are supplied as standard equipment by many auto manufacturers. Protection can be added to secondary wires by jacketing them in tubing made of glass cloth that is highly resistant to heat, the most common cause of premature wire failure. MSD offers glass-cloth tubing and a self-vulcanizing silicone rubber tape that can be wrapped around the wires to secure the cloth tubing or to add more heat protection at critical points, especially around header tubing. High engine compartment temperatures bond the tape permanently to the ignition wires, improving their insulation resistance to both heat and high voltage.

Larger-diameter distributor caps are generally preferred to help prevent spark scatter by placing the terminals farther apart. The low-profile crab-style cap is smaller in diameter, but made from the best materials so spark scatter is not an issue.

146 COMPETITION ENGINE BUILDING: ADVANCED ENGINE DESIGN & ASSEMBLY TECHNIQUES

IGNITION SYSTEMS

High-voltage coils are essential to provide reliable spark energy in a high-compression, high-RPM environment. Coils like this MSD HVC II unit produce in excess of 44,000 volts with great consistency.

Many speed shops sell a variety of great-looking colored plug wires. Some of these wires are much better suited to racing use than others. Carefully examine the core and the insulation before you buy. If they have a carbon-string core, either put them down or resign yourself to replacing them every year. Make sure the plug wires are insulated with temperature-resistant silicone rubber.

Keep in mind that wire manufacturers can claim they use silicone insulation as long as the jacket material is composed of only some silicone rubber. Cheaper wire sets do not withstand racing-level heat radiated from headers. The best include top-of-the-line wires from MSD, Mallory, Accel, Moroso, and others designed for serious racing applications.

Race Engine Ignition Tips

A racing ignition system should generate a rock-solid timing mark at all engine speeds. There should be no visible signs of widening, spreading, or jumping. Most of these problems can usually be traced to several mechanical and/or electronic sources, but the most common causes are a loose timing chain, worn distributor bushings, or a sticking mechanical advance. In addition, since the oil pump is driven off the bottom of the distributor, spark scatter can often be traced to pressure pulses generated by the oil pump, especially when high oil pressure is used. Also, big-block and small-block Chevy V-8 racing distributors incorporate a pair of rubber O-rings around the base of the distributor just above the distributor gear. These seal the oil passage around the distributor and prevent loss of pressure due to excessive leakage.

As a rule, use spark plugs with the coldest heat range that support complete combustion without fouling under race conditions. Pay particular attention to the routing of the spark plug wires. Make certain that the wires do not touch anything (such as a hot header), and that they are actually routed as far as possible from any heat source that could damage them.

Power time the engine at a speed above the point of any mechanical advance, or at least 2,500 rpm if the advance is fully locked out.

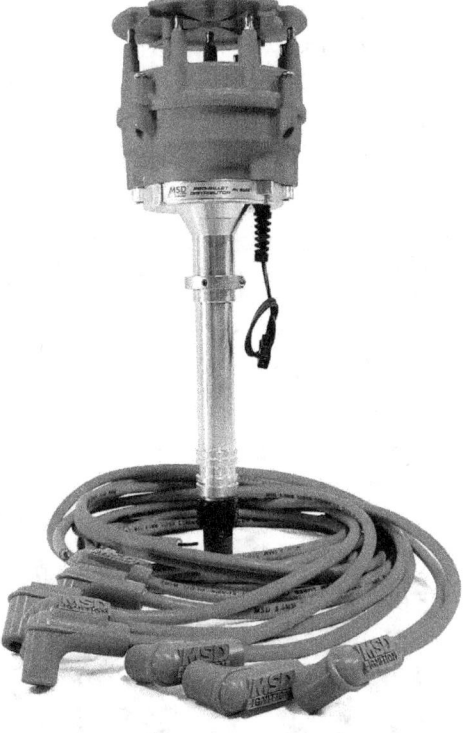

MSD's Pro Billet series racing distributors feature larger-diameter caps and adjustable collars to aid in setting up the correct distributor depth for proper oil pump driveshaft engagement.

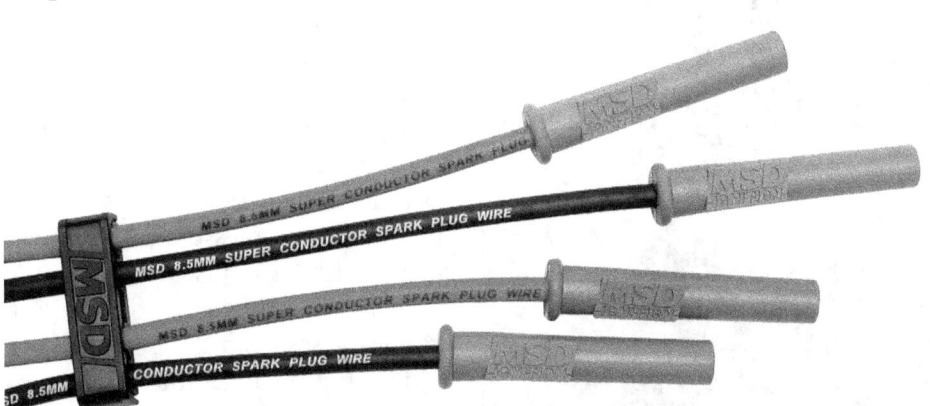

Race-quality plug wires are necessary for adequate spark energy to the plug. To ensure best results use 8-mm or larger high-quality wires as shown in this MSD selection. For added protection, cover the boots and wires with temperature-resistant sleeves.

COMPETITION ENGINE BUILDING: ADVANCED ENGINE DESIGN & ASSEMBLY TECHNIQUES

CHAPTER 14

Exhaust Systems

All top engine builders recognize that the exhaust system exerts tremendous influence on engine performance, particularly with regard to breathing efficiency and torque curve positioning within the required RPM range. Thoughtful exhaust tuning can often promote additional torque production and the enormously valuable ability to position that torque in the most favorable part of an engine's operating range based on the final application. Header primary tube cross-sectional area and length are the core contributors to this strategy and they must be sized accordingly to complement inlet tract dimensions, cam timing, and engine speed as they relate to the final application in terms of the overall powerband and the specific placement of torque and power within the vehicle's required operating range.

So how do you determine the correct header size for any given engine combination? Off-the-shelf headers are, at best, a compromise that can't possibly meet the broad application specific requirements of all the engines they support. Wave tuning theory has long been a popular method, and there are many good engine simulation software programs designed to help you pinpoint the ideal dimensions for your particular application.

In short, wave tuning seeks to take advantage of oscillating pressure pulses within the exhaust stream to aid cylinder scavenging. The goal is to time the waves or pulses so that a reflected low-pressure pulse arrives at the cylinder at just the right time to lend its energy to discharging exhaust gases from the cylinder. The critical timing is a function of primary tube length, and is affected by the point at which the pulse reaches atmospheric pressure at the end of the tube. It is most effective at one particular engine speed, and its value

Header configuration and dimensions significantly influence an engine's powerband. Accordingly it pays to construct the best header possible by precisely pre-modeling the layout and dimensions.

EXHAUST SYSTEMS

is well illustrated in top-level engine simulation packages such as Performance Trend's Engine Analyzer Pro, Motion Software's Dynomation 5, and the PipeMax program that calculates the optimum pipe dimensions based on the engine builder's specified parameters.

The quick and easy way to calculate the ideal primary header pipe diameter for effective performance is based on engine displacement, engine speed, and VE. Performance authority Jim McFarland provides a simple formula for calculating the optimum cross-sectional area (c/s) of a header primary tube or pipe. This method optimizes for the engine's torque peak, which is the point of maximum VE and thus the point of maximum generated exhaust volume. At engine speeds above the torque peak, cylinder filling decays proportionately with RPM (time) because there is progressively less time available to fill the cylinder on each intake event. There are more power strokes per minute, but proportionately less exhaust volume to evacuate due to declining VE with increased engine speed.

Optimizing for the torque peak provides the ideal primary pipe diameter and since peak power is usually no more than 1,500 to 1,750 rpm above the torque peak, the selected pipe size has no trouble accommodating an exhaust volume that essentially flat lines and begins to fade rapidly. The RPM spread between the torque peak and the power peak is largely influenced by the engine's rod to stroke (R/S) ratio. Shorter rods tend to broaden the separation between the torque peak and the power peak. Similarly, longer rods tends to move the peaks closer together. The previously stated range applies for most of the stroke lengths and rod lengths commonly used by performance enthusiasts.

A formula can be written two ways—one to solve for primary pipe cross-sectional (c/s) area when the torque peak RPM is known or anticipated, and the other to predict torque peak engine speed based on a primary pipe cross section that is under consideration.

To accommodate specific cylinder volumes, the formula considers a single cylinder only, so you have to divide your known or anticipated displacement by the number of cylinders to determine single-cylinder volume.

Cylinder Volume = displacement ÷ number of cylinders
c/s = (cylinder volume x RPM) ÷ 88,200
RPM = (c/s x 88,200) ÷ cylinder volume

Where:
c/s = primary pipe cross-sectional area
Cylinder volume = volume of a single cylinder
88,200 = mathematical constant
RPM = RPM at torque peak

Once the calculated c/s area is known, the corresponding primary pipe diameter to the nearest available pipe size can be calculated.

If area = diameter^2 x .7854, then pipe size equals the square root of the previously calculated c/s area times the reciprocal of the constant .7854.

Pipe Size = √[A x (1÷7854)]
Pipe Size = √(A x 1.273)

If you're solving for a torque peak RPM based on contemplated primary pipe size, calculate the c/s area by squaring the inside diameter (ID) of the pipe and multiplying by .7854. To determine the true inside

Exhaust primary tube cross section determines the torque peak RPM while length influences the shape of the torque curve. Glowing headers look cool in photos and may indicate very high power under heavy load, but in many cases it indicates retarded timing with fuel still burning in the pipes.

diameter of a pipe for the purpose of calculating c/s area, use the measured outside diameter (OD) minus twice the wall thickness of the pipe.

$$ID = OD - (2 \times \text{wall thickness})$$

For example, the ID of a pipe with a 1.75-inch OD and a wall thickness of .040 inch is calculated to be:

$$ID = 1.75 - (2 \times .040) = 1.67 \text{ inches}$$

For many applications header pipe size selection based on manipulating peak torque RPM outweighs the pursuit of absolute peak power. This often suggests erring on the small side of primary pipe selection to preserve velocity with the minimum c/s required to service maximum exhaust volume at peak torque, hence the formula for c/s area is based on engine speed, cylinder volume, and VE. Additionally, tuned induction systems generate their own torque curves that contribute independently and proportionately to an engine's "net" torque curve.

PipeMax Header Software

Meaux Racing Heads PipeMax program is a popular exhaust system dimension calculator. It is primarily a header design program, but it incorporates enough user data to also function as a partial engine simulation program. It also calculates torque and horsepower output based on VE and the recommended header specs. It provides a wealth of information about header dimensions and the proper design of headers to accommodate wave tuning.

You input all the usual engine information along with details about the cylinder heads and camshaft and it calculates the optimum primary pipe diameters, cross-sectional areas, primary tube lengths, and collector specifications for optimum performance. The results screen displays dimensions for a single primary pipe or a two- and three-step header designs. It provides recommended pipe diameters and lengths for the primary pipes and the collectors. It also displays the best and worst specifications (so you can avoid them). It calculates primary pipe harmonics for the first through eighth reflected wave and collector harmonics with mufflers and tailpipes.

All of these specs are delivered in standard (U.S.) and metric units automatically. The program is based on projected VE and consequent exhaust volume and it can estimate VE for your particular engine specs. It allows you to select a dyno acceleration rate for the simulation and you can specify the mean flow velocity to be used in cross-sectional area calculations.

It is inexpensive, very thorough, and makes a perfect complement to other simulators you might be using. It pinpoints ideal header dimensions for an engine and simplifies header design. It teaches you a lot about the effects of pressure wave activity in the engine's exhaust system.

Step Headers

The steps in a stepped header design tend to reduce flow resistance along the specific length of the pipe, but they must be strategically placed to take maximum advantage of pulse reflections and minimize velocity loss within the pipe. Considerably more effort is currently being directed at understanding the dynamics of stepped header performance and how it applies to specific applications. Each step presents an area change that reflects a smaller-magnitude, negative pressure pulse back toward the valve while diminishing the intensity of the positive pulse that continues down the pipe toward the next step or the collector.

Steps also function the opposite way, returning both positive and negative waves down the pipe. This disrupts their strength, speed, and overall effect. They are commonly thought to constitute functional reversion dams on milder applications with a broader RPM range and are generally considered unnecessary on higher-powered applications with narrow powerbands.

Larger steps intended to reduce flow restriction are typically more effective when employed on a 4-into-1 system than on a 4-into-2-into-1 arrangement. In effect, however, it is relatively easy to get lost in the dimensional mathematics of pulse tuning so it is often more beneficial to size the cross section to adequately service maximum exhaust volume based on actual VE at the torque peak RPM. Hence, the growing popularity of merge collectors, which provide a restriction or choke to attenuate the pulses and minimize their effect in favor of dimensionally correct collectors that optimize the effectiveness of properly sized primary pipes.

The merge collector works by maintaining maximum system velocity until the exhaust encounters atmospheric pressure. Maintaining exhaust velocity and pulse strength in the pipe is often more beneficial than using steps to reduce flow restriction. Larger steps tend to require longer primaries to compensate for velocity loss regardless of powerband width.

EXHAUST SYSTEMS

The position of the first step provides an area increase that generates the first reflected pulse and influences how quickly the pulse arrives at the valve—the closer the step, the lower the mean velocity in the pipe.

Exhaust gas temperature also influences pulse timing. Higher EGTs (within reason) increase the speed of the pulse and improve scavenging if the pulse can be properly timed. This is relatively critical to calculate and I believe that optimizing the cross-sectional area with a single-dimension (no step) pipe length that tunes to the second or third reflected pulse adequately services 90 percent of most racing applications.

A cross section that satisfies the discharge requirement of the engine's exhaust volume at peak VE provides an ideal header dimension to position the torque peak for maximum effect. Beyond that, primary pipe length can be adjusted accordingly to provide a torque boost above or below the peak as required by the specific application.

When multiple steps are positioned at various lengths along the primary pipe the area increase at each step creates another reflection point. There are typically only one or two steps in most stepped header designs. Each reflection point along the pipe delivers progressively weaker pulses returning to the valve. The closer the first step is to the valve the sooner it returns a pulse, which is typically the highest-intensity pulse with the greatest scavenging effect. Pulse strength diminishes accordingly at each successive step, making it critical to properly locate the first step to take maximum advantage of its strength. Where there is only one step, the step is typically positioned approximately halfway along the total length of the pipe.

On two-step systems, the pipe lengths after the first step usually split the difference of the remaining length. So you might have an initial step at something like 11 to 12 inches and two secondary steps approximately 6 inches long. One reason for this is to reflect more pulses sooner because it takes progressively longer for each pulse to reach the valve, primarily because they are weakened when they encounter the first step. Hence, multiple pulses are continuously reflected up and down the pipe at supersonic speed that varies according to specific exhaust gas temperature.

You can do more harm than good here if you're not careful. That's why I recommend a properly sized (cross-section) non-stepped pipe for most applications. If you run a stepped header, consult PipeMax to calculate the optimum step lengths.

Another thing to consider is the initial cross section of the pipe relative to the size of the exhaust port. If the cross section of the pipe is considerably larger than the port, it tends

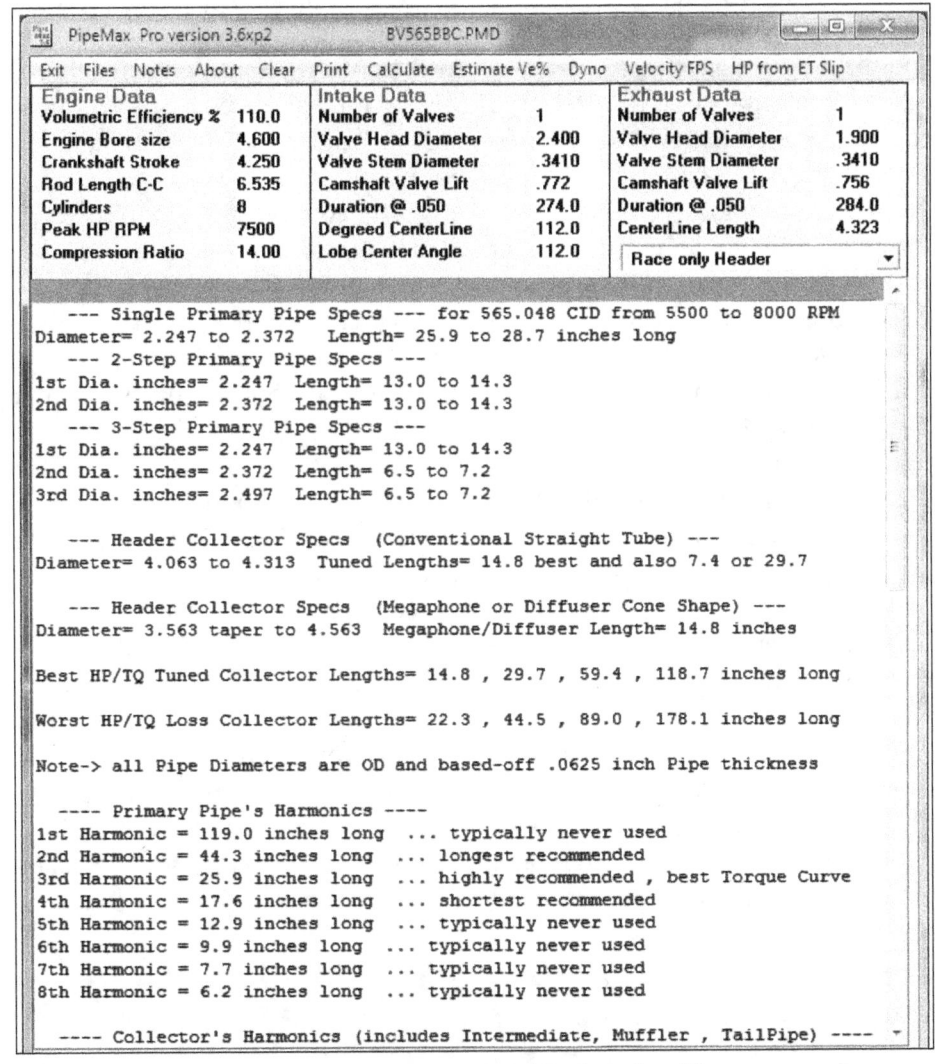

Note PipeMax calculations for our sample 565-ci engine. The program is recommending a 2.25-inch-diameter primary tube 25.9 to 28.7 inches long. The recommended choice for best torque is 25.9 inches.

to function as a very short first step, or what is commonly thought of as a reversion dam. The large area change reduces flow velocity, particularly if it departs too far from the mathematically correct cross section required to process the engine's exhaust volume at maximum VE.

Many applications, particularly those with broader powerbands, are better served by closely matching pipe size to port size to preserve flow energy at lower engine speeds. This often requires altering the cam specs to deal with any reversion tendencies. Wave tuning software such as Dynomation 5 graphically predicts reversion problems if provided with very precise camshaft data. You can use this to successfully choose alternate cam timing that helps reduce or eliminate reversion.

Header Design Kit

Once the importance of constructing exhaust headers with dimensions specifically targeted to improve and position torque is recognized, you must construct dimensionally correct headers that actually fit the chassis. To help accomplish this, icengineworks offers a header design and modeling kit to help build headers to fit any particular chassis requirement. These clever kits are like nothing you've seen before. They provide a complete set of ABS plastic modeling blocks shaped exactly like header tubing of the appropriate size. Each block is exactly 1 inch long and they come in straight and curved versions that provide 2-, 3-, 4-, and 6-inch-radius bends at the centerline. You snap these blocks together in any desired combination and rotate the curved pieces to achieve the required configuration and radius.

The kits allow you to piece together a full-scale model header that exactly fits your engine and chassis combination. Each individual piece is clearly marked with multiple indexing arrows and witness marks so you can easily duplicate the sections in metal tubing using lengths of straight, J-bend, or U-bend tubing.

The witness marks are spaced 30 degrees apart providing exact positioning references for transferring the design to metal. The Pro Kit version includes block adapters, which lock the blocks in expandable starter tubes so the initial blocks do not move during the process. The beauty of this system is that it allows you infinite freedom to rotate, extend, or shorten any segment into the desired shape and length you need. This makes it particularly easy to model your way around various chassis obstructions and still achieve an equal-length header or a multiple-length header with perfectly aligned joints and bends.

The company also offers construction aids in the form of a special pivot table for making precise tubing cuts, starter block accessories, and special tack welding clamps that facilitate precise joints for final welding.

You can purchase a kit for just one side or both sides of a V-8 engine. Once you have created a perfect model header and transferred it to metal, you can disassemble the model and store the kit until the next header project comes along. The math involved is easy and straightforward, consisting primarily of counting the segments and noting the appropriate lengths and radii. It can turn an amateur into a first-class header designer almost overnight.

TECH TIP

Header Selection Criteria

- Calculated Torque Peak
- Calculated Header Size
- Powerband RPM Range
- Primary Cross Section
- Primary Length
- Primary Wall Thickness
- Port Exit Dimensions
- Engine Displacement
- Collector Diameter
- Collector Length
- Collector Type
- Valve Overlap
- Cam Timing Events
- Exhaust System Specs
- Thermal Coatings
- Header Material
- Ground Clearance
- Minimum Pipe Radius

CHAPTER 15

ENGINE BUILD TIPS

The engine assembly stage typically includes multiple mock-ups or pre-assembly stages where the fit and compatibility of all internal components is checked and verified. Care must be taken to prevent component damage during mock-up, fitment, and final assembly. Prior to final assembly, perform a thorough cleaning and layout of all engine components to eliminate the possibility of dirt contamination and to ensure that all components are present, spotlessly clean, and ready for assembly. To prevent mistakes due to distraction it is also important to have on hand and lay out all of the necessary assembly lubricants and sealers and the various tools required to properly assemble an engine. The following are typically required for most engines.

- Torque Wrench
- Ring Compressor
- Dial Indicator
- Dampener Installation Tool
- Rod Bolt Stretch Gauge
- Cam Installation Tool
- Engine Assembly Oil
- Engine Oil
- ARP Ultra-Torque Lube
- Anti-Seize Compound
- Loctite Thread Sealant
- Loctite Threadlocker
- RTV Silicone
- Carb Cleaner
- Brake Cleaner
- Thread Tapping Lube
- ARP Thread Sealer
- Non-lint Paper Towels
- Magnifying Glass
- Engine Stand

Engine building requires attention to small details such as installing pin oiling jets in the main bore saddles prior to assembly. These preliminary preparation steps are often essential for maximum power and durability.

CHAPTER 15

Proper engine assembly tools help maintain focus while building a racing engine. For this build we're using a selection of engine building tools from ARP, Comp Cams, Proform, Snap-on, and Summit Racing. They include a set of micrometers, a cam installation tool, universal cam checking tool, digital scale, rod balancing tool, valvespring-height mic, digital calipers, electric piston ring filer, and deck bridge.

Dart's Big M Sportsman block features siamesed 4.600-inch bores and 9.800-inch deck height with ductile iron four-bolt main caps, priority main oiling, minimum .300-inch wall thickness, and clearance for up to a 4.500-inch stroke.

Assembly Procedure

Our sample engine build is a 565-ci big-block Chevy based around a Dart Big M cylinder block and Dart Big Chief Pro 1 aluminum cylinder heads. Following the step-by-step procedures is designed to simplify the mating of all the important components.

Oil Gallery Plugs

After thoroughly cleaning the cylinder block and all of the individual engine parts you are ready to begin the final stage of engine assembly.

Begin by installing the oil gallery plugs. Every engine is different, so be sure to identify the correct plugs for your particular engine.

Apply a small amount of ARP Thread Sealer to each plug and install it snugly with a hex key wrench.

At this time you may also want to install the core plugs in the cylinder block. Apply sealer lightly to each core plug and drive into the appropriate openings.

A rotating adjustable engine stand with 360-degree cranking head plate from Summit Racing makes it easy to adjust a block to any desired position without requiring the usual large pry bar to rotate the engine.

ENGINE BUILD TIPS

The initial step in block preparation includes chasing all threaded holes with thread-chasing taps from ARP. This is particularly important to ensure proper seating of main cap and cylinder head studs.

Check the depth of all head bolt holes to ensure adequate depth when head bolts are being used. Too little clearance can prevent proper clamping and initiate a blown head gasket.

Cam Bearings

Carefully install the camshaft bearings. Our sample big-block Chevy is fitted with Comp Cam's Composite Coated cam bearings. To help start the cam bearings, the cam housing bores were pre-chamfered with a 2½-inch ball hone attached to a drill motor. Carefully align them and drive them in place.

Main Cap Studs

You can upgrade to ARP main cap studs for added crankshaft stability. To maintain proper fitment Dart recommends that the main caps and block mating surface be lightly deburred upon removal to ensure that the correct main size is maintained.

To check the work, run a straight-edge through the housing bores and check all of them with a dial bore gauge prior to removal. These measurements are then compared to new ones taken after the main studs were installed and torqued. The goal is to maintain the proper housing bore measurement and the existing housing bore alignment. In our case, Dart's precise main cap fit allowed us to make the swap with no misalignment.

Main Bearings

Install the grooved upper main bearing shells into the block and verify alignment of the bearing insert oiling hole with the priority main oiling hole in each main web housing bore. Some builders grind the opening to match the bearing insert if the hole is partially blocked by the bearing being misaligned.

On our build the bearing feed hole did not exactly match the opening in the block, but once the feeder grooves were cut for the pin oiler inserts, it all matched up correctly.

COMPETITION ENGINE BUILDING: ADVANCED ENGINE DESIGN & ASSEMBLY TECHNIQUES

CHAPTER 15

Some builders are careful to countersink the head-bolt holes after decking and surfacing to prevent misalignment and/or cracking.

Carefully deburr the bottom of the cylinders after honing to remove sharp edges.

ARP instructs that main studs and the corresponding threaded holes in the cylinder block be thoroughly cleaned. Then install the main studs finger tight. Do not overtighten them. If the studs do not fit properly, chase the threads with an ARP thread-chasing tap.

The upper main bearing is always grooved. Inspect the back of the bearing for dirt or damage, then install it in the housing bore, pressing it down firmly by the parting lines. Install the ungrooved mate in the main bearing cap.

Install the lower half-shells (ungrooved) in the appropriate main caps.

During initial engine mock-up, the proper clearances were determined, and a combination of standard and 1-under Calico coated main bearings were used to achieve .003-inch clearance. Although we are using Calico coated engine bearings for added protection, high-pressure assembly lube on the bearings for the crank installation is still used.

Once the bearing's shells are properly seated in the housing bores, apply lubricant and set the crankshaft in place. Rig a dial indicator to read off the front of the crank snout or from one of the crank throws and check the crankshaft thrust clearance.

Crankshaft

After numerous mock-ups with setup bearings, the crank is usually contaminated. Clean it using small Moroso cleaning brushes available from Summit Racing. Brush all of the oil passages thoroughly. A common trick is to stand the crank upright in a rack and spray it down thoroughly with brake cleaner. It leaves no residue and the journals can then be wiped carefully with soft, shop (blue) paper towels that don't shed.

When you are satisfied that the crank is clean, install the rear main seal. If you have a two-piece seal, clock one half of it in the block so that one side protrudes by about 3/16 inch.

Lubricate the upper main bearings and carefully lower the crank in place.

Clock the other half of the rear main seal in the opposite direction in the rear main cap, apply a thin bead of sealer to the parting faces, and carefully work the seals together as you install the cap.

ENGINE BUILD TIPS

A convenient place to check the crankshaft thrust is off the rear main crank throw adjacent to the thrust bearing. Rig a dial indicator horizontally and zero it at the top. Then use a pry bar to move the crank forward and backward to check the thrust. This crank checked at .0075 inch.

Even lightweight big-block cranks like this Scat Pro Comp unit are heavy and difficult to handle. To minimize the chances of damage, have an assistant help lift the crank and lower it carefully into the main bearings.

Apply assembly lube to the lower rear main bearing and install the rear main cap. Torque to recommended specs and turn the crank to ensure that it spins freely.

Install the lower main bearings in each of the other main caps using assembly lube for lubrication.

Torque all studs to spec and check the crank for freedom of movement.

Camshaft

Lube the cam bearings and carefully slide the camshaft into the cylinder block taking great care not to scratch the cam bearings or nick the lobes on the block. For best results use a camshaft installation tool like those sold by ProForm. These tools bolt to the front of the cam and provide a cushioned handle that offers additional leverage so you can guide the cam easily into the block.

Break-in motor oil is used for a lubricant because this particular engine has a roller camshaft. Flat-tappet camshafts normally require the application of a special camshaft break-in lubricant to the lifters and cam lobes to protect them upon initial engine startup.

Many builders wait until the very end to install the rear cam plug, but it is better to install it early on to prevent accidental contamination via the exposed rear cam journal. Most engine stands permit this.

Cam Drive

Belt drives are the preferred cam drive device for most racing applications. They deliver rock-solid timing and are very durable. Care must be taken to provide proper camshaft thrust clearance and proper belt alignment by making sure that the crank drive pulley is fully seated against the shoulder on the crank snout. The lower pulley incorporates drive guards to prevent belt walk.

The reciprocating portion of our power system is a formidable combination that includes Ross Pro Mod Nitrous pistons with high-strength pins and pin buttons, scat H-beam connecting rods, Calico coated rod bearings, and Speed Pro HellFire piston rings.

A ProForm cam installation tool provides a sturdy grip and the necessary leverage to carefully guide the cam into the bearings without damaging them.

COMPETITION ENGINE BUILDING: ADVANCED ENGINE DESIGN & ASSEMBLY TECHNIQUES

CHAPTER 15

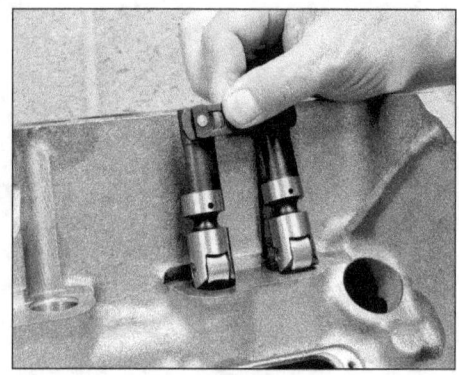

The Dart block requires .300-inch-taller lifters. Note that the lifter tie bar installs to the inboard side toward the valley.

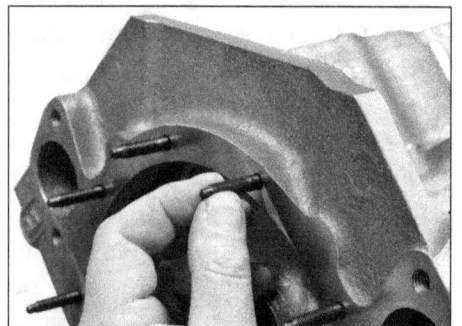

ARP makes a stud kit for Jesel-equipped Chevy belt drives. It works just fime with Comp belt drives too.

Big-block Chevy drive uses an idler pulley to maintain tension and promote stable timing. When the upper pulley (red) lock nuts are loosened the cam remains stationary while the crank position is altered as required.

Cam thrust on the Comp Cams belt drive is adjusted via three inclined ramps with corresponding ramps on the cover plate. As the plate rotates, cam thrust is increased or decreased depending on the rate of ramp incline.

When the desired amount of cam thrust is set, an indicator mark is placed at the top and the three button-head screws lock the cover in place. Multiple holes allow for an infinite range of cam thrust adjustment.

Adjustable pointers like this Moroso unit can place the timing indicator in the exact proper position for accurate timing adjustments.

Check out ProForm's timing pointer with built-in timing light.

ENGINE BUILD TIPS

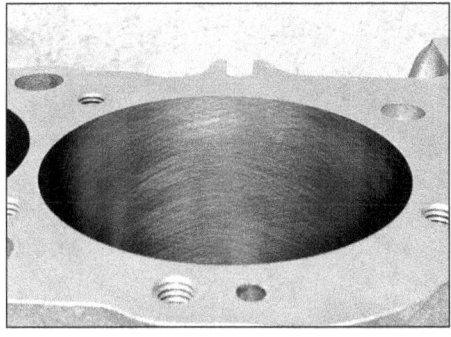

The cylinder bores are finished to .008-inch piston-to-wall clearance with 200-grit, then 280-grit, and finally 400-grit.

A ProForm digital scale is essential for accurately weighing pistons, pins, piston rings, rods, bearings, and other components for balancing.

ProForm's connecting rod balancing jig uses the ProForm digital scale to accurately obtain rod balancing weights.

A Summit Racing tapered ring compressor allows easy ring installation.

The sliding ring support platform has an adjustable cam and a locking device to help position the ring end face perfectly parallel to the grinding wheel surface.

Precise piston ring gapping is easily obtained with a ProForm electric ring filing tool. Piston rings are clamped in place on the sliding ring platform and the handle is used to guide the ring end against the grinding surface. A dial indicator shows the amount of material being removed.

CHAPTER 15

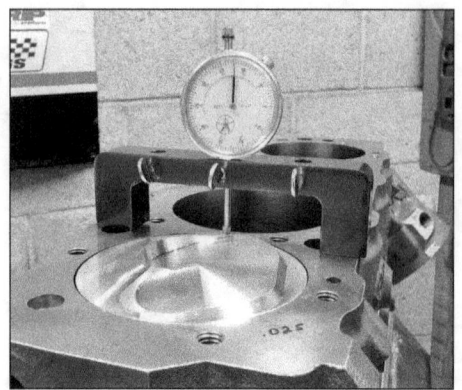

A ProForm deck bridge makes quick work of checking piston deck height.

Rod side clearance on our sample big-block was measured at .021 inch.

When properly aligned, the belt runs true with minimum drag.

Cam timing adjustments are performed by loosening the six bolts on the upper pulley and using a locking lever to hold the cam still while the crankshaft is rotated. This rotates the upper pulley in relation to the camshaft, altering their relative position and thus the actual camshaft timing. Only very minute movement of the crank is required to effect a 2-degree advance or retard of the camshaft. The drive permits up to 10 degrees of advance or retard, but if it takes more

The ARP rod bolt stretch gauge indicates .0065-inch stretch as recommended by ARP.

than 4 degrees, you probably have the wrong cam.

Pistons and Rings

File fit rings are always used on racing engines. They permit the most precise ring end gaps for maximum sealing. An electric ring filing tool such as that made by ProForm is recommended. The tool allows you to lock the ring in position so the end face is square to the grinding surface. Then the sliding mount platform allows you to move the ring against the grinding wheel while a dial indicator shows the amount of material you have removed.

Square each ring in its respective bore and then use the ring grinding tool to achieve the correct end gap. Once the rings are properly gapped, assemble them onto each piston carefully. Most builders gently twist them on by hand.

In our sample big-block, the Ross pistons use pin buttons to hold the piston pins in the pin bore. Once the piston is installed, the buttons are captured in the bore, providing the proper end clearance as preset during engine mock-up. In this type of assembly the pin buttons are added last, just before the assembly is inserted in the cylinder bore.

We used a Summit Racing tapered ring compressor to compress the ring pack to the proper diameter to slide into the bore. With the crank properly positioned, the assembly is easily pressed down in the bore until the rod bearing insert is guided carefully onto the rod journal.

As each piston is installed, lubricate the rod journal and install the rod cap with the appropriate bolts. Some builders torque each pair of rod bolts as the pistons are installed. Others pull them up snug and then set the proper bolt stretch on each individual bolt. Use an ARP rod bolt stretch gauge to measure the bolt stretch.

Measure the static length of each rod bolt and then slowly tighten each bolt until the recommended stretch is obtained. In this case we strived for .0065 inch using ARP Ultra Torque lubricant on the threads and mating surfaces.

Oil Pump and Drive

Many builders install the oil pump, drive, and oil pan at this point, but this may not be the best practice since it is still possible that some small component might be accidentally dropped down the distributor hole or the camshaft gallery. This requires removing the pan to retrieve it. On our example a block-off plate on the rear main cap oil pump mount was installed since a dry sump system is being used. Then the oil pan was installed and the appropriate precautions on the top of the short block were taken to prevent accidental transfer of small parts to the pan. A cork in the distributor hole and tape over the cam and lifter gallery did the trick.

ENGINE BUILD TIPS

Small-diameter (6¼ inch) BHJ dampener for internally balanced applications features internal elastomer construction for optimum damping properties. The dampener must be honed for a .0015- to .0020-inch fit.

The Moroso dry sump pump and drive mandrel must accommodate the dampener, crank trigger, and a Weiand Action Plus water pump. Front block plates add dimensional complication to the setup. Drive belt must run straight and true via guides on the drive mandrel.

Since the dry sump pump and attending drive hardware require considerable setup, the short block was finished and then we concentrated on fitting and plumbing the dry sump system with appropriate consideration for the chassis fitment requirements. This engine uses a Jegs front motor plate for chassis placement, so mounting the dry sump pump was problematic until the appropriate opening in the plate was measured and cut to provide full movement of the pump assembly and attending hardware.

This installation requires that the crankshaft dampener be fully seated on the nose of the crank so that the crank trigger wheel and the drive mandrel assembly can be properly fitted. Consideration must also be given to fitting the Weiand Action Plus mechanical water pump and drive pulley assembly.

Our Moroso drive mandrel incorporates multiple spacers to properly position the various drive pulleys.

Instead of installing an oil block-off plate on the rear main cap for dry sump systems, some builders tap and plug the oil feed gallery in the block.

Plumbing your dry sump and fuel systems is easy to accomplish with high-quality stainless braided hose, nickel plated fittings, and AN wrenches from Jegs Performance Products.

COMPETITION ENGINE BUILDING: ADVANCED ENGINE DESIGN & ASSEMBLY TECHNIQUES

Once the drive assembly was properly fitted, attention was turned to plumbing the lower portion of the dry sump system. A selection of nickel plated hose fittings and braided steel hose were used, direct from the Jegs Performance catalog.

Assembling these components is as easy as cutting the appropriate hose lengths and installing the ends using a Koul Tools assembly kit from Jegs. Braided hose assembly is typically complicated by the difficulty of inserting the rough cut hose into the hose fitting. The Koul Tools assembly guides have a tapered cone that squeezes the hose end to a smaller diameter so it inserts easily. It all happens inside the tool so that any frayed bits of hose cannot cut your fingers, or try your patience.

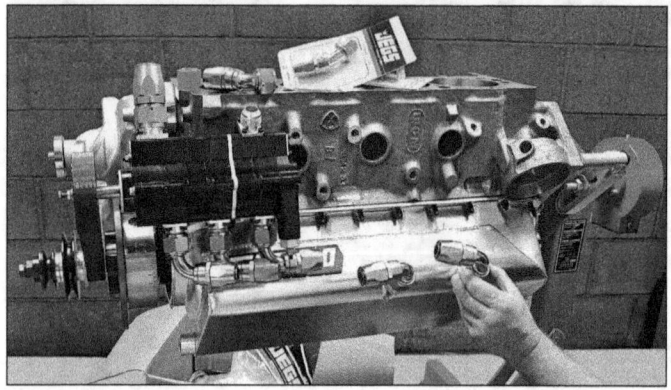

With Moroso pump and dry sump pan installed setup plumbing begins with trial fitment of nickel plated AN fittings and braided hose from Jegs Performance. A combination of 45-, 90-, and 120-degree fittings normally accommodate most chassis fitment requirements.

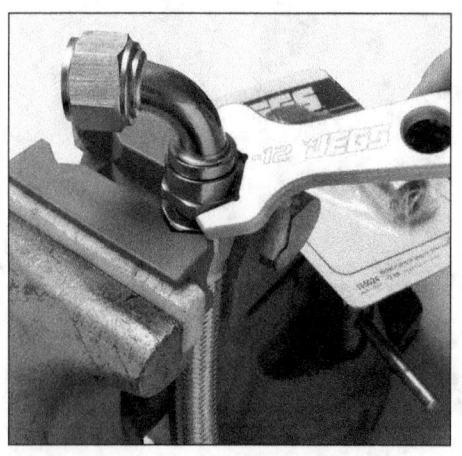

Nickel-plated hose fittings from Jegs provide superior protection against galling. After lubing the inner hose and applying anti-seize to the threaded fitting, place the fitting in a set of Jegs protective vise guides and tighten the fitting with the appropriate-size Jegs AN wrench as shown.

With the Jegs motor plate installed, mock-up essential plumbing like this CV Products remote oil filter mount with a Wix race filter.

Koul Tools braided hose assembly kits from Jegs Performance incorporate assembly guides for all popular hose sizes. With hose fittings placed inside the split assembly guide the tapered cone reducer guides the hose into the fitting without interference or personal injury from frayed braided hose ends.

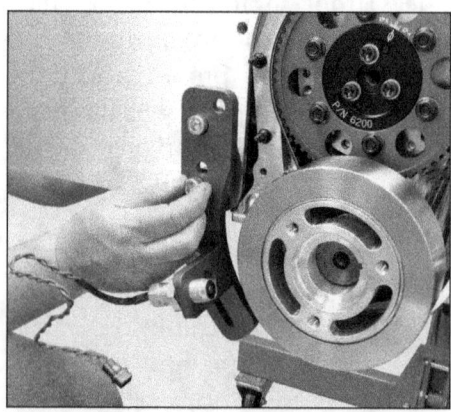

Moroso's dry sump tank is positioned to accommodate hood clearance and still provide gravity feed to the Moroso dry sump pump.

Motor plates also require precise fitment of the crank trigger ignition pickup. Spacers are used to position the pickup mount. The pickup flange incorporates two mounting positions to make precise alignment easier with a wide variety of setup requirements.

ENGINE BUILD TIPS

Dart recommends machining a .150- by .350-inch bullet to center each head stud.

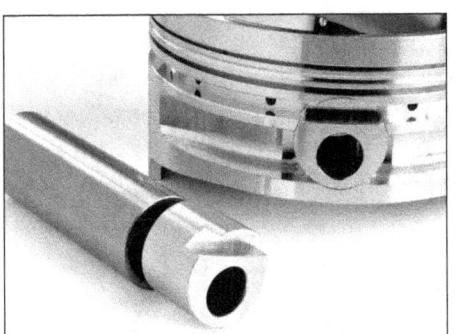

Ross Pro Mod nitrous pistons use inboard bosses with shorter, lighter pins and pin bushings with oil ring grooves to locate the pins and support the oil ring where the pin bore extends into the oil ring groove.

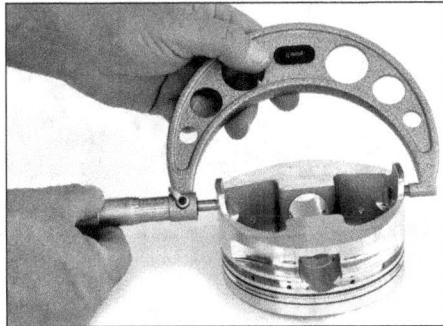

Measure the skirt diameter on Ross Racing pistons with a ProForm 4.00- to 5.00-inch micrometer. Ross and other manufacturers specify the exact location where the piston diameter should be checked.

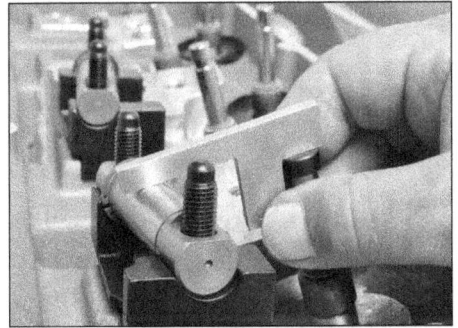

T&D precision rocker arm installation begins with the rocker setup tool. Shims are adjusted under each rocker stand until one end of the gauge fits squarely on top of the lash cap when the other end just touches the bare setup shaft setting in the rocker-stand cradle.

When T&D rockers are properly installed this proper geometry is achieved. Include the lash cap if using titanium valves. Roller is positioned slightly inboard of the valve centerline to provide proper motion. Note the adjustment shims underneath the rocker stand.

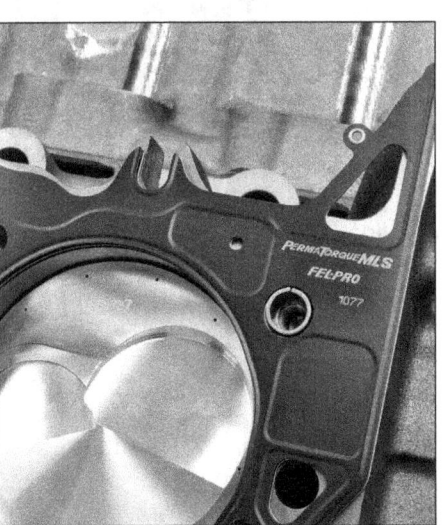

Fel-Pro's #1077 MLS head gasket features .041-inch compressed thickness. Note precise fit to cylinder bore.

The MLS (multi-layered steel) head gasket incorporates embossed layers with flat inner layers to provide the seal.

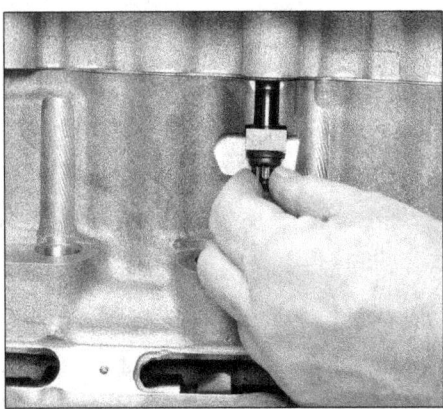

The Dart Big M block and Big Chief head employs two inner head studs per side to ensure even clamping force.

COMPETITION ENGINE BUILDING: ADVANCED ENGINE DESIGN & ASSEMBLY TECHNIQUES

CHAPTER 15

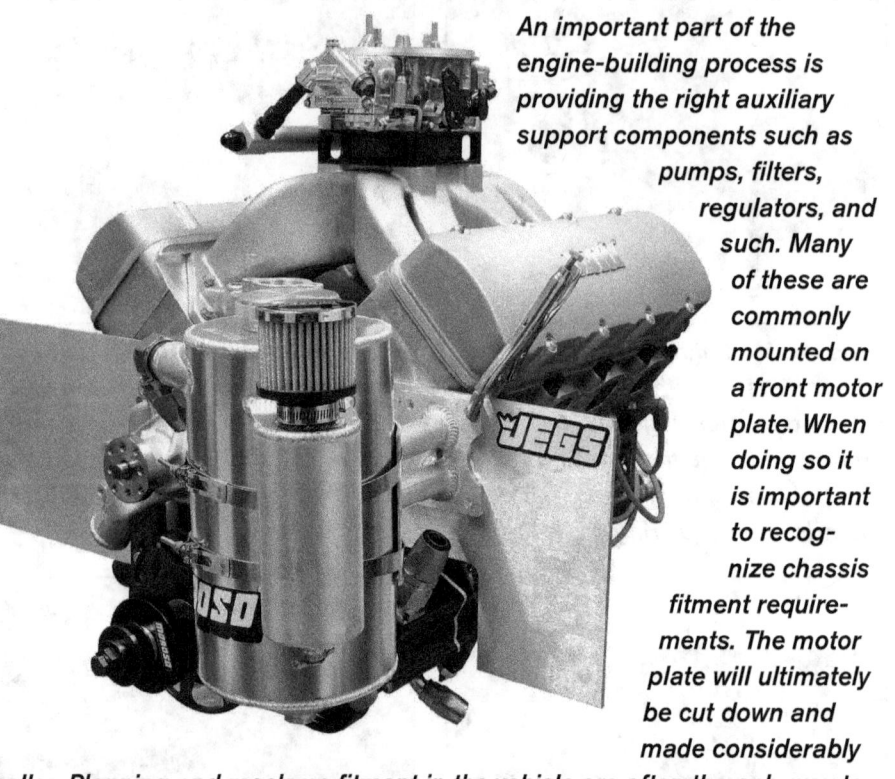

An important part of the engine-building process is providing the right auxiliary support components such as pumps, filters, regulators, and such. Many of these are commonly mounted on a front motor plate. When doing so it is important to recognize chassis fitment requirements. The motor plate will ultimately be cut down and made considerably smaller. Planning and mock-up fitment in the vehicle are often the only way to ensure the final compatibility of all the necessary components.

Cylinder Heads

Dart 18-degree Big Chief heads (PN 18475136) with titanium valves were tapped for this build. These heads feature 2.400-inch intake valves and 1.900-inch exhaust valves with CNC'd chambers and bowls and basic Sportsman porting at the port entry (see Chapter 8). Cylinder head preparation requires considerable setup work to set all the spring heights and pressures and rocker arm geometry.

Top-notch valve gear in the form of T&D Machine shaft rockers (PN 3036) was used here. T&D rockers provide rock-steady valve motion when set up according to recommended specs. Each rocker sets on an individual rocker stand that is adjusted via shims under the stand. A setup gauge is provided to ensure the correct geometry. The gauge must sit squarely on top of the valvestem while just touching the top of a setup shaft installed in the rocker stand. Each stand requires its own shim pack to achieve optimum geometry.

The more time and care you devote to getting this right, the more stable the valvetrain will be. You have to get the setup correct before you can determine the optimum pushrod length. You can establish all of this during mock-up assembly so that final assembly only requires checking for proper fit and clearances.

We used ARP cylinder head studs and Dart's auxiliary inside head stud kit to secure the heads with Fel-Pro .041-inch MLS head gaskets. Dart recommends that head studs be further machined with a bullet of .350-inch

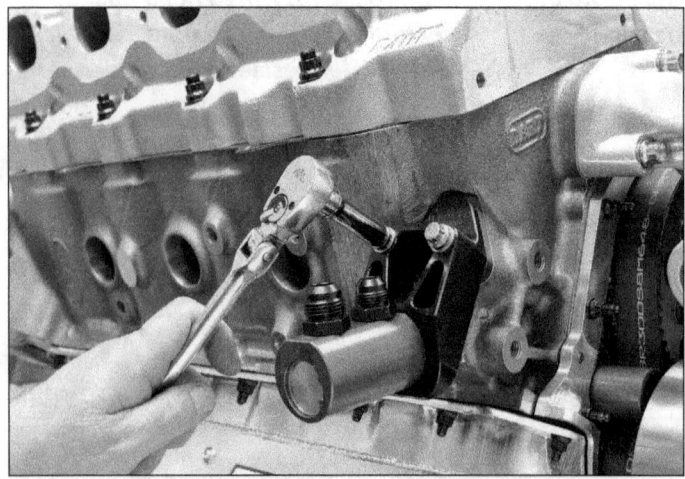

The Race Pumps fuel pump mounts behind the motor plate, hence the regulator mounts on the back of the plate with appropriate plumbing to the distribution block on the front of the plate.

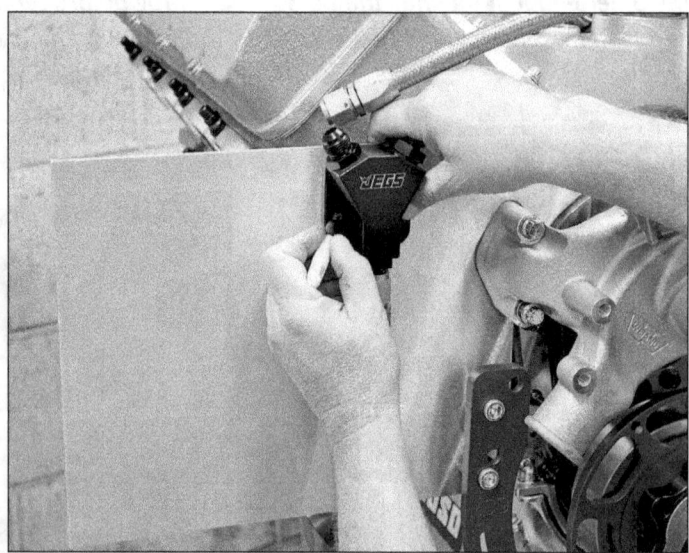

Jegs Performance fuel distribution block is mounted on the front next to the Weiand water pump.

diameter and .150 inch tall on the block end to help center the stud in the hole. This provides more stable stud seating and makes it easier to install the heads because they are all perfectly aligned to the head. ARP Ultra-Torque lubricant was used on the nuts and washers to ensure proper torque and the desired clamping force.

Cam and Valves

This is a straightforward operation that all engine builders are familiar with. Installation began with the cam straight up according to the specs on the Comp cam card as shown in Chapter 11. The exhaust opening/intake closing method was used to establish the clearance for initial startup. The important thing here is the initial lubrication of the lifters, pushrods, and rocker arms. Make certain all components are well lubricated prior to starting the engine.

Intake Manifold

The intake manifold is a Dart single 4-barrel (PN 43124000) spread-port design to match the spread-port cylinder heads. In addition to the proper port alignment established during mockup, you must ensure that the end rails do not contact the top of the block and prevent it from seating properly on the cylinder heads. Never use the end rail gaskets. Use a bead of silicone sealer after trial fitting the manifold to ensure proper contact. Unless you are absolutely certain the water passages do not leak, a thin bead of silicone around them helps ensure the integrity of the seal. Many manifolds are capable of warping during installation. Applying proper torque to the intake manifold bolts helps ensure even gasket compression and proper sealing.

Carburetor

The carburetor is a Holley Ultra HP 1150 CFM Dominator (PN 0-7320-2RD), installed on top of a Wilson Manifolds 1½-inch spacer using ARP carb studs. Fuel feed is accomplished via a Race Pumps fuel pump (PN 1600) and regulator (PN 5014), a System 1 fuel filter (PN SOF-202-201408), and a Jegs fuel distribution block mounted on the motor plate. A Jegs Performance adjustable aluminum fuel log made specifically for Holley Dominators was installed at the carburetor.

Valve Covers

Dart valve covers were installed with no modifications and no breathers since a dry sump system is being used. ARP makes a valve cover stud kit specifically for this application, and a Fel-Pro 1664-1 valve cover gaskets was used for a secure seal.

Accessories

We also installed the MSD crank trigger assembly (PN 8620) along with a MSD Digital 6AL ignition control (PN 6425) and Power Grid controller (PN 7730). The distributor is a crab cap-style MSD race unit (PN 8486, see Chapter 13) connected to an HVC II coil and MSD race wire set (PN 31239).

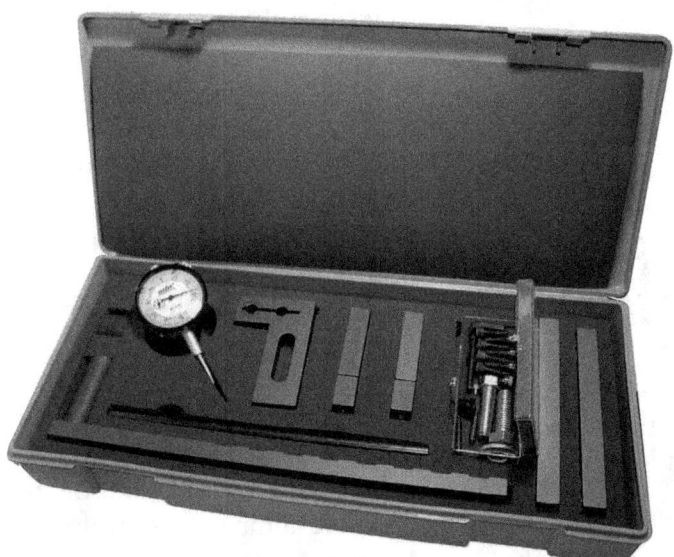

T&D Machine Products sells this cool all-in-one DIY engine blueprinting kit.

The Fel-Pro #1893 oil pan gasket offers precise fit for leak-free operation.

CHAPTER 16

ENGINE STARTUP AND MAINTENANCE

Initial engine startup and break-in procedures are vital to the success of every new racing engine. Many top engine builders treat initial startup and break-in with nearly the same respect as with a NASA shuttle launch. Countless hours of preparation and a substantial amount of money have been invested to build the best possible engine.

Engine maintenance includes appropriate initial starting procedures at each event. For example, even a used engine benefits from pre-heating and pre-oiling prior to the first restart at a new event. Some builders take great pains to keep the engine and the oil warm (at least 140 degrees F) at all times so the engine is never started cold.

If you subscribe to the theory that all of this is beneficial to long-term performance, you're exactly right. You can never do enough to support the precision assembly of parts in any racing engine.

Startup and Break-In

Initial startup is not the time to rush. Each engine is a precision assembly of expensive components fit together with critical operating clearances. Although every effort has been made to ensure the integrity of critical component relationships, innumerable things can go wrong in an instant if proper care is not exercised. This sort of thing often happens when you get caught up in the rush to hear it run.

To ensure consistent results, it is advisable to establish a universal checklist that can be applied to every engine. This guarantees that you don't skip crucial steps that may affect the component health of your engine and ultimately its real world performance potential. Numerous checks and verifications must be performed prior to initial engine

Dyno testing is the final step prior to installation in the car. Here, a 300-mph, 1,400-hp twin turbo small-block Chevy endures the break-in process at Mike LeFevers' Mitech Racing Engines facility in Placentia, California.

ENGINE STARTUP AND MAINTENANCE

startup. Many of these steps will not be required once you establish the engine's operational well-being, but they are critical to preventing unexpected damage when you first fire the engine. Some of them also address the important issue of ring seating during those first few critical moments of engine operation.

Assembly Lubrication

The first line of defense against initial startup damage or follow-on damage during the engine break-in period is the use of proper assembly lube during engine construction. High-pressure engine assembly lube is favored by most professional engine builders although there are still diehards who only use engine oil on everything except cam lobes.

Most builders use high-pressure lube on bearings, lifters, pushrod tips, rocker arms, and (on most) bolt assemblies to ensure proper torque and bolt stretch. Others favor straight engine oil or automatic transmission fluid (ATF) on the cylinder walls for assembly and they coat piston rings and skirts with engine oil. Some builders still use assembly lube on piston skirts, but oil is perfectly adequate especially now that many pistons are prepared with coated skirts. High-pressure lube is also appropriate on wrist pins and many builders approve of it for coating oil pump gears and the distributor drive gear as well.

The former practice of heavily coating everything with moly lube has fallen out of favor now that high-pressure lubes and special break-in oils are available. Moly lube takes a long time to work its way out of the system and it tends to plug filters. Builders used to find globs of it in various locations such as cylinder heads and the bottom of the oil pan; it's nothing to worry about, just messy.

Modern high-pressure lube is vitally important for the initial break-in of flat-tappet cam lobes. Flat tappets have virtually vanished from most modern production engines, hence commercial motor oils are no longer formulated with the critical friction inhibitors that provide protection to sliding components experiencing high-contact loads. Older motor oil formulas used a high zinc content to provide this protection. Modern oils don't use it, primarily because it damages oxygen sensors and throws production cars out of tune. Fortunately most racing lubricants and break-in oils are formulated with high zinc and phosphorous contents to resist friction damage between sliding components.

Break-in oils are expensive, but they have largely displaced additives used to supplement conventional motor oils. They include ingredients expressly designed to protect engine bearings and promote ring seating during the critical break-in process. Many of these oils emerged from the early break-in practices of Pro/Stock drag racing and other venues that began using oils formulated for severe-duty diesel engines that are vulnerable to high-pressure friction conditions. Shell Rotella T was a favorite for many years as were Mobil Delvac 1300 Super, Castrol Tection Extra, and Chevron Delo 400—all 15W-40 multi-grade Diesel engine oils. Performance suppliers like Comp

Quality break-in oil with high zinc and phosphorous content is essential for proper engine break-in. Do not attempt engine break-in with off-the-shelf regular or synthetic motor oils that are not formulated for the high-friction environment of initial engine startup.

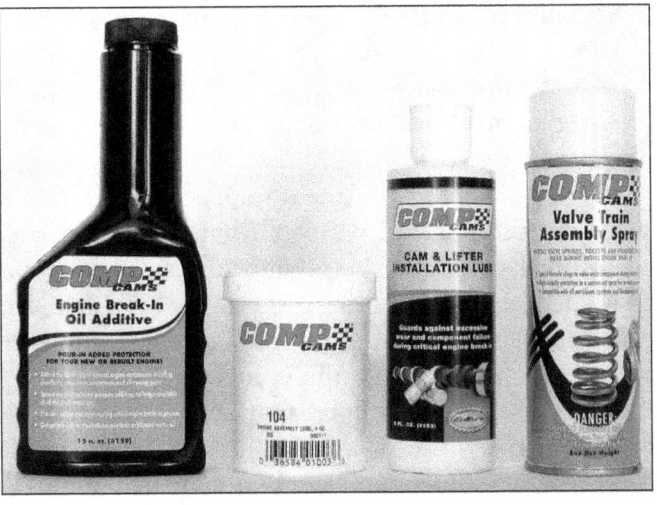

Proper assembly lubrication is essential to prevent engine damage upon initial engine startup. This includes assembly lube, cam and lifter lube, engine oil break-in supplement, and valvetrain assembly spray, among others.

Cams, Joe Gibbs, and Red Line now offer similarly formulated break-in oils specifically for race engine use. Once the engine is properly broken in, racers can switch directly to their preferred synthetic engine oil with complete confidence.

Valvespring Pressure

Precautions are especially necessary to prevent damage to flat-tappet camshaft lobes during initial startup. Valvespring pressures designed to support high RPM are excessive for the initial contact and break-in period. Even with high-pressure lube coating the cam lobes, it is possible to wipe out cam lobes during the initial fire-up session. Solutions include substituting lower-rate break-in springs for the initial break-in. Depending on the application, some builders feel it is sufficient to remove the inner valvesprings from multiple spring packages for the break-in period.

To ensure success with this method, it is necessary to further quantify the startup spring package on a spring tester. Since startup and initial break-in procedures rarely exceed 3,500 to 4,000 rpm, it is safe to employ springs that provide adequate operational pressure, but not so much that it wipes out cam lobes. About 100 pounds on the seat usually suffices.

If removing the inner springs from the spring pack proves to be insufficient, try using the outer springs only from a well-used spring set that has substantially less spring pressure. Once you have completed the break-in process you can install the correct spring package designed for your camshaft without consequence. Because of the very high spring pressures used on some modern cams, many engine builders routinely run break-in springs even on engines equipped with roller cams. They don't want to overstress the roller axle until it has been fully lubed and has some operational time on it.

Break-In Rockers

Comp Cams sells low-ratio break-in rocker arms (1.2:1) for small-block Chevys. The low-rocker ratio minimizes valve motion and protects the cam from exposure to excessive spring rate on initial start-up. Engines run just fine with these rockers for break-in. Comp only makes them for small-block Chevys, but in some cases you may be able to identify a lower-ratio rocker that works temporarily if you have a different engine. If not you can use the valvespring substitution method.

Low-ratio rockers work by limiting valve motion to the point that the spring never approaches full compression thus placing minimal load on the cam lobe to lifter interface. While these rockers permit the engine to run smoothly at lower engine speeds, it is important not to overload them. Always change back to the correct springs and rockers immediately after a break-in session and verify that all components have been switched out prior to running the car or tuning the engine on a dyno. Failure to do so may cause damage to the cam or valvetrain if you exceed the safe engine speed. Even if you only damage the break-in components, some metal will likely deposit in the engine and eventually circulate to the bearings. Consider 3,500 to 4,000 rpm the redline when working with specialized break-in components.

Wet Sump Tips

Some builders using deep-sump oil pans like to add an extra quart of oil for break-in, thinking it provides additional splash lubrication to the cylinder walls, but the practice is generally self-defeating. If the cylinder walls, pistons, and rings were properly lubricated during assembly it is generally unnecessary and may actually inhibit ring seating due to excessive lubrication. The only time you might consider it is if the engine had been stored for an extended period prior to startup. Even then it is largely unnecessary and most builders simply squirt some light oil through the spark plug holes prior to starting.

Some builders find it comforting to pull the pan after break-in to clean out any trash that may have accumulated (not that any should) and to take a look at the bearings. With a wet sump system it is best to pre-fill the oil filter and then pre-lube the engine using a sturdy 1/2-inch drill motor and the appropriate oil pump drive rod until oil is confirmed coming out of every rocker arm.

Dry Sump Tips

Dry sump systems require pre-lubing to ensure that the pressure line from the pump and all internal oil passages are full. Then the proper level in the supply tank can be established.

For the initial start-up remove the drive belt from the pump and give the engine one final pre-lube just before starting. Then closely monitor oil pressure and oil level in the supply tank during warm-up and cam break-in. Be sure to pre-lube the pump with a light coat of high-pressure lube during installation.

ENGINE STARTUP AND MAINTENANCE

Valve Lash

While exact valve lash is not absolutely critical during break-in, engine components do expand with heat and valve lash typically increases. As a rule you can set the lash .002- to .004-inch tighter on engines with iron blocks and aluminum cylinder heads. You can close it up even more on all-aluminum engines, which tend to grow considerably more with temperature. Don't overdo it, but the lash should grow into the correct clearance range for your particular valvetrain. When you perform the first check after warm-up you should find all lash settings relatively close to the specified clearance.

If running break-in springs, initial lash should be close to what you will eventually run. Watch it closely to make certain it doesn't tighten or loosen excessively, which indicates a problem. While rarely used in true racing engines, hydraulic lifters are sometimes specified in lower sportsman classes. Here it is important to establish proper lifter pre-load so the lifter absorbs dimensional changes as the engine gains temperature.

Typically zero-lash plus 1/8 to 1/4 turn down on each lifter provides the desired pre-load to absorb thermal growth and prevent lifter pump-up later when the engine is run under full power. At this point it is wise to mark each pushrod with a vertical line (white or silver marker on dry surface) to track pushrod and lifter rotation with flat-tappet cams. If the lifters are rotating properly all the marks have rotated to different positions during engine warm-up. If they haven't moved, investigate thoroughly before you go any further.

Magnets and Filtermags

Some engine builders running iron blocks and iron cylinder heads place small engine magnets in the lifter valley and the cylinder heads to catch errant metal debris that may be floating in the oil supply. These magnets also capture microscopic metal (ferrous) particles and can provide additional wear protection depending on the source and severity of the contaminants.

Every race engine should have a Filtermag attached to the oil filter. This draws any ferrous metal particles to the edge of the filter can where you can easily judge their importance when you cut open the filter after break-in. Using magnets is a detail that is frequently overlooked, but it is difficult to see how they could do any harm. Even if you remove them after engine break-in, you still have the benefit of their protection during the engine's initial run-in. Some builders don't believe in magnets and feel it is sufficient to practice strict clean assembly procedures and keep a sharp eye out for metal during the first inspection after engine warm-up. In my experience, this practice is acceptable because precision assembled race engines rarely shed much metal. Post-startup oil changes used to be favored because builders expected to find a certain level of trash left over from assembly. Proper clean assembly techniques dictate that this shouldn't occur and that you should be able to run the break-in oil and filter for the entire break-in period.

Instant Fire

Adjust the engine's initial timing and fuel delivery so that it fires instantly or with very minimal cranking. A favored tactic is to rotate the engine by hand to about 25 to 30 degrees BTDC, then adjust the crank trigger or the distributor reluctor so the engine fires at that point with the distributor locked down. This provides sufficient advance for starting and warm-up prior to initial inspection.

Perform all of your checking for WOT prior to filling the carburetor with fuel. Once the bowls are full every little throttle movement sends a small shot of fuel into the plenum. Most new engines fire on one moderate pump shot of fuel just before you hit the starter. You should easily be able to start the engine and take it right to the desired break-in speed (typically 2,000 rpm) in only a few seconds.

After the warm-up, cam break-in (if required), and initial inspection, you can readjust the timing to your anticipated base setting prior to further break-in and certainly before beginning initial torque checks and final tuning procedures.

A Filtermag attached to an engine's oil filter is strong insurance against engine damage from dislodged or undetected metal particles in the oil supply.

CHAPTER 16

Engine Pre-Lube

Fill the engine with the appropriate amount of break-in oil. Make certain to use one of the quarts of oil to pre-fill the filter depending on how the filter attaches to a particular engine. Immediately prior to initial engine startup, pre-lube the engine for 3 to 5 minutes, or longer if necessary. Do this by spinning the dry sump pump with the belt off or, on a wet sump engine, remove the distributor and install a suitable pre-lube tool to engage and spin the oil pump.

It is best to use a heavy-duty 1/2-inch drill motor that does not overheat during the extended pre-lube period. You will feel the drill bog down and create torque when the pump first gets a bite of the oil supply. Continue pre-oiling until oil is smoothly flowing from all of the pushrod tips and lubricating the rocker arms. This indicates that all the oil passages are full and that oil has reached every internal part of the engine. This often takes some time and it is helpful to rotate the engine with a large breaker bar every minute or so to expose all the oiling passages in the crankshaft to the feed holes in the bearings.

Once the pushrods and rockers are oiling you can be pretty certain the lifter galleries are full. Continue pre-oiling for another minute or two until the rockers are thoroughly covered and all air has been forced from the oil passages. Then install and pre-time the distributor and fire the engine ASAP. Remember oil pressure on a gauge doesn't always mean that oil has reached every part of the engine. Full oil pressure for five or more minutes with frequent engine rotation and verified oiling at the rockers is a much safer indicator.

Flooding

On carbureted engines, check float levels and fuel pressure carefully to ensure that flooding does not occur. Observe the carburetor carefully when you first apply fuel pressure to it to ensure that a stuck float or needle-and-seat assembly does not cause overflow into the engine. Visually verify this on each venturi bore. Don't pump the throttle to observe accelerator pump operation. A very slight stroke to verify pump shot is sufficient. The engine should start with as little fuel in the manifold as possible to prevent fuel wash on the rings and cylinder walls.

For EFI applications, verify correct fuel pressure and check for line leaks and injector leaks. A stuck injector could flood the engine so turn off the pump as soon as you verify pressure and check your gauges to see if they register fuel flow with the engine off. Don't turn the pump on again until you are ready to fire the engine.

Cylinder Heads

Although most gaskets do not require a re-torque after initial firing, many engine builders still prefer to re-torque the heads. There is no hard-and-fast rule here and it often boils down to personal preference. If you do prefer to re-torque the heads you must wait until the engine has cooled to room temperature. Hot torquing only leads to false results and could cause engine damage.

Maintenance Program

A regular maintenance program can help ensure the health and longevity of your racing engine. With the exception of unexpected catastrophic failure, engines normally exhibit distress symptoms that indicate the onset of potential problems. Regular checkups and maintenance catch these indicators and help you preserve engine performance.

Keep a logbook and note critical symptoms and abnormalities after every event or at some reasonable time later. In addition to logging the number of miles, runs, or laps, check and record the following regularly.

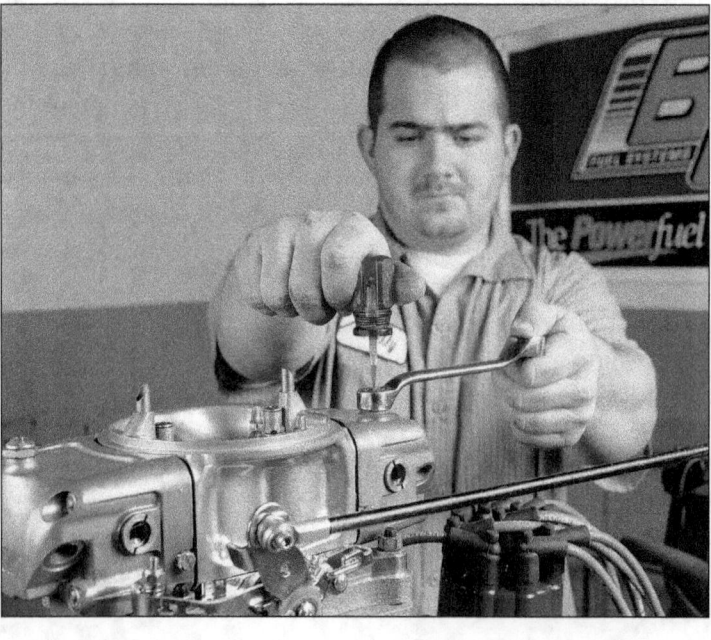

Adjust the carburetor float levels to recommended specs. Run the fuel pump until the bowls are full and no fuel is leaking or discharging into the engine prior to startup.

ENGINE STARTUP AND MAINTENANCE

Timing

One of the easiest checks to make is ignition timing. Check timing before and after an event. Testing should have established the engine's preferred timing setting. Check it prior to every event to make certain that the engine performs as expected and to verify that the distributor or crank trigger has not been accidently moved in the shop or during transport. Checking timing before a race verifies that the ignition system is functioning properly. Checking it after a race may reveal potential problems.

A simple mark on the distributor housing and the manifold indicates your preferred setting. If it has moved during the race you may have failed to tighten the distributor clamp or the crank trigger pickup securely. The crank trigger may have been struck by track debris or it may have moved because of a vibration.

If the checks seem correct but the engine timing still fluctuates, you may have a worn or failing timing chain, loose components in a gear drive, or slippage in the adjustment mechanism on a belt drive setup. A failing cam or distributor drive gear could also contribute to unexpected timing changes.

Investigate timing abnormalities carefully to determine not just the change, but also what caused it. A loose distributor or crank trigger pickup is one thing, failing parts is quite another.

Valve Lash and Valvesprings

If timing seems in order, pull the valve covers to check the springs and valve lash. Take note of the condition of the residual oil in the cylinder head. Look for debris, water, or any radical color change. Oil naturally darkens with use, but it should still exhibit some level of transparency and no debris whatsoever. If in doubt, try to identify the problem. Don't just change the oil and hope it clears up. It won't! This is a good time for another filter check.

If the condition of the oil is satisfactory you can begin checking springs and valve lash. Examination of the oil in the cylinder head should only take a moment or two so the engine still has temperature in it for the lash check. Log each lash setting in your notebook.

Operational changes in valve lash can indicate spring problems or potential failure in the rest of the valvetrain. Any change of more than .002 inch should be investigated carefully. Modern valvetrain components for racing engines are very good. They tend to maintain lash setting very well unless aggravated by other influences. If the lash is moving around, get to the bottom of it or else the engine will ultimately experience a catastrophic failure.

Normally, lash may tighten slightly as the valve settles into the seat, but this should be no more than .001 to .002 inch. If the lash is tightening more, you may have a valve or seat problem or a valve lock that is moving in the retainer. Investigate. If the lash is opening up, you may have loose components, pushrod deformation, or a failure in the roller lifter assembly, a rocker arm problem, or some bit of abnormal contact between various valvetrain components including the cylinder head. This may be a retainer or a lock moving around in the spring and contacting the inner surface of the rocker or any number of subtle and often hard-to-identify valvetrain problems that require patience and keen eyes to detect.

Careful measurements and observation for damage or witness marks usually reveal the problem. If in doubt, remove the rockers one at a time and carefully examine them, the valvestem tip, pushrod cup, and both ends of the pushrod for signs of distress.

Check for pushrod-to-cylinder-head contact or guide interference and evaluate the contact pattern on top of the valvestem.

Examine the roller and bearing and check for contact marks on the bottom of the rocker.

Valve lash distress could also mean problems with lifter or pushrod rotation or a loose roller lifter tie bar that is allowing a small degree of lifter rotation on a roller lifter. This leads to massive failure pretty quickly and is certainly worth investigating even if you have to pull the manifold.

If you don't observe any valvetrain problems, check the springs and log their pressures. Your logbook should have a record of spring pressure at assembly, during testing, and after every event. Some builders like to fire an engine before every event and check springs after warm-up or practice. Moroso, Proform, L&K, and other manufacturers sell heads-on spring testers that make the procedure quick and easy. Race springs lose a slight bit of pressure and take a set after break-in and a few power runs on the dyno. Observe this carefully.

As a rule, springs relax about 5 percent, but you won't know if there is a bad one unless you check and recheck regularly. Log all spring pressures during and after dyno testing, during track testing, and after every event. Some racers only spot check springs, but that's not good enough for a precision race engine. It only

The initial valve lash always changes and must be re-adjusted after the initial warmup. Set the lash to recommended specs as noted on the cam card provided by the camshaft manufacturer.

takes a few moments longer to check and log every spring.

When you find a weak spring, it is likely time to change the whole batch. Others may be on the verge of losing pressure or failing on the very next lap or run down the drag strip. Why take the chance? Besides, springs that don't hold pressure are probably not controlling the valve properly and performance degrades prior to failure. If the valvesprings can't control the valve bounce, you're not getting all the power available from your race engine.

Oil Filter

An oil filter check should be performed after every race. Purchase a filter cutter and open the filter for examination. Pry open all the pleats and check for debris. If you find any, determine the likely source depending on whether it is aluminum, iron, silicone, gasket material, dirt, or otherwise.

If you use a Filtermag (and you should) check the inside of the filter canister. Excessive magnetic material here may indicate a looming failure somewhere in the engine. A very light spread of metallic particles is normal, but be wary if the pattern of trapped particles seems excessive. If you run an Oberg-style screen filter examine it closely for material.

This is also a good time to examine any engine magnets you may have placed on the heads or lifter valley to see if they have collected any ferrous material. Any time you find a significant amount of collected material, consider it a warning shot and get to the bottom of it. Some racers have been known to attach small magnets to the exterior of their dry sump tank near the outlet to the pressure pump to catch metallic debris before it can enter the pump. Examine the oil you drain from the engine. If it smells burned and no longer feels slippery, a problem may lurk within. You can't change the oil often enough, but it won't save the engine if the problem is serious. You have to find the source of the debris and correct it, if it's not already too late.

Engine Temperature

If an engine has been run hot, numerous problems accrue. Excessive component growth may have caused damage via contact with other components. It causes bearings to lose their crush and spin. It also causes fasteners to relax and lose torque, particularly cylinder head and intake bolts. Check cylinder head and manifold bolt torque and log them in your book.

If the engine was only slightly overheated and corrected relatively quickly you may have dodged a bullet. If it really got hot, consider yourself lucky to have escaped with all your parts still inside the block. Cylinder walls may be scored, piston skirts galled, and numerous other problems are likely present. A full teardown is warranted.

Recommended Maintenance

After each race many builders take additional steps to preserve the integrity of internal engine components. One popular practice is to back off all the rocker arms so that no rocker arms or springs are in compression between races. This releases all valvesprings to their normal seat pressure. It is good practice since a stored engine always has some valves partially or fully open, which can place full valvespring pressure against any given retainer, rocker arm, and/or related components. Another favored procedure is to perform a full leakdown test while the engine is still warm. This provides an immediate indication of the engine's post race health and can indicate whether damage has been sustained during the race. Careful leakdown procedures can pinpoint potential problems specific to any given cylinder and suggest the nature of the problems and how you should proceed. Consider it good insurance for any high-dollar engine. An example might be a turbocharged high-boost engine that has just completed a run at Bonneville. No doubt the engine builder would like to verify every cylinder prior to the next run.

Other post race techniques include cylinder lubrication to protect the cylinders between races. Some builders like to crank the still warm engine while spraying WD-40 down the carburetor to lube the cylinder walls. Not all builders subscribe to this technique, but it is hard to see how it can do any harm unless the engine is stored for a very long time. Others like to cover the exhaust collectors or stuff rags up in them to prevent moisture from finding its way to the valves via the headers.

Another popular and essential post-race procedure includes fuel pump and fuel system maintenance. Depending on the length of time between races, race gas can gel in the pumps and lines, clogging them and leaving harmful residue that could later clog injectors, jets, needles, seats, and so on. Post-race procedures often include running some pump gas through the fuel system to remove all the race gas. Running pump gas through the system flushes the fuel supply and ensures that all components function properly on the next startup. The engine will not object to this under low or no load conditions. After this step it is also a good idea to clean or change the fuel filter and, depending on the length of time between events, you might also consider draining the carburetor float bowls. These steps are more important than you might suspect, especially if there is a lengthy period between races. And of course all of these steps should be performed if you are planning on storing or shipping the engine.

Engine Dyno Testing

All racing engines should be tested and broken-in on an engine dyno. Dyno testing fosters proper engine break-in procedures and it makes it easy to spot and correct potential problems ranging from valvetrain issues to simple oil leaks. Most top engine builders insist on dyno testing to certify their work. Even independent builders not equipped with their own dyno facilities take their engines to a reputable shop to check and validate their work.

It's important to remember that the dyno is a comparative device whose accuracy is only as good as the data used to program it. It requires accurate atmospheric data and consistency of operation. You can't really compare power numbers from one dyno to another because there are too many variables. Stick to one dyno source and make sure it is well maintained, regularly calibrated, and competently operated. Make sure the operator follows your instructions and records the data you are seeking. Most dynos are capable of recording every possible bit of data about your engine if equipped with the proper sensors.

Consistent testing procedures and spot-on calibration are imperative. Because dynos often "seem" to give consistent results, some operators become complacent and fail to regularly verify proper calibration. Many dyno operators are capable of providing considerable help and insight about how the engine is performing, but the best ones ask you exactly what you want every step of the way. A dyno operator who doesn't really listen to you probably isn't qualified to test your racing engine. Never let the dyno operator rush you. A dyno operator who is more concerned about lunch or what time he is going home probably isn't concerned about properly evaluating your engine.

Don't wear the engine out on the dyno. Do most of the initial testing at or below the torque peak while establishing optimum spark and jetting. Ask the operator for a full printout including all of the raw, uncorrected numbers. The correction factor means very little to most engine builders; the uncorrected number is what the engine really delivers for any prevailing conditions. The uncorrected data establishes a benchmark and permits accurate analysis of fuel usage and BSFC numbers. If you're seeking or selling numbers the correction factor is your co-conspirator. If you're an engine builder validating your combination, uncorrected numbers tell you everything you need to know.

The chances of the engine running with the same conditions as the correction factor are slim to none, so what's the point? Magazine testers use corrected numbers because they are impressive. Real engine builders glean everything they need to know from the raw data. Most dyno facilities can provide you with a disk or a a thumb drive of all your data plus a simple software program that allows you to read, graph, and evaluate the tests on your home PC where you can study them at your leisure.

Consistency in how the raw data numbers are obtained is important. Well-maintained dynos are very repeatable tools as long as the operator maintains consistent environmental conditions and runs all the tests at the same oil and engine coolant temperature and repeatable atmospheric conditions.

Many operators insist on running tests at coolant temperatures far below actual race operating conditions. To some degree this is a function of the dyno cooling sytem, which is not often adequate for running at race engine temperatures. You must decide what serves your needs best and try to test at a temperature that works for you.

Since dyno tune-ups rarely transfer well to the track, it's generally not necessary to pursue absolute power numbers on the dyno. Its more immportant to establish the engine's operational health and to generate data that allows you to verify the powerband and how well the engine meets your requirements.

Testing at lower temperatures makes it easier to generate big power numbers and the operator doesn't have to be as careful. Experienced dyno operators can quickly spot any inconsistencies and verify whether they are due to the dyno or an engine problem. More often than not it's not the dyno but rather a tuning or mechanical issue that can be pinpointed by thoughtful evaluation.

In a sense, repeatability is more important than accuracy. If the dyno reports that you made 825 hp, you can't really be sure if that is a truly accurate number. But if it repeats within 1 hp over and over then you're accomplishing something because you can accurately judge the effect of any changes you make. The engine may actually only make 795 hp, but if it repeats and shows you gains or losses from your benchmark, the specific number is less critical than the degree of gain or loss and what the instrumentation tells you about fuel flow, air/fuel ratio, EGTs, and other factors that relate according to the changes made and the subsequent results.

One important factor is the data filtering method used to smooth the curves on test graphs. Those smooth curves look impressive, but in reality a "zoom in" of the data reveals numerous peaks and valleys in the overall curve based on inconsistent fuel delivery, mixture quality, ignition scatter, and other intermittent interference all affecting the quality of the measured power curve.

Dyno testing can easily go on forever if you don't establish some goals and parameters. Unless you are testing different cams, carbs, manifolds, or headers to ascertain the differences, you're better off focusing on establishing the engine's powerband and the operational integrity of all the critical components. Don't rush the testing. After the proper break-in and fluid changes, do some checkout pulls at a safe RPM and examine the valvetrain carefully for signs of distress. When you are absolutely confident of the engine's mechanical integrity you can make a couple short sweep tests across the range of the anticipated torque peak. Once you pinpoint it, you can begin evaluating fuel ratios and spark settings. Since the torque peak is the point of highest efficiency, tuning efforts here establish the optimum spark lead and jetting requirements that allow you to fine tune the top end with the high-speed air bleeds.

Don't beat the engine to death on the dyno. You're going to have to establish a track tune wherever you go so it's relatively pointless to tune the engine repeatedly on the dyno. Once you know the engine is healthy, pack it up.

SOURCE GUIDE

Altronics, Inc.
1411 S. Roselle Rd.
Schaumburg, IL 60193
888-464-2587
www.altronicsinc.com

Audie Technologies
23 N. Trooper Rd.
Norristown, PA
610-630-5895
www.audietech.com

Automotive Racing Products
1863 Eastman Ave.
Ventura, CA 93003
805-339-2200
www.arp-bolts.com

Automotive Specialists
4357 Triple Crown Dr.
Concord, NC 28027
704-786-0187
www.automotivespecialists.com

Autotronic Controls, MSD Ignition
1490 Henry Brennan Dr.
El Paso, TX 79936-6805
915-857-5200

BHJ Inc.
37530 Enterprise Ct.
Newark, CA 94560
510-797-6780
www.bhjproducts.com

Big Stuff 3
4352 Fenton Rd.
Hartman, MI 48353
248-887-5636
www.bigstuff3.com

BMS Machine
1904 Riverview Dr., Unit 101
San Bernardino, CA 92408
909-799-7770

Calico Coatings
6400 Denver Industrial Park Rd.
Denver, NC 28037
704-483-2202
www.calicocoatings.com

Comp Cams
3406 Democrat Rd.
Memphis, TN 38118
800-999-0853
www.compcams.com

CV Products
42 High Tech Blvd.
Thomasville, NC 27360
800-448-1223
www.cvproducts.com

Drag Racing Pro
www.dragracingpro.com

Duttweiler Performance
1563 Los Angeles Ave.
Ventura, CA 93004
805-659-3648

Edelbrock
2700 California St.
Torrance, CA 90503
800-416-8628
www.edelbrock.com

Federal-Mogul Corp.
26555 Northwestern Hwy.
Southfield, MI 48033
800-325-8886
www.federalmogul.com

Filtermag, Inc
13260 West Foxfire Dr., #7
Surprise, AZ 85374
623-556-4201
www.filtermag.com

SOURCE GUIDE

Fuel Air Spark Technology
33400 Democrat Rd.
Memphis, TN 38118
901-260-3278
877-334-8355
www.fuelairspark.com

Holley Performance Products
1801 Russellville Rd.
Bowling Green, KY 42101
270-781-9741
www.holley.com

JEGS High Performance
101 JEGs Pl.
Delaware, OH 43015
800-345-4545
www.JEGS.com

Moroso Performance Products
80 Carter Dr.
Guilford, CT 06437
203-453-6571
www.moroso.com

Motion Software
222 South Raspberry Ln.
Anaheim, CA 92808-2268
714-231-3801
motionsoftware.com

NDT Systems, Inc
17811 Georgetown Ln.
Huntington Beach, CA 92674
714-893-2438
www.ndtsystems.com

Performance Distributors
2699 Barris Dr.
Memphis, TN 38132
901-396-5782
www.performancedistributors.com

Performance Trends, Inc.
Box 530164
Livonia, MI 48153
248-473-9230
www.performancetrends.com

Pipe Max
9827 Hwy. 343
Abbeville, LA 70510
337-652-6220

ProRacing Sim
535 W. Lambert, Bldg. E
Brea, CA 92821-3911
714-255-2931
901-259-2355
www.proracingsim.com

Race Pumps
222 Hillcrest Dr.
High Point, NC 27262
336-476-9720
www.racepumps.com

Racing Systems Analysis
www.racingsecrets.com

Ross Pistons
625 S. Douglas St.
El Segundo, CA 90245
310-536-0100
www.rosspistons.com

Scat Enterprises
1400 Kingsdale Ave.
Redondo Beach, CA 90278-3983
310-370-5501
www.scatcrankshafts.com

Sealed Power Corp.
100 Terrace Plaza
Muskegon, MI 49443
616-724-5200
www.federal-mogul.com

Sonny's Racing Engines
352 Training Center Rd.
Lynchburg, VA 24502
434-239-1009
sonnysracingengines.com

Specialty Auto Parts
P.O. Box 306
Roseville, MI 4806
586-774-2500
www.proformparts.com

Summit Racing Equipment
P.O. Box 909
Akron, OH 44309-0909
800-230-3030
www.summitracing.com

T&D Machine Products
4859 Convair Dr.
Carson City, NV 89706
775-884-2292
www.tdmach.com

Weiand
1801 Russellville Rd.
Bowling Green, KY 42101
270-781-9741 tech Line
www.weiand.com

Wilson Manifolds
4700 N.E.11 Ave.
Ft. Lauderdale, FL 33334
954-771-6216
www.wilsonmanifolds.com

World Products
35 trade Zone Dr.
Ronkonkoma, NY 11779
631-981-1918
www.worldcastings.com

www.ingramcontent.com/pod-product-compliance
Lightning Source LLC
Chambersburg PA
CBHW051407070526
44584CB00023B/3324